# AMERICAN JOURNEY

# AMERICAN JOURNEY

On the Road with Henry Ford,

Thomas Edison, and

John Burroughs

## WES DAVIS

**W. W. NORTON & COMPANY**

*Celebrating a Century of Independent Publishing*

For information about permission to reproduce selections from this book, write to
Permissions, W. W. Norton & Company, Inc., 500 Fifth Avenue, New York, NY 10110

For information about special discounts for bulk purchases, please contact
W. W. Norton Special Sales at specialsales@wwnorton.com or 800-233-4830

Manufacturing by Lake Book
Book design by Chris Welch
Production manager: Louise Mattarelliano

Library of Congress Cataloging-in-Publication Data

Names: Davis, Wes, author.
Title: American journey : on the road with Henry Ford, Thomas Edison, and
John Burroughs / Wes Davis.
Description: First edition. | New York, NY : W.W. Norton & Company, [2023] |
Includes bibliographical references and index.
Identifiers: LCCN 2022060080 | ISBN 9781324000327 (hardcover) |
ISBN 9781324000334 (epub)
Subjects: LCSH: United States—Biography. | Burroughs, John, 1837–1921—Travel—United
States. | Ford, Henry, 1863–1947—Travel—United States. | Edison, Thomas A. (Thomas
Alva), 1847–1931—Travel—United States. | Automobile travel—United States—History—20th
century | United States—Description and travel. | United States—History—1901–1953.
Classification: LCC CT220 .D38 2023 | DDC 917.3048—dc23/eng/20230313
LC record available at https://lccn.loc.gov/2022060080

W. W. Norton & Company, Inc.
500 Fifth Avenue, New York, N.Y. 10110
www.wwnorton.com

W. W. Norton & Company Ltd.
15 Carlisle Street, London W1D 3BS

1 2 3 4 5 6 7 8 9 0

For Lola Kelchner and Ronald Davis

*Owning a car was still a major excitement,*
*roads were still wonderful and bad.*

—*E. B. White*

# Contents

*Prologue*                                                          xiii

1. THE SPARK                                                        1

2. COMPENSATION                                                     25

3. TRIAL RUNS                                                       44

4. THE PALACE OF INDUSTRY AND THE
   GARDEN OF EARTHLY TREASURES                                      86

5. SEPARATE WAYS                                                    121

6. SUNBURNED AND FULL OF VIM                                        139

7. AT SEA                                                           163

8. A GREAT SLICE OF OUR GEOGRAPHY                                   186

*Epilogue*                                                          279
*Acknowledgments*                                                   307
*Notes*                                                             309
*Selected Bibliography*                                             339
*Illustration Credits*                                              347
*Index*                                                             349

# Prologue

---

## Summer 1918

On the afternoon of August 20, 1918, an open-topped, four-door Simplex touring car angled off the rutted dirt road it was traveling along and trundled to a stop on the edge of a cornfield situated half a mile outside the remote mountain village of Lead Mine, West Virginia. From the back seat emerged a frail, white-haired man, looking weary and uncomfortable. He wore a cloth driving cap, wire-framed goggles, and an ankle-length duster made of beige linen. A snowy beard cascaded onto his chest. The man's name was John Burroughs. He was a well-known nature writer and the nation's foremost expert on birds. For several days now, he had been traveling with a party of friends in a caravan composed of the Simplex and a Packard touring car, a pair of Model T Fords, and a White truck loaded down with camping and cooking gear. The trip thus far had not been an easy one, and the strain of the journey was beginning to wear on Burroughs.

As he eased his sinewy, 128-pound frame down from the running board, he could not help feeling that he lacked the youthful anatomy that might make long-distance automobile travel more nearly endurable. "You have good cushions," he had told the stouter of his traveling companions the day before, after a particularly forceful bump had bounced him out of his seat. "My cushions must have disappeared long years ago," he decided, "and it seems pretty rough to me." One thing Burroughs knew for certain: at the age of eighty-one he was too old a man to be wondering where he was going to spend the night or how far he might have to walk when the car broke down—again.

Earlier in the trip, as the caravan approached the town of Connellsville, Pennsylvania—a hamlet of some thirteen thousand people situated along the Youghiogheny River, fifty miles southeast of Pittsburgh—the Packard car in which Burroughs was then riding with two of his friends had rattled to a halt. The cooling fan, they discovered when they raised the hood, had torn itself apart and punctured the radiator. One of Burroughs's companions, a rangy, middle-aged mechanic from Dearborn, Michigan, managed to make a temporary repair on the spot, and the party limped on into town, where they soon found a garage. But while a crowd quickly gathered to gape at the travelers and offer advice, there was no one in evidence who could actually make the necessary repairs. Finally, Burroughs's Dearborn friend again took matters into his own hands. Working with a handful of tools he had gathered in the garage, he removed the fan and radiator and began to rebuild both piece by piece. Three hours later he had the car reassembled and running again.

That afternoon Burroughs was taking no chances. Wearied by another day's driving and eager to see the party encamped for the night before anything else could go wrong, he had called for a halt the moment he spotted a suitable-looking field near the road. Now, with his duster flapping around his ankles, he went in search of the farmer to ask for permission to set up camp. To his disappointment he found that the taciturn widow who owned the place was not inclined to accept a ragtag band of drifters on her land. Burroughs imagined that she must have had trouble from parties like his in the past, but he hoped he could find some way to reassure her.

He watched as the mountain woman's skeptical gaze swept from him to his companions, now beginning to tumble out of their odd assortment of cars and trucks. Then he saw her eyes turn from his friends to the field of sweet corn just beginning to ripen under the August sun. Suddenly Burroughs understood the problem. The woman was worried that the boisterous camping party would trample her corn.

A farmer himself, as well as a renowned naturalist, Burroughs might have traded on his own name in the confidence that his reputation as a conservationist would win any landowner's trust. Instead, he decided to bank on the fame of his companions. Perhaps the widow had heard of his friends, he suggested, gesturing toward his stout, cushiony companion from New Jersey and the lanky mechanic from Dearborn.

Their names, Burroughs said, were Thomas Edison and Henry Ford.


How had these titans of industry come to join a venerable naturalist on such an unlikely road trip? As it happened, several stories—both personal and cultural—had converged to put John Burroughs and his new friends together on the dusty back roads of the Appalachian South that summer.

The proximate cause lay in the budding relationship between Burroughs and Ford, which had begun by chance at the end of 1912, when Ford happened across an article in which Burroughs seemed to disparage the automobile, complaining that the rapid spread of the new technology could only have a negative impact on the natural world and America's appreciation of its riches and wonders. Ironically, it was the car itself that would bring the two men closer together, when their shared interest in Ralph Waldo Emerson's philosophy of self-reliance led them to set out in one of Ford's Model T cars to visit the house where Emerson had lived and explore the old Transcendental-ist's New England. By the time that excursion ended, a lasting friend-ship between the two men had been established and so had the habit of traveling by car.

Around the same time, a change was underway in the long-standing friendship between Ford and Edison. Over the course of their acquain-tance, neither of these industrious men had been inclined to take much time off from work. Since the era of their first meeting, in 1896, both had been single-minded in the pursuit of their respective visions—the internal combustion automobile for Ford and the work of his lab-oratory for Edison. By the middle years of the 1910s, however, each found himself at a career pinnacle. Ford's Model T was the fastest-selling automobile in the United States, while Edison had become the nation's inventor—credited with the incandescent lamp, phonograph, and motion pictures—and the man the public most trusted to drive the engine of American progress and to solve whatever problems they faced. When the organizers of the 1915 Panama–Pacific International Exposition, being held in San Francisco, proposed setting aside a day to honor Edison at the fair, where the achievements of Ford's motor company would also be on prominent display, Ford persuaded his old friend to make the journey to California. The trip proved a great suc-cess, not least because both men took a ready interest in the secrets and methods of any kind of manufacturing and production. Strolling through the exhibits at the fair, the two friends gained a broader per-spective on their own accomplishments and the modern industrial world they had helped create. While the majority of the fair's exhibits emphasized the triumph of industrialism, however, others played up the agrarian values that had always stood at the other pole of Ameri-can idealism. These gardens and agricultural displays also attracted the attention of Ford and Edison, amplifying, it seems, their nostalgia for the rural experiences of their midwestern childhoods and propelling them on side excursions to visit Luther Burbank's gardens in Santa Rosa and to explore the farmlands of Southern California. As the party boarded the train to return to the East Coast, Edison, who liked to proclaim that he had not taken a vacation in years, proposed that they reassemble soon for another expedition.

While Ford and Edison traveled to the fair by train, two of their sons, Edsel Ford and Theodore Edison, each caught up in the first blush of the country's dawning enthusiasm for long-distance automobile travel, had separately made their way to San Francisco by car, braving the perils of a still-primitive network of roads and sleeping out at night. When they came to tell the stories of these adventures, their enthusiasm was transmitted to the older generation, leading Edison, when he began to flesh out a plan for the trip he had proposed, to conclude that he and his friends must travel the nation's back roads by car and camp under the stars. In 1916 this plan was put into action on a small scale, and although Ford was not able to join the party, he put Edison in touch with Burroughs and Harvey Firestone, a longtime friend of Ford's and the founder of the Akron-based tire and rubber company that supplied tires for the Model Ts. This group, along with Firestone's son Harvey Jr., explored the Adirondacks of New York and the Green Mountains of Vermont, setting a template for the expedition that would take them through Southern Appalachia in 1918.

In many ways their timing could not have been worse. With war raging in Europe and an influenza pandemic that had already claimed thousands of lives abroad beginning to take hold in the United States, it was an inopportune moment for travel. Nevertheless, each of the men who took part in the 1918 journey would subsequently point to it as the most memorable vacation of their lives.

What follows is a chronicle of that epic trip and the far-flung adventures that prepared the way for it. The contours of the story are distinctly American, shaped by the push of industry as much as the pull of the farm; its fuel is a spirited blend of modern bustle and the dream of agrarian stability, faith in progress and nostalgia for the lost Eden once promised by the image, false though it was, of a verdant, empty continent.

# AMERICAN JOURNEY

# 1

○———○

# THE SPARK

It looked like 1912 was going to be a banner year for Henry Ford. In the newspapers that January, reporters were singing the praises of the Model T, the automobile Ford had introduced in 1908 at a starting price of $850. The Ford Model T was by no means the fastest car on the road nor the most powerful. The nimble Mercer Raceabout could more than double the Ford's top speed, while the six-cylinder Simplex Model 50 boasted more than twice its horsepower and, in the 1912 model year, came with a warranty that provided free maintenance for two years. The Babcock Electric, a vehicle powered by a six-cell Edison battery, held the record for range, having been driven from New York to Philadelphia, a distance of just over a hundred miles, on a single charge. Another electric car, the Baker Model V, put the Ford to shame when it came to comfort, providing passengers with a salon-like cabin outfitted with embroidered upholstery, lounge seating, flower vases, and electric sconces. But with the Model T, Henry Ford seemed to have hit the sweet spot of value, simplicity, and efficiency. His was the car more and more Americans wanted to own.

The development of the Model T had been accompanied by a number of innovations that were transforming the automobile industry— lighter and stronger steel alloys than American automakers had ever used before, a four-cylinder engine block cast as a single unit, a magneto-driven electrical system, body panels pressed several at a time from sheets of steel, and parts milled to such precise standards as to be interchangeable without filing and fitting at the time of assembly. It was Ford's aim to make not just the parts but the cars themselves interchangeable. He wanted "to make them all alike," as he put it, "just as one pin is like another pin when it comes from a pin factory." But the manufacturing plant Ford built to produce the Model T was no mere pin factory. It was the largest and most advanced industrial facility the world had ever seen.

In the months leading up to the Model T's debut, Ford had also fought and defeated a consortium of Wall Street chiselers who had tried, on the strength of a single bogus patent, to charge automakers a licensing fee on the very idea of the gasoline-powered automobile. At the same time, he had wrested control of his own company from financial backers who did not share his vision of an affordable automobile for the people. Now, with demand for the Model T doubling every year, Ford was beginning to perfect the assembly-line production process for which he would one day be known. Already Ford cars were rolling off the factory floor at a rate of more than two hundred a day.

"Ford Car a Paradox," proclaimed the headline of a typical newspaper article published that winter. The account, which appeared in the *Salina Evening Journal*, went on to ask how other manufacturers got away with selling vehicles at much higher prices when they were manufactured using cheaper basic materials than the Model T, which was built on a frame of technologically advanced vanadium steel. The *Boston Globe* struck a similar tone, calling the latest Ford model "one of the small-car sensations of the present season" and praising the quality of service Ford provided to keep its vehicles on the road. "Nothing irritates an owner of a car as much as his inability to use it for the want of some trivial part," the article noted. "With a Ford owner the minute anything happens, recourse to the telegraph or the telephone to the nearest Ford branch will bring any needed part in a few hours at most."

All of this was music to Ford's ears, and no doubt he had helped orchestrate the tune, feeding material to the news and editorial departments of the nation's newspapers. But pleased as he was with the progress of his company, he wanted more. Over and above his obsession with building a superior yet affordable vehicle, Henry Ford was fixated on the idea that his Model T would improve the lives of ordinary people in rural America. The press often played along in this as well, nurturing a faith in progress that appealed to the average journalist as much as to Ford. The editor of one midwestern newspaper announced at the end of 1911 that the Model T had doubled the area of the country. "Until the advent of the motor car," he argued, "there was at least half of the United States that might as well have been in the Fiji Islands for all the good it did the rest of the country." The lightweight, affordable Model T had, from this point of view, suddenly made it more attractive to live and work the land in areas not conveniently served by rail lines. It had also opened up the natural beauty of the nation, its remote mountains and lakes, for the enjoyment of ever-greater numbers of Americans. When he heard talk like that, it sounded to Henry Ford like the fulfillment of the dream he had had growing up on his family's farm in Michigan.

Ford's car was not without its naysayers, however. The proliferation of cheap automobiles was a menace to pedestrians, some claimed. Others pointed to the alarming effect noisy automobiles had on the horses that were still a significant presence on the streets of American cities. As the number of automobiles grew, so did the number of incidents in which they played a role. A 1907 court case stemming from an automobile accident put forward the notion "that automobiles are to be classed with ferocious animals, and that the law relating to the duty of the owners of such animals is to be applied." A counterargument suggested that it was "not the ferocity of automobiles that is to be feared, but the ferocity of those who drive them. Until human agency intervenes, they are usually harmless." Neither point of view cast the automobile in a particularly favorable light. A piece that ran in *Life* in 1912 put the point more succinctly still. "I don't claim that every man who runs an auto is a jackass," its author declared, "but I do claim that every jackass runs an auto." Whether to take the sting from his criticism or to highlight his authority in the matter, the author added, "I run one myself."

Henry Ford had a gift for tuning out these voices. But as 1912 progressed, one critic began to cut through the chorus of praise, speaking to Ford as he had perhaps never been spoken to before.

In the second week of January, Ford's wife, Clara, received a sizable bill from the Houghton Mifflin Company of Chicago. Over the previous few months, while Henry worked at the Ford Company plant or tinkered in the machine shop he had installed over the garage of the couple's Tuscan-style brick house on the corner of Edison Street and Second Avenue in Detroit, Clara had busied herself outfitting the house with a substantial library of British and American classics in deluxe editions.

Building a library was a natural outgrowth of Clara's own literary interests, as well as a matter, she felt, of middle-class uprightness. But it was also something more. Clara had long ago pledged in her own mind to tend the fire of her husband's genius. Henry, she imagined, might well be inspired by the sentiments of those geniuses who had come along before his time, and she intended to introduce him to as many of them as she could.

Although Clara was by nature a frugal woman, in this new

endeavor she spared no expense. She was a lifelong reader and had always loved books, but she had not always been in a position to collect them. When she and Henry first moved to Detroit in the fall of 1891, the forty-five-dollar paycheck Ford brought home each month from his job at the Detroit branch of the Edison Illuminating Company had barely covered the couple's household necessities: rent, food, and tools for Henry's home workshop. Buying books was out of the question. But Clara quickly found her way to the public library and became such a frequent visitor that she was soon on friendly terms with the staff. She carried home novels by James Fenimore Cooper and Sir Walter Scott, among others. Even then, at a time when Henry was working twelve-hour shifts to keep the power generators turning at the nearby Edison substation, Clara had made an effort to share her literary tastes with her husband, sitting him down in the evening and reading to him from Charles Dickens novels—stories of hardscrabble Londoners that Ford seemed to enjoy. Left on his own, Henry was still more inclined to delve into *Mechanics Journal* than *Great Expectations*, but Clara, undaunted, began surrounding him with more and more books. She had faith in their transformative power. "When I visit Mrs. Ford," a friend remarked, "I see almost as many dictionaries as Bibles around the house."

It was not surprising that the first order Clara placed for her new library included Dickens's complete works, in a handsome set of thirty-two volumes bound in red leather with marbled endpapers and titles embossed in gold lettering. Now she and Henry could always enjoy the company of the Dickensian friends they had made during the couple's first difficult months in Detroit.

Clara went on to order the works of the American philosopher John Fiske, bound in maroon silk, which included an everyman account of Darwin's theory of evolution, as well as a volume in which Fiske argued that religion and science were perfectly compatible—a view with which Ford sympathized. A twelve-volume set of Ralph Waldo

Emerson—burgundy Morocco leather—soon followed. Clara knew better than anyone that Henry Ford was inclined to distrust anything he had not learned through firsthand experience, but she hoped this collection of Emerson's essays, evoking as they did themes of self-reliance and American values, might capture her husband's attention. As it turned out, Emerson's way of looking at the world would come to have a more profound effect on Henry Ford's thinking—and on the economy of the United States—than Clara could possibly have imagined. But that was all in the future.

By the time the bill arrived from Houghton Mifflin, Clara had spent nearly three thousand dollars outfitting the couple's library with eight new sets of books. Among them was a fifteen-volume set of the works of John Burroughs, a writer whose essays and poems Ford had first encountered in the McGuffey readers he fondly remembered from his boyhood.

As his automobile company flung the nation into the future, Henry Ford himself had begun looking toward the past, back to the youth he spent in the farmland of eastern Michigan. With his fiftieth birthday little more than a year away, Ford was growing more and more fixated on the patterns of rural American life that seemed to be slipping from his grasp.

He was preoccupied in particular by one especially beguiling childhood memory—in fact the earliest experience he could recollect. His father, without telling him why, had once led him out into the fields of the farm where he grew up. They came to a clearing, a hundred yards or so from their house, where a large oak tree had fallen. Ford's father knelt down and, beckoning Ford to kneel with him, drew the boy's attention to a nest that a sparrow had built under the great stricken trunk. "I remember the nest with 4 eggs and also the bird and hearing it sing," the middle-aged Ford now recorded in a shirt pocket–sized notebook he had previously used only for phone numbers and business notes. "I have always remembered the song, and in later years found that it was a song sparrow."

He could still recall just where the log had fallen and how long it had lain there undisturbed in the fields. He also remembered a lesson titled "Don't Kill the Birds" that he had come across in the McGuffey reader he had used as a schoolboy in those same distant days. For whatever reason, these birds, flighty and ephemeral creatures that they were, had begun to feel like a solid link to the rural life that Ford feared was fading away. As his own past receded in time, the rural footing of American life seemed to grow more distant as well. When the Republic was founded, only one in twenty new Americans lived in cities, but now, even in Ford's Midwest, nearly half the citizens lived urban lives, while in the Northeast cities claimed three-quarters of the population. If Ford did not know these numbers, he certainly sensed the shift. It felt as if a curtain were closing on the country's agrarian past.

At the end of March 1912, the Detroit *Free Press* ran an article that resonated deeply with Ford: a celebration of the achievements of John Burroughs on the occasion of his seventy-fifth birthday. Ford had long been aware of the man known throughout the nation as John O'Birds. Indeed, Burroughs was then at the peak of his fame as a naturalist and bird-watcher. He had written more than two dozen widely read books on nature and natural themes, a number of which had recently been adapted into new textbooks that, like the McGuffey readers in which his writing had appeared during the previous century, spoke to the hearts as much as the minds of schoolchildren, who now regularly lined up in the hundreds to catch a glimpse of the white-bearded Burroughs when he toured the country.

As a young man in the 1860s and 1870s, Burroughs had been on close terms with Walt Whitman and Ralph Waldo Emerson—so close that Whitman had found inspiration for several of his own poems in

Burroughs's journal. More recently, Burroughs had befriended Teddy Roosevelt, accompanying the president in 1903 on a widely publicized camping excursion in the newly designated Yellowstone Park, where the two outdoorsmen waged a friendly contest to see who could identify more species of birds. (John O'Birds won but by the slim margin of a single species.) Their rivalry resumed a few years later at a White House luncheon, where the president's other guests were surprised to find themselves ignored while Roosevelt engaged in a protracted debate with Burroughs on the number of notes in the call of a common songbird. "Mr. President," Burroughs had been heard to say, "you must be mistaken. It was not a chippy sparrow if it sang twee, twee. The note of the chippy sparrow is twee, twee, twee."

The *Free Press* article recounted Burroughs's early life, from his education in a one-room schoolhouse outside Roxbury, New York, through his employment as a teacher in a similar rural school, to the birth of his career as a writer, which had begun with the publication of an essay titled "Expression" in the *Atlantic Monthly* in 1886. Burroughs had so deeply absorbed the style and sentiments of his hero Ralph Waldo Emerson that the editor of the magazine first balked at the young writer's submission, thinking it was an Emerson essay passed off as a new work. And he was not the only reader who noticed the resemblance. Thomas Hill, the president of Harvard, quoted from "Expression" soon after it appeared and went so far as to attribute the quotation to Emerson; even Poole's Index, the standard scholarly reference to periodical literature of the time, listed the essay as one of Emerson's works. Burroughs would go on to develop a style uniquely his own—more minutely attentive to the day-to-day realities of nature than Emerson had been—but he never put aside the Emersonian spirit with which he had begun.

Burroughs had used his early literary earnings, the *Free Press* article went on to say, to buy seventeen acres of tangled forest and swampland along the Hudson River near West Park, New York.

He had drained, cleared, and cultivated the land, and built a stone house, which he called Riverby, where he still lived with his wife, Ursula.

Ford read this as a triumphal account of rugged American individualism. It was the sort of effort, undertaken alone against the challenges of nature, that he admired. At the same time, he could not help imagining that Burroughs's effort to wrest farmland out of unimproved wilderness would have been abetted by the kind of technology that begat his Model T.


In the wake of the *Free Press* article, Ford began to thumb his way through the volumes of Burroughs's essays that lined the shelves of Clara's new library. He threw himself into reading more earnestly than he ever had before, and Clara, noticing her husband's deepening interest, was as surprised as she was pleased by the result. The books had "quite a marked effect" on Ford's thinking. "They started new currents in him," Clara believed, "and he was no longer utterly absorbed in his car."

A few months later, Ford came across a new essay Burroughs had written for the September issue of the *Atlantic Monthly*. He was dismayed to see that his new hero seemed to believe, as Ford put it, "that the automobile was going to kill the appreciation of nature." In the *Atlantic* essay Burroughs admitted that science and industry had given us certain advantages; employment of what he termed the scientific "habit of mind" had "made the earth a much more habitable place than it was in the pre-scientific ages." But technological advancement of the kind represented by the automobile had come at a cost. "It practically abolishes time and space," Burroughs argued, "while it fills the land with noise and hurry." And as he saw it, the trouble went still deeper. In our obeisance to the businesslike yoking of science to industry, we were trading deep culture for surface facts, hard-won wisdom for mere knowledge, "because," as Burroughs put it, "wisdom cannot or will not come by railroad, or automobile, or aeroplane, or be hurried up by the telegraph or telephone. She is more likely to come on foot, or riding on an ass, or to be drawn in a one-horse shay, than in any of our chariots of fire and thunder."

Ford, needless to say, disagreed. He felt that Burroughs had let his "emotions" carry him away "on the wrong tack." But he soon formulated a plan to set the naturalist back on the right course.

"I had a surprising letter," Burroughs told a friend that December. "Mr. Ford, of automobile fame, is a great admirer of my books—says there are few persons in the world who have given him the pleasure I have." What's more, it appeared that Ford wished to return the favor. "He wants to present me with a Ford automobile, all complete."

Ford's letter and its proposal of what was to Burroughs both an extravagant and an unwanted gift bewildered the old naturalist. "I didn't know what in the dickens to think," he recalled. After discussing the matter with his family and friends, however, he eventually sent back a favorable reply. "If it would please Mr. Ford to present me with one of his cars, it would please me to accept the car," Burroughs wrote.

The first day of the new year 1913 dawned fair and mild. Burroughs spent the Wednesday morning writing in his study at Riverby, but in the afternoon the warmer-than-expected weather lured him outside. He walked through the woods along a rambling footpath that mounted to a plateau some two miles above Riverby to visit the rustic cabin he had built as a retreat from the more constraining domesticity of life at the main house. He had named the retreat "Slabsides," partly as a nod to its cedar log construction and partly as a signal that here he intended to put aside any pretense of formality.

"Some folks object to the name of my little house," Burroughs liked to say, "but it's a rough-and-ready place so why shouldn't it have a rough-and-ready name?"

Burroughs loafed on the porch through the afternoon, soaking up the winter sun and watching the activity of moths that were unseasonably busy in the bushes nearby. The following morning he and his wife moved to a house on Cannon Street, in the nearby town of Poughkeepsie, where Ursula preferred to spend the harshest months of winter. By that evening it had turned cold.

On Friday, Ford's agent, a man named Glen Buck, arrived to deliver the promised Model T. Buck was a witty advertising man from Chicago who had recently taken over the editorship of the *Ford Times*. He had a sturdy, athletic build and a shock of dark hair that fell in a clump over his forehead. It was Buck who a year earlier had designed the winged pyramid logo affixed to the new Model T. Buck called the design "a happy combination of two of the oldest Egyptian symbols—the pyramid symbolizing strength and stability—the scarab wings symbolizing lightness and grace." Although he presented himself as a man of business, Buck was a businessman like none Burroughs had met before. "The best piece of business literature," Buck maintained, "is Thoreau's 'Walden'—and there's not a word of business in it." Burroughs liked Buck immediately.

Henry Ford had chosen an ideal middleman to lay the foundation for his relationship with Burroughs. Buck was "big, artistic, prophetic, poetic and practical," as a journalist had recently described him. He balanced a potent blend of contradictions. On the one hand, he shared Ford's mechanical sensibility. "The man who today doesn't understand mechanical things," Buck argued, "is just as ignorant as the man who doesn't understand literary things." Buck's personal philosophy had been shaped by the automotive industry he found himself working in. But he also had a humanist streak that appealed to Burroughs. "The fool," Buck once quipped, "keeps his automobile in repair and allows his friendships to go to the scrap-heap." He held writers in particularly high esteem—"The writer is the world's secretary," he maintained—though he had little patience for highbrow posturing. "If books do not help you in your business," he had been heard to say, "they will help you to forget your business—and that is more important." Before the day was out, Burroughs was already hoping he would see Buck again.

That afternoon Buck gave Burroughs's son, Julian, his first driving lesson. The family had agreed that the thirty-four-year-old Julian should be the primary driver of the car, and it would be up to him to train his father in its operation. Buck showed Julian how to set the choke control by means of a pull ring that extended between the radiator and the passenger-side fender at the front of the car, and then slowly turn the starting crank to draw fuel into the carburetor. Then Buck led Julian to the driver's seat, pointed out the ignition key, and showed him how to set the timing stalk to retard the spark to allow for a smooth idle on starting. "A spark may consume a city, break a heart, or start an automobile," Buck liked to say.

Then it was back to the front of the car, where Buck demonstrated the proper technique for cranking the engine over, grasping the crank with the left hand—always the left because a backfire could send the crank flying back in a way that was more likely to break the right arm—and pulling it clockwise through a sharp half turn. If the engine caught, you then quickly began to adjust the choke, gradually opening up the airflow to avoid flooding the carburetor. The speed of the engine was controlled by a throttle lever to the right of the steering wheel. On the floor the right pedal operated the brake, while the left controlled the transmission. Pushing the transmission pedal all the way to the floor put the Model T in first gear. All the way out was second gear, while halfway out disengaged the transmission. A third pedal mounted between the brake and the gear selector was used to put the car in reverse.

When Julian had mastered the basic operation of the car, the party, including Burroughs and Julian's children, took the new Model T on its inaugural outing.

The Ford car quickly became a fixture of the life Burroughs led in Poughkeepsie that winter. On January 11, Burroughs and Julian took the Model T out for an afternoon drive along the improved state road that ran north along the Hudson River. A light rain was falling. Burroughs, however, was strictly an open-air motorist; neighbors who watched him spinning over the roads around Roxbury rarely saw the top up on his Model T touring car. Whether a day brought sun or showers, Burroughs faced it in the automobile much as he would on foot, head on, with no shelter other than his hat. On this occasion Burroughs enjoyed motoring over such a fine road and gave the rain no mind.

On a whim he decided to continue on to Rhinecliff, some twenty miles from Poughkeepsie, to pay a visit to a former student from the one-room school on Tongore Brook in the Catskills where Burroughs had held his first teaching job nearly sixty years earlier. The two had fallen out of touch, until the previous spring, when the student, who had been a boy of eleven when Burroughs last saw him, sent him a letter. Burroughs expected a warm reunion with his former pupil, but when he and Julian arrived in Rhinecliff they found the man on his deathbed. In the months since he had sent his letter to Burroughs, he had developed stomach cancer and now had only days to live. Despite his condition the dying man clutched warmly at Burroughs's hand, told his old teacher how important he had been to him as a youth, and how often he had recalled Burroughs over the years. "It was a pathetic meeting," Burroughs told a friend later, but its effect was surprising. "What a vista the incident opened!" he went on to exclaim.

His own past had been brought back to life—"a world as far away as Uranus suddenly made real to me." It was not lost on Burroughs that the gift from his new friend Ford had made this unanticipated encounter with the past possible.

As heartbreaking as the experience in Rhinecliff had been, Burroughs found that both his health and his mood began to improve in its wake. He had gained four pounds since the car arrived. He attributed that to a change in his diet and the warmer conditions provided by the house in Poughkeepsie. But he also found that he was feeling "unexpectedly contented." It seemed that Henry Ford's plan was working. The mobility the Model T provided was giving Burroughs a new enthusiasm for the world around him. "We go out nearly every day in our Ford chariot," Burroughs wrote to a friend on January 12.

Two days later the old naturalist convinced his wife to accompany him and Julian on a motor excursion to Staatsburg, some ten miles north of Poughkeepsie. The weather was clear and crisp, with a light haze over the Hudson, and the route provided breathtaking views of the river. Ursula, however, was unimpressed. She waited out the journey with no sign of enjoyment, "silent as a sphynx," as Burroughs recorded in his journal that evening. But if Ursula was impervious to the charm of the Ford car, Burroughs was hooked. On Wednesday, January 15, he passed up an invitation to dine in New York with Irving Bacheller—a prominent novelist and newspaperman whose syndicate had serialized the work of writers like Stephen Crane, Joseph Conrad, and Arthur Conan Doyle—in favor of another outing in the Model T. Although Bacheller was good company and Burroughs had recently enjoyed a few days with him at his camp in the Adirondacks, the naturalist now preferred to go for a drive. That afternoon he and Julian motored south beyond Wappingers Falls to Fishkill, a round-trip run of thirty-odd miles. Warmer temperatures had brought farmers out into the fields, and Burroughs was pleased to find them at work—"hauling stone, manure, digging drains"—in advance of the coming spring. On January 21 he and Julian motored south as far as Newburgh, twenty miles below Poughkeepsie—"a fine ride." The next day they drove up to West Park to observe the bluebirds.

Within a few weeks Ford's Model T, and the assembly-line system that produced it, seemed to be giving a new shape to Burroughs's thinking on other matters. "Modern surgery does indeed show man to be a kind of machine," he wrote in his journal on January 27. "It mends him and tinkers him up, putting in new parts, splicing his nerves, patching his skin, plumbing his arteries, fixing his bones . . . all mechanical procedures." But the old naturalist kept open the idea of an animating force that gave the physical body its higher life. "It is a machine," he concluded, "plus something else."

Still, he viewed the car as a means to an end, particularly once he learned to drive it himself. All his life he had attended to the progression of the rural seasons—the arrival of the robin in the spring, summer thunderstorms, the cutting of hay at the end of the summer. His new Ford car allowed him, despite his age, to cover as much ground in making these observations as he had in his youth. Although he had been an enthusiastic walker all his life, Burroughs found that the automobile could carry him into remote country he did not otherwise have the leisure to reach. He could drive from one bird-watching haunt to another and thereby canvass the feathered population of the whole countryside in half a day. And he found to his surprise that he enjoyed the sensation of motoring effortlessly over the hills where he had once laboriously driven oxen as a boy.

But his relationship to the Model T was neither purely mechanistic nor particularly friendly. To hear him mutter as he drove along, one might well have thought his mode of transportation was the swaying back of a recalcitrant mare. When his own inattention allowed the car to drift toward the edge of the road, he would correct it with a rebuke followed by a mighty jerk on the wheel that more often than not sent the spindly vehicle careening too far in the other direction. "The trouble with driving," he was heard to complain, "is you have to keep your eyes glued to the road all the while." Friends who rode with him wished he would more closely adhere to his own advice.

As Burroughs took over more of the driving from Julian, who was busy with a new job that spring, automotive mishaps became more frequent occurrences. One chilly afternoon in early April, after Burroughs had again set up house at Riverby, he was returning home from a drive to Port Ewen and noticed as he passed through the gate at the entrance to his property that he had steered the Model T dangerously close to one of the gate supports, which stood adjacent to a locust tree. "I looked back, as I came through the gate, to see if I was going to hit," Burroughs noted in his journal, "and the little beast sprang for that tree like a squirrel." The tree he collided with was not significantly damaged. But the impact mangled the starter spring on the Model T. The lesson was clear to Burroughs. "Never look back while driving your car."

A few weeks later, after a brief but fraught morning drive, Burroughs vented his frustration: "The blind, desperate thing still scares me; how ready it is to take the ditch or a tree or a fence! I fear I have not the mechanical type of mind to ever feel at my ease with it, or to feel the perfect master of it."

But when he took the car out for another drive that same afternoon, his experience could not have been more different. "A run to Highland in the car, through the fresh, fragrant May air in the mid-summer heat. A golden border of dandelions to the roadsides, the apple orchards a mass of pink and white bloom, the fragrance of lilacs streaking the air; the grass lush in the meadows; a thick mist of foliage in the woods and wayside trees; the delicate maple fringe hanging beneath its canopy of leaves; plowing and hoeing going on in the vineyard; swallows darting in and out of the empty barns; and

*John Burroughs behind the wheel of his Model T touring car, Roxbury, New York, 1913.*

the entrancing beauty and suggestiveness of May over all—the calm, waiting, unfolding May."

Mr. Ford's Model T, after disappointing Burroughs in the morning, had in the afternoon given him a veritable magic carpet ride into the kind of rural paradise he had sought out and relished all his life.

But not everyone was pleased by the change in John O'Birds's attitude toward the automobile. When a photo of Burroughs piloting his Model T made its way to the press that April, a journalist writing for the Omaha *Bee* wondered what the great outdoorsmen and naturalists who had known Burroughs in the previous century might have had to say about "the degeneracy of . . . John Burroughs riding around in an automobile."


June 3 arrived cloudless and warm at Riverby, with an intermittent breeze drifting up from the river. It was the kind of early summer day that Burroughs enjoyed most. "Clover blooming, locust bloom dropping, young robins and phoebes and sparrows out of their nests." Burroughs spent part of the day packing and in the evening traveled to New York to catch the train to Detroit. With some trepidation he had accepted an invitation to visit Henry Ford.

Glen Buck met Burroughs at the station when he arrived in Detroit the next day and later took him to see Ford. A meeting had been arranged at the two-story bungalow Ford had built on two thousand acres of farmland in Dearborn, along the Rouge River to the east of the city. Although the situation was unusual—a meeting of two strangers whose initial contact was triggered in part by a basic philosophical difference—any awkwardness quickly evaporated. Burroughs was immediately taken with Ford, and he felt the sympathy was mutual. "Mr. Ford pleased with me and I with him," he later confided in his journal.

The two men soon found their way outdoors and spent their time strolling through the fields and woodlands that surrounded the house. Ford surprised Burroughs with his knowledge of the local wildlife— birds in particular. He was familiar with dozens of species, from myrtle warblers and juncos to goldfinches, nuthatches, and downy woodpeckers. He could even distinguish one sparrow from another— the vesper sparrow, the field sparrow, the white-throated and white-crowned sparrows, and, of course, the song sparrow whose nest he had identified as a boy.

Birds were so much a part of the fabric of Ford's thought that he even dated the occasion of the inaugural operation of his first gasoline vehicle, the quadricycle, by the fact that it coincided with that year's springtime arrival of a particular migratory songbird. "I was running it when the bobolinks came to Dearborn," Ford recalled, "and they always come on April 2nd."

As he and Burroughs toured the farm, Ford pointed out the shelter boxes he had placed around the property to encourage nesting. There were some five hundred of these, he told Burroughs, along with dozens of feeding stations, suspended on iron bars meant to deter hungry squirrels.

More than twenty-five years in age separated the two men. One lived in a rural retreat in the Catskills and had moved in the company of Transcendentalists like Emerson and Whitman, while the other stood at the center of America's burgeoning industrial tumult. And yet they hit it off at once. Ford struck Burroughs as an "earnest, big-hearted man," and he liked Ford's unassuming manner. "He'd never lost the simplicity of his early plain living on the farm," Burroughs felt. "Ford was the real thing, a man of sterling quality."

Near the end of the visit Ford took Burroughs to see the Highland Park plant where the Model T was being manufactured. The newly opened factory was housed in a massive, low-slung structure of brick, reinforced concrete, and glass—there were fifty thousand square feet of windows—that enclosed some forty acres of what had once been a cornfield at the end of a country road on the northern outskirts of Detroit. The sheer "magnitude" of the setup astonished Burroughs. The sprawling facility looked to him like "a wilderness of men and machinery."

But the really impressive developments at the plant were as yet operating on a relatively small scale, in an out-of-the-way corner of the building. In the department that built the magnetos used to power the car's electrical system, Burroughs saw that Ford was experimenting with a new assembly process. Workers perched in a row alongside a steel counter situated a little above waist level. Along this shelf a motor-driven conveyor belt carried magnetos in various stages of completion. At each station a man added a part or two—a magnet here, a bolt or clamp there—until, as it neared the end of the line, a finished magneto took shape. With this system Ford's men could construct a magneto in five minutes, less than a quarter of the time the same job had required a few months earlier. It was the first time such a moving assembly line had ever been employed. And it had proved such a success that Ford was already expanding the process to the construction of the transmission and the engine itself. Eventually, the entire assembly process would be automated from bumper to bumper. At Highland Park it seemed that Ford was producing not just a new car but a new kind of world.

If Ford had impressed Burroughs with his knowledge of birds, it was now Burroughs who displayed a surprising aptitude for matters outside his own field. As the pair ambled through the various departments that made up the factory, Ford was "astonished" by the old Transcendentalist's "quick conception of things mechanical." Glen Buck noticed this too. "So interested was he," Buck later remarked, "that he could scarcely be gotten to leave long enough for luncheon."

When Ford showed Burroughs the original quadricycle, the first gasoline-powered vehicle he had built, the two men clambered aboard the spindly contraption and sat for a while discussing Thomas Edison. Burroughs had crossed paths with the inventor once or twice and hoped to get to know him better. Ford had known the inventor since 1896, when he was an employee of Edison's electric generation company and the boss had encouraged the young mechanic's effort to build a gasoline-powered automobile. In the intervening years he had come to think of him as a close friend, though he still referred to him as "Mr. Edison." Little did Ford suspect that afternoon that his burgeoning friendship with Burroughs would serve to deepen his relationship with Edison and that the three would soon find themselves exploring the country together.

As Ford and Burroughs continued their tour through the plant, the two new friends also talked of Emerson and Whitman. Ford expressed his admiration for those giants of Transcendentalism but insisted that his own favorite writer was John Burroughs. For the most part, though, it was the astonishing operation of the factory that held their attention that day.

*Henry Ford and John Burroughs seated in Ford's 1896 quadricycle, June 1913.*

Yet even here, at what was likely the world's most advanced manufacturing plant, Burroughs found evidence of the other side of Ford's
personality—the man who had not forgotten the plain life of his boyhood. Although Ford was rarely to be found in the wood-paneled office
assigned to him as president of the motor company, there was one
feature that made him enjoy stopping by from time to time: next to
the immense window at one end of the office he had set up a telescope

that allowed him to observe the birds that made their home on the farmland that lay beyond the factory walls.

As the two men left the Highland Park plant that afternoon, they paused for a moment to watch the finished Model Ts emerging from the far end of the assembly line. "The Ford cars grow before your eyes," Burroughs wrote in his journal. Ford's pride in the efficiency of the production line, and in the product itself, was evident.

"While we stood looking at the cars as they rolled forth," Burroughs recalled, "he pointed to one that was a little finer in its fixings and said, 'That's for you.'" Burroughs protested, reminding Ford that he had already given him a car. But Ford wouldn't hear it. Even a Ford car would not last forever, he said. Besides that, he wanted to do it. "Giving away a car is no more to me than giving away a jackknife would be to most men," Ford told Burroughs.

Not long after he had watched the trim, newly built cars emerging from Mr. Ford's factory, Burroughs underwent an experience that left him with an entirely different feeling about the Model T.

He was staying at the time in the house he called Woodchuck Lodge, a rustic, two-story cabin a mile or so away from the family homestead near Roxbury, where Burroughs had grown up. His older brother Curtis had built the house and taken on ownership of half the family farm when Burroughs was a boy and had then fallen into financial difficulties. Burroughs had since made several loans to his brother to help maintain the house and keep it and the farmland that went with it in the family. For the last several years Burroughs had used Woodchuck Lodge as his summer house.

"The place is still home to me and always will be," he told his friend Clifton Johnson. "The air seems to agree with me better than that down by the Hudson, and how restful the long, flowing lines of the landscape are! No other region on earth compares to this for me."

On the evening of June 28, Burroughs awoke in the middle of the night with a concern about the car. It had been a warm afternoon, and he had driven to Roxbury and back, which must have put the Model T in his thoughts. But it was not the drive he thought of now: it was the way he had to park the car on returning home.

"When I'm up in the Catskills at Woodchuck Lodge," he later explained to Johnson, "I keep the car in an old barn and have to run it up a steep rise to get in the door. I was always timid about that on account of the power I had to use and the necessity of shutting it off properly." Burroughs was well aware of the danger if he failed to handle the car just right. "I told myself, 'If you lose control you'll smash right through the other side of the barn, where there's a fall of fifteen feet down onto some rocks—and there you'll be!"

When Burroughs found himself worrying about this problem in the predawn hours, he determined to remedy the situation by securing a rope across the back of the barn to serve as a safety barrier. That idea eased his mind enough for sleep, and in the morning he thought no more of it.

That afternoon, a lovely warm Sunday, he drove his son, Julian, to the train station. It was a pleasant drive, but as he returned home Burroughs let himself get "rattled" and lost control of the vehicle. "I went into the barn as if the devil was after me." The Model T accelerated wildly, and the next thing Burroughs knew "it burst through the side of the barn like an explosion."

To Burroughs's surprise and relief, the car came to an abrupt halt. The front axle was hanging over the drop, and the shaken driver could see the rocks below. But as the front wheels dropped over the edge, the Ford's flywheel had crashed into the floor of the barn, stopping its wild forward momentum just in the nick of time. "Only for that I'd have been in eternity," Burroughs believed.

"I just got rattled and couldn't stop the cantankerous beast," Burroughs later explained to his Roxbury neighbor Harriet Shatraw.

Burroughs recalled the story with an air of humor, laughing as he re-created the scene. But he knew it had in fact been a close call. "It was a humiliating experience," he said at last. "Yes! Yes! A very humiliating experience."

His humiliation stemmed in part from the fact that Burroughs had violated one of the two cardinal rules of driving that Ford himself had set down for him: "You mustn't go fast in ticklish places, and you mustn't take your hands off the steering-wheel to point." At least, Burroughs could console himself, he had not been pointing.

The day after the accident a few friends turned up to help Burroughs haul the dangling Model T back from the precipice into the barn. He found that the radiator had been crushed, but there was less damage than might have been expected, and the car still ran. Nonetheless, Burroughs was a chastened man. He hired a local garage operator to give driving lessons to a young friend who was visiting Burroughs for the summer. Burroughs himself would be a passenger from now on—or for now at least.

# 2

# COMPENSATION

With stocks and bonds in a steep decline during the summer of 1913, the press was beginning to take still greater note of the success Henry Ford had made of his automotive concern. An article in the *Wall Street Journal* observed that over the previous five years Ford had turned himself into the nation's most successful industrialist, reporting that he "is said to have more actual cash on deposit than any single individual in the United States." And with Ford sales booming—two hundred thousand cars in the previous twelve months—his wealth would only rise, while speculators on Wall Street watched theirs evaporate. It was rumored that Ford Motor Company would soon pay stockholders a dividend of some ten million dollars, of which Ford himself, as majority shareholder, would receive somewhat more than half.

In Dearborn, Ford signed a contract in July to build a two-million-dollar mansion on the three-thousand-acre estate where he and Burroughs had enjoyed a bird-watching walk together. He also began making plans to visit his new friend at Burroughs's family farm in Roxbury, New York.

Meanwhile, newspapers across the country were quoting Ford's prediction that lightweight vehicles would one day soon achieve what were currently unheard-of speeds. "Lightness is what we are striving for more than any other thing," Ford had said. "It will not be long before the present 1300 pound motor car will be reduced in weight to 500 pounds. This will mean greater speed and a somewhat lower price. . . . Although I am not a speed enthusiast," he continued, "I see no reason why motor cars should not eventually attain a speed of 150 or 200 miles an hour."

At Woodchuck Lodge outside Roxbury, the latter half of July remained warm and dry. By the end of the month John Burroughs was beginning to worry that the spring that supplied the house with water might soon be depleted. What was worse, his literary well-spring seemed to have already dried up, despite the cooperation of the local wildlife: on one walk he had spotted a weasel, a hawk, a mother grouse and her brood, an ailing bluebird, a queen bumblebee, and a pair of phoebes' nests, and had gathered a pint of raspberries. Still, since he had finished work on his latest book, *The Summit of the Years*, earlier in the summer, he had found himself lacking inspiration. He also lacked a place to write.

When he stayed at Woodchuck Lodge, Burroughs liked to set up his writing desk in the hayloft, but since the hay had been cut for the season, the bales of sweet grass had crowded the writer out of the barn. On August 2, a warm Saturday, Burroughs built himself a writing camp at the edge of the tree line on the hillside above the lodge. He named the place Bush Camp. It was a simple lean-to structure, open at the front, with a frame of branches and a canvas tarpaulin for a roof. Burroughs lined the two sides with boughs to form a windbreak. An upturned crate served for a desk. It was a fine place to work, but the dryness, of both sorts, persisted.

Then, on August 7, Burroughs was returning from a hot and dusty drive through the Catskills and was caught in a rain shower. "A fine rain," he wrote in his diary that night. It continued for an hour and a half after he reached Woodchuck Lodge. "Raised the spring a little and relieved the drought."

A few days later Burroughs built a campfire at Bush Camp and lingered there through the evening as a light rain fell. The next afternoon, after a cool and clear morning, found him writing again.

Henry Ford and Glen Buck arrived at Woodchuck Lodge on August 27. Burroughs was extremely pleased to see them both. It was Ford's first opportunity to pay Burroughs a visit and see the old naturalist in his own element. By this time he had read his way deep into Burroughs's accounts of his boyhood, and he was eager to explore the rocky three-hundred-acre homestead adjacent to Woodchuck Lodge, where the old naturalist had grown up. Burroughs was happy to indulge his friend's interest, particularly on a subject so close to his own heart.

Burroughs had been born on this farm in 1837, on April 3, a birthday, as he liked to point out, that he shared with that great storyteller of the Catskills, Washington Irving. Burroughs was the seventh of ten children. The house at that time had been a modest, unpainted affair of a story and a half, planted between the road and the hill that rose steeply to the north. This tree-lined mound Burroughs and his family always referred to as "Old Clump." Water was supplied by a spring some distance up the hillside and piped to the house by a system involving logs that had been bored out with an auger. Burroughs could remember digging up the logs to replace them when they rotted out every few years and began to leak. There were two barns, one across the road from the house, the other in the next field over. It was the young John Burroughs's job to clean out the stables where cows were kept, a chore he found all the more difficult because he viewed both barns as the haunt of hobgoblins. "I would enter the barn with fear and trembling," he recalled.

In retrospect Burroughs did not think he had been much of a hand at farmwork, though he had pitched in with his brothers and sisters and seldom complained. Even unsavory jobs like spreading manure he undertook with a cheerful spirit, while other tasks, like tapping the maple trees that proliferated on the farm and boiling their sap into sugar, he genuinely enjoyed. Burroughs was permitted to tap a few trees for himself, on top of the family sugaring enterprise, and he could still recall the satisfaction he derived when he sold the sugar in the village. "Money I get now doesn't stick to my fingers as that did," he mused. "I used to carry the sugar money around a month or two till the novelty wore off before I began to spend it."

When Burroughs was around thirteen years old, his family, having outgrown the original farmhouse, moved it and built the house that stood on the property now. So massive an undertaking as moving a house had stuck in his memory. "We pried it up and underneath put runners that consisted of two long straight tree trunks, and these rested on skids made of green poles. All the neighbors came to help and brought their oxen." The oxen were hitched to the runners by means of heavy log chains, and, with a great deal of "bellowing, hawing and geeing," they hauled the old house to a new spot in the orchard. That original house no longer stood in the orchard, but the image of its short journey that day remained.

Ford's second day on the farm dawned clear and warm. He and Burroughs took the opportunity to inspect the region's trout streams and hayfields. They tasted milk fresh from the cow and sat together on a shaded porch.

Ford's nostalgia for his own rural boyhood allowed him to settle naturally into country life at Woodchuck Lodge. He chopped wood and cleared debris from Burroughs's spring. When Ford noticed that a nesting box Burroughs had set up for wrens had been invaded by English sparrows, he could not let the matter rest until he had redesigned the box. His modification worked perfectly: wrens came and went at their leisure, but the sparrows could not get in at all. "They tried it and then scolded us for the rest of the day," Burroughs later recalled.

When Burroughs took Ford for a walk to a grove of beech trees that had long been a favorite spot of his on the farm, they found, to Burroughs's dismay, that his nephew, who now owned the farmhouse and the surrounding farmland, was beginning to clear the trees to make way for a new field.

"This is the first place where I ever studied the nature of birds," he told Ford.

To Ford the answer was simple. "Well," he said, "then the grove ought to stay here. Don't let 'em cut it."

Burroughs explained that the ownership of the farm had passed to his nephew. "We'll fix that," Ford said. Before long, negotiations were underway for Ford to buy the farm for Burroughs. His nephew and his wife were to remain there as tenants, and the beech grove where John O'Birds had begun his ornithological studies would remain standing. If Burroughs had reservations about putting himself in Ford's debt, they were outweighed by his devotion to the farm and the faith he had already developed in the automaker's character.

On the evening of August 28 there was rain and the rumbling of thunder, which Burroughs listened to with pleasure, imagining the good it would do for his spring. The next morning at 11:00, he, Ford, and Buck departed for Boston. They motored east fifty miles to Catskill, New York, where they crossed the Hudson River and turned north.

Burroughs had first visited Catskill as a boy of ten or so. Every November his father would transport a load of butter to sell in the town, and one year he took young John along "to see the world." It was his first real glimpse of a world beyond the farm, and it made a lasting impression. "I saw the Hudson and I saw a steamboat, and I saw a railway train, though it was far off across the river," he recalled. "Catskill seemed to my eyes a big city."

Once, leaving the hotel where they had stayed for a night, Burroughs's father had handed John the reins and instructed him to steer the wagon out of the barn. "I started the horses," Burroughs recalled, "but in the doorway I miscalculated and let the hub strike. And there I stuck." His father was angry, and Burroughs was humiliated. It was, in retrospect, the start of a checkered career as a driver—especially where barns were concerned.

In Burroughs's youth the fifty-mile wagon journey from Roxbury to Catskill had taken him and his father nearly two days. Now, traveling by motor car at a leisurely pace, Ford, Burroughs, and Buck covered the same ground in three-and-a-half hours.

By 6:30 p.m. the Ford party had reached Pittsfield, Massachusetts. The weather had turned threatening, and they decided to stop for the night. Burroughs, despite his recent automotive mishaps, found himself enjoying the ride. "A fine drive," he noted in his journal.

They were on the road again by 9:00 the next morning, heading east through mountainous terrain toward Northampton. As the car emerged from a stretch of road shaded by woods, Burroughs noticed a ruined farmhouse by the side of the road, still smoking from the fire that had destroyed it. When they neared the house, Ford and Burroughs saw an elderly farmer and his wife sitting beneath a tree in the yard. Ford stopped the car and approached the couple, asking what had happened. It seemed that lightning had struck the house, and the couple had lost everything in the fire that followed. Burroughs watched as Ford "fumbled in his pocket and took out a hundred-dollar bill and gave it to them." Still, he stood looking at the ruined house, then asked the couple if they had any children. Before he finally turned to leave, he pulled out a second bill and gave them that, too.

Burroughs watched the old couple hesitate, unsure whether they ought to accept so extravagant a gift. When they finally did, Burroughs was standing close enough to see tears running down their faces as they thanked Ford. Later, Ford dismissed the gesture as "nothing" to him. But Burroughs was beginning to feel there was a real altruistic streak in Ford, however much he liked to downplay his own generosity.

Just past Northampton the party made a stop at the tiny village of Hockanum, on the Connecticut River. Burroughs wanted to call on his friend Clifton Johnson, who lived on a farm near the village, and introduce him to his new friend Ford. When they arrived, Johnson treated their visit like a grand event, calling his sons in from their work in the fields, something he rarely did, to greet the visitors. A well-traveled man himself and the author of many travel books, Johnson was always pleased to welcome wayfarers, whether eminent or ordinary. But a visit by Henry Ford and John Burroughs was something to remember.

Burroughs was in his element now. "The moment you strike New England you strike a different atmosphere," he maintained. "The people are alert, they discuss, they have literary clubs." To his mind this was in marked contrast to his own native state. He had created a stir some years earlier when Johnson, writing for a journal called *Outlook*, had quoted Burroughs saying that the people of New York "read nothing but dime novels and the Sunday papers."

The party stayed only a short time, however, since Ford wished to reach Worcester that evening. They pressed on and by 7:00 p.m. they were checking into their hotel.

The drive from Worcester to Concord was thirty-five or forty miles, and by the time they arrived the following day, it was already growing warm. Burroughs was surprised to see how the once sleepy town had changed; now there was "a stream of motor cars all day to the historic places." If the proliferation of automobiles bothered Burroughs, he was nonetheless pleased to be in Concord with his new friend. While the older naturalist had nothing like the industrial operation at Highland Park to reveal to Ford, he did have something commensurate to offer. He could take Ford on a tour through what amounted to the foundries of American literature and philosophy. Ford had arranged to stay in Boston that night, but they tarried in Concord long enough to call on Burroughs's old friend Franklin Sanborn and arrange for him to meet them the next day to guide them around the town's historic sites.

In the evening the party drove on to Boston, where Ford had reserved rooms at the Hotel Touraine, an elegant gray limestone-and-brick building perched at the southeast corner of Boston Common. Outside, a fleet of chauffeured cars standing ready at curbside gave the hotel a modern air. The first impression on entering the building, however, was that one had stepped back in time. The architecture was inspired by a sixteenth-century French château, and the management had gone to some lengths to conceal the conveniences of a modern hotel while still providing the same services. The newsstand was tucked into a hidden corner, and the building's boilers and generators were housed in a separate structure, as was the service staff. Everything in evidence was Siena marble and mahogany, and the fleur-de-lis motif was ubiquitous. Even the ranges, roasting ovens, and broilers in the kitchen were of French design. There was a reception parlor, an elaborately decorated oval ladies' parlor, a music room, barber shop, barroom, café, and grand dining saloon, as well as a separate dining room for children. The hotel even had its own library of more than 2,500 volumes, catalogued and shelved by category— which included history, poetry, fiction, travel, and reference books. Another "feature" touted as a particular refinement when the hotel opened was "the absence of a billiard room."

The *Boston Globe*, in an early review of the Touraine, had called it the "most superb and complete hostelry of modern times" and "a princely abode." Burroughs was astonished at the extravagance of the arrangement. "There was a little party of us," he told Clifton Johnson later, "and our suite of rooms cost forty dollars a day."

After a night of luxury, Ford, Burroughs, and Buck drove back to Concord where they met Sanborn for lunch. A somewhat gaunt, dry man now in his eighties, Sanborn was a longtime resident of Concord and had been on friendly terms with many of the town's illustrious Transcendentalists, including Emerson and Henry David Thoreau—though his insistent proposals of marriage to Emerson's daughter had for a time soured that friendship. He had occupied himself over the years as an editor, teacher—for a while he ran a school where he taught three of Emerson's children—and social scientist. Sanborn had also been an ardent abolitionist in the years leading up to the Civil War. During the trial of John Brown, following the failed raid at Harpers Ferry, with which Brown and his followers had hoped to launch a slave uprising, it came out that Sanborn had been a member of the group, known as the Secret Six, that had provided financial support to Brown. When federal marshals arrived in Concord to arrest Sanborn, more than a hundred citizens of the town turned out to assist their homegrown abolitionist. One young woman went so far as to throw her own body into the marshals' carriage to hinder their efforts to carry Sanborn away. In later life Sanborn had written biographical studies of Emerson, Thoreau, Nathaniel Hawthorne, and other literary figures, as well as of John Brown.

Burroughs had first made Sanborn's acquaintance in 1877 through their mutual friend Walt Whitman. On the way to Canada for a three-week tour that included a week of camping in the woods north of Quebec, Burroughs had stopped off in Concord to see the home terrain of his hero Emerson. Whitman, who had been present at Sanborn's trial for his involvement in the Brown affair, encouraged Burroughs to call on him while he was there. On that occasion Sanborn had shown Burroughs the house where Thoreau had lived in town and had taken him to Sleepy Hollow Cemetery, where Thoreau and Hawthorne were buried. Along the way they passed the house where, at the time, Emerson still lived. Burroughs was by then developing his own literary style, but he remained an Emersonian at heart, and he recalled the powerful effect his discovery of Emerson's essays had once had on him: "I was like Jonah in the whale's belly—completely swallowed by them." To drop in on Emerson at home was more than Burroughs could muster the courage to do. Sanborn did not offer to take him inside for an introduction. So Burroughs took a moment and "admired his wood pile," as he told Whitman later, and the two passed on by. "I like Sanborn," Burroughs added, "all except his lofty coldness & reserve."

After lunch the now elderly Sanborn led Ford, Burroughs, and Buck out to Walden Pond, where Thoreau had undertaken his experiment in living deliberately, spending two years in his cabin there, an experience he then condensed into the yearlong narrative of his book *Walden.* Later they strolled along the leafy pathways of the Sleepy Hollow Cemetery, where Emerson's grave now lay close by Thoreau's and Hawthorne's. The highlight of the day, for both Ford and Burroughs, was a visit to the white clapboard house in Concord where Emerson had lived and written his most influential essays.

Sanborn had first visited this house on a June day sixty years before, when he was still a sophomore at Harvard College. He had heard Emerson lecture a number of times and was on friendly terms with a few of the writers in Emerson's circle. But he had never met the man himself until a chance opportunity arose that summer.

"I had walked up from Cambridge to Concord," Sanborn remembered. He had been on his way to visit a friend in nearby Sudbury, and as he passed through Concord, around 11:00 in the morning, it struck him that he was walking by Emerson's house. He knew it stood where the Cambridge Turnpike met the Lexington Road. Unlike Bur-

*Henry Ford, John Burroughs, and Glen Buck explore Walden Pond, 1913.*

roughs on his first visit to Concord, Sanborn worked up his nerve, turned off the road, and went to the door.

"I rang the bell," he recalled, "and was shown at once into the study, where Emerson sat in his accustomed chair."

Emerson, who had evidently been busy reading or writing, nevertheless welcomed the young visitor who had turned up with no letter of introduction and nothing but the name of one of Emerson's friends to recommend him. Emerson had then just turned fifty, and Sanborn remembered him as a slender, plainly dressed man, vigorously healthy, "with abundant dark hair, no beard, but a slight whisker on each cheek." "His striking features," as Sanborn pictured them, "were the noble brow, from which the hair was carelessly thrown back, though not long, and the mild and penetrating eye."

Despite his aura of gravitas, Emerson had put his young visitor at ease, "except in those moments," Sanborn added, "when he seemed to be removed to an infinite distance from human companionship, and hardly to recognize the presence of those with whom he seemed to be conversing." (Burroughs might well have said something similar of Ford.)

Sanborn attributed those episodes of withdrawal to Emerson's "high poetic nature, to which the phenomenal world presents itself as a phantasm, rather than a fact." He liked to quote a famous passage from Emerson's 1836 essay "Nature" to illustrate the point. It described the feeling of transcendence, when mundane distractions fall away.

"All mean egotism vanishes," Emerson had written, "I become a transparent eye-ball. I am nothing. I see all. The currents of the Universal Being circulate through me; I am part or parcel of God." In transcendent moments like those, Emerson had concluded, "The name of the nearest friend sounds then foreign and accidental."

For Burroughs there was something of that feeling of transcendence brought on just by standing in the great man's house. Although he had eventually met Emerson and come to think of him as a friend, he had never lost his sense of reverence for the Sage of Concord. And here in the house everything had been preserved just as Emerson left it. "His dining-room, his study, library, his bedroom—all look like Emerson," Burroughs thought, "the home of a scholar and thinker."

Returning to the house was a reminder for Burroughs of the role Emerson had played in his own awakening as a naturalist. It also reawakened the feeling of loss he had felt when news of his death reached him thirty years earlier. "With Emerson dead," Burroughs had told a friend at the time, "it seems folly to be alive."

For Ford, it was at Emerson's house that the writer Burroughs talked about with such enthusiasm seemed to take shape as a man. Ford had been, up to that time, neither a great reader nor a profound thinker. Burroughs, for all his fondness for Ford, was not blind to this weakness. "He was a mighty good talker in his own field," Burroughs confided to Clifton Johnson, "but crude in his philosophy. His philo-sophic ideas were those of a man who'd turned his attention in that direction late in life."

But as he and Burroughs made their way around Concord, Ford was more and more enthralled by what the old naturalist had to say about Emerson. "He had so saturated himself with Emerson that at one time he thought as he did and even fell into his mode of expres-sion," Ford told a friend later. "He taught me to know Emerson."

What most captivated Ford in Emerson's philosophy was the notion that every man contained divinity within himself. Ford liked the idea that this divine nature could be brought out not by formal education or religion—neither of which he had much faith in—but by spontaneity and accession to one's own individual genius. He later highlighted passages in Emerson's essays that reflected the mood of individual-ism he was already soaking up secondhand from Burroughs. "With exercise of self trust, new powers shall appear," ran one passage, while another held that "a man contains all that is needful to his gov-ernment within himself." Ford was especially pleased to learn that Emerson believed "machinery and transcendentalism agree well."

Burroughs explained that Emerson thought of technological inno-vations as simply "new and necessary facts." The impact they had on the natural world was good or bad, depending solely on the use to which they were put. Machines like the "telegraph, loom, press, and locomotive" had been shaped by their human inventor "in his own image," Emerson believed. "But in these, he is forced to leave out his follies and hindrances, so that . . . the machine is more moral than we." It is the machine's human operator who bears responsibility for its effects. And what's more, Burroughs and Ford could now agree, if Emerson were alive to see it, he might well view the Model T in the same light.

To Ford's mind, Emerson was speaking directly to the condi-tion of men like Ford himself. "To be great is to be misunderstood," announced one passage he would later mark as noteworthy. At the same time, the altruistic upshot of this philosophy was beginning to tug at his thoughts. Emerson maintained that the "class of men" who were (like Ford) "endowed with insight and virtue" received along with those natural gifts a certain responsibility to others. Ford later underlined a passage that spelled out the terms of this contract. "It is as easy for a strong man to be strong as it is for the weak to be weak." The strong, it seemed, were obliged to use that easy strength in aid of the weak.

As the two men lingered with Glen Buck and Sanborn looking at the gravestones in Sleepy Hollow Cemetery, Burroughs thought it "the most beautiful cemetery I ever saw, a fit place for the last resting-place of Emerson." For Ford, however, Emerson, dead more than thirty years, was just now coming to life.

After their tour of Concord, Ford and Burroughs returned to Boston for a day or two. They met with two of Burroughs's literary friends, J. T. Trowbridge and Nixon Waterman, and later went to the Plymouth Theatre on Stuart Street to see the Canadian actress May Irwin playing a singing teacher in a musical farce called *A Widow by Proxy*—"laugh a good deal," Burroughs noted in his journal.

On September 3 they crossed paths with Thomas Edison and his wife, Mina. When Burroughs had first made Edison's acquaintance several years earlier, he had found him an exasperating man to talk to because of his deafness. "You have to get up close to his ear and howl into it," he once told Clifton Johnson. But now he discovered another side to the famous inventor. "If you happen to touch the right string, and the company suits him, he talks freely, with wisdom and humor."

Burroughs could see right away that Ford and Edison were "warm friends." But to him they represented very different types. Ford was, of course, "the more practical man of business." Edison, in contrast, reminded Burroughs of the eminent naturalist Louis Agassiz, who had once said, "I can not afford to waste my time in making money."

It was a brief meeting—Burroughs and Ford had to catch a 2:00 train for Albany that afternoon—but it set the stage for the blossoming of a three-way friendship that was to last for many years.

In Albany, Ford and Burroughs parted ways, Ford bound for Dearborn, Burroughs first to Riverby in West Park and then back to Woodchuck Lodge.

When Burroughs reached home, he found a letter waiting for him from his friend William Sloane Kennedy, who wondered if the old naturalist had been following the outrageous woodland adventures of artist Joe Knowles that had gripped Boston during his stay there with Ford. Knowles, according to an article that ran in the *Boston Post* on August 10, had ventured naked into the wilds of northeastern Maine "to live as Adam did."

Knowles had asserted, "I am not interested in money and my purpose is entirely scientific. I shall enter naked and take with me absolutely nothing. I shall see absolutely no one." He was to leave records of his adventure, scratched on birch bark with a piece of charcoal, in a cache where they could be retrieved by a trapper and forwarded to the *Post* in time for each Sunday issue. The story grew more sensational each week, and by the time Burroughs and Ford returned to Boston from Concord, Knowles had reportedly killed a deer with his bare hands, trapped a bear, and fashioned himself a bearskin suit.

Burroughs was dismissive. "The artist Knowles, to whom you refer, is unknown to me, and the articles in the Boston *Post*, of which you speak, I have not seen." He had encountered his share of hucksters out to make a buck from nature stunts or literary accounts that misrepresented the natural world. In this case again Burroughs's instincts were sound. It would later emerge that the story of Knowles's wilderness adventures was a fiction and that his only real achievement was lifting the *Post*'s circulation by more than thirty thousand copies.

Knowles's stunt emphasized the way Americans, growing increasingly accustomed to the comforts provided by modern technology—

often the products of Ford's factory or Edison's laboratory—were coming to view nature as something exotic, if not downright danger-ous. It was separate from their daily lives, so that becoming reac-quainted with it seemed a momentous and perhaps risky undertaking.

With Concord and Emerson still in his thoughts, Burroughs had no patience for the carnival view of nature Knowles's stunt implied; he was eager to change the subject back to the Transcendentalist past he had been pleased to reencounter with Ford. "Mr. Ford is the man who gave me my car and took me on a week's tour through New England," he told Kennedy. "We spent two days at Concord, and I got many new impressions of that historic town." It would soon become evident that the visit to Concord, and particularly to Emerson's house, had made a deep impression on Henry Ford as well.

When Ford returned to Detroit that September, he plunged back into the work of refining his moving assembly line. All through the autumn the time it took to manufacture a complete Model T plum-meted, as more and more of the car's components were assembled in the new manner. Despite the success he was enjoying, however, Ford found that his mind kept returning to Emerson. He read the essays Burroughs had recommended and could even be heard quoting the so-called Sage of Concord to friends and interviewers. Perhaps inevita-bly, Emerson's philosophy began to influence the way Ford conducted his business.

A few days before Christmas, Ford was inspecting the Highland Park factory in the company of his twenty-year-old son, Edsel, who had recently begun to learn the automobile business. As Ford and Edsel walked through the assembly area, they came across two of Ford's production workers "trying to bash each other's brains out." Ford stopped the fight but found that he could not let the episode go. When he asked himself what it was that drove men to behave in such a way, the answer he came to was poverty.

Many of his employees were stuck in a condition that brought out the weakest elements of their nature. What men like this needed, as Ford recalled Emerson saying, was someone to inspire them to become the best they could be. In an essay titled "Compensation," which was becoming Ford's favorite piece of Emerson's writing, the philosopher spoke even more directly to the question Ford was confronting. "In labor as in life, there can be no cheating," Emerson warned. "The swindler swindles himself." What, Ford began to wonder, was a fair price for a man's work?

Less than a week into the new year of 1914, Ford announced that he would begin paying his workers five dollars for a day of work, more than doubling the going rate. He was also reducing the workday itself from nine hours to eight. It was a move that stunned the nation. Even members of Ford's own staff predicted that it would bankrupt the company, if not the entire industry.

Soon after the wage hike was announced, a reporter from the pro-labor *Chicago Day Book* turned up at Ford's Detroit office to ask the question on everybody's mind: "What made him do it?"

The reporter found Ford unruffled by the developments that were causing such a stir in the world beyond his office. "Today he is just as he was a week ago," she wrote of the automaker. Even with the eyes of the nation upon him, Ford's manner remained "unpretentious," his appearance that of "a man who works at least a part of the day until the sweat is on his brow."

It was only when Ford looked out through the enormous window from which he ordinarily observed his birds that the reporter saw a ripple of emotion pass over his face. Outside could be seen "great crowds of needy men, most of whom bore unmistakable signs of impoverishment." Word that Ford intended to hire thousands of new employees at the five-dollar wage had brought these men to his door in the hope of improving their lot in life. In answer to the reporter's question of why, Ford simply said that paying a reasonable wage was "an act of social justice."

The photograph Ford handed over to accompany the *Day Book* article was a recent shot that showed him seated in the passenger seat of the first Ford automobile, a boxy, open cart on spindly wheels that he had pieced together in 1893. His arms were crossed and a half smile played on his face. In the driver's seat, his white beard flowing onto his chest as he looked off into the distance, sat Ford's new friend John Burroughs. It was the naturalist's hand rather than Ford's that gripped the rudimentary tiller that steered the vehicle.

More than anything he had done previously, the announcement of the new wage scheme brought Ford into the public eye. Over the next three months the *New York Times* would publish more than thirty articles about Ford and the operation of his company. Not all of the press was favorable. A piece that ran in the *Wall Street Journal* referred to Ford's changes to the company's compensation plan as "economic blunders, if not crimes."

But the news landed well at Woodchuck Lodge. Burroughs felt that Ford's decision to pay the men fairly and share the company profits was a true act of benevolence. When the two friends discussed the matter, Ford refused to take credit, saying the decision was just good business. "It gives him the pick of the workers in the labor market," Burroughs explained to Clifton Johnson. "The business is theirs as well as his, and they are stimulated to do their best."

To a dyed-in-the-wool Emersonian, it looked as if Ford had taken seriously the Concord sage's rejection of the market view of success. "If the gatherer gathers too much," Emerson had cautioned in "Compensation," "nature takes out of the man what she puts into his chest."

Whatever else it had accomplished, the pilgrimage to Emerson's Concord had cemented the friendship between Ford and Burroughs. "I guess you and I are in the same 'vibration,'" Burroughs had written to Ford in the wake of the trip. "I feel so much at home with you. We certainly see things through with kindred eyes. Why should not serious-minded men—lovers of truth and excellence—have much in common? At any rate I trust we will meet again many times and see more of the world together."

In the coming years Ford and Burroughs would indeed see more of the world together. But they would not always see eye to eye.

# 3

○━━━━━○

# TRIAL RUNS

A t Henry Ford's Fair Lane farm on the outskirts of Dearborn, Michigan, the morning of Thursday, June 17, 1915, dawned clear and unseasonably cool after two days of showers. Ford's son, Edsel, now twenty-one, and four of his young friends had been eyeing the weather warily on Tuesday and Wednesday as they sorted through camping gear and made ready for what they expected to be a monthlong excursion. There had been tents to prepare, along with bedrolls, kerosene lanterns, foul weather gear, cooking equipment— and ammunition. Because they would be traveling through stretches of rugged, unsettled territory where wildlife still had the upper hand, they intended to arm themselves with a rifle and pistols.

But Edsel and his friends were not bound for the wild timberlands of northern Michigan's Upper Peninsula, where the Fords liked to camp and fish. Instead, they were striking out on a new kind of out- door adventure, one that few Americans had yet experienced. It might even be said that it was only thanks to Edsel's father, among a handful of other automotive pioneers, that such an undertaking was now becoming possible. Edsel Ford was about to embark on a road trip.

In one sense this was all old hat to Edsel. Automobiles were in his blood. When Henry Ford tested his first internal combustion engine in 1893, clamping it to the kitchen sink in the family's Detroit apartment and running a wire from a light fixture to power the spark plug, Edsel, not yet two months old, had been lying in his crib in the same room—until, that is, his mother whisked him upstairs to escape the exhaust fumes. As a toddler he had been taken for rides along the wagon-rutted roads between Detroit and Dearborn in the first vehicle his father built, the spidery, two-cylinder, three-and-a-half-horsepower contraption Ford called the "quadricycle." When he was ten, Edsel had watched Ford build an eighty-horsepower racer that he would later use to set a world speed record, clocking a run at nearly a hundred miles an hour across a frozen lake. Earlier that same year, Ford had given Edsel his first car, a red 1903 Model A runabout that he was able to drive wherever he wanted, provided he could find someone to do the heavy work of starting it for him. By the time he entered high school, Edsel was zipping around Detroit in a more powerful four-cylinder Model N, expertly dodging the streetcars and carriages that still made up the bulk of the city's traffic.

Nevertheless, a month on the road was a daunting prospect in 1915, even to Edsel Ford. Roads, although often well constructed and carefully maintained in larger towns and cities, rarely provided an easy way to travel between cities. And automobiles, even those manufactured by Henry Ford, required a great deal of maintenance and tinkering to keep them functioning smoothly—maintenance that was not always easy to do while traveling long distances. Edsel had already acquired some hard-knock experience in cross-country motoring. In 1910, when he was just sixteen, he and a schoolmate had decided on a lark to drive the Model N from Detroit to Chicago and back. Edsel's fellow motorist had already had a firsthand brush with the risk involved in piloting an automobile over city streets: earlier that spring his car was all but destroyed by a Detroit streetcar when the motorman failed to obey a traffic officer's signal. Still, neither boy expected the Chicago excursion to be as arduous as it turned out.

The 600-mile round trip had taken them four days. Just getting as far as South Bend, 180 miles west of Detroit, turned into an ordeal. Near the Indiana line the travelers had encountered a washed-out bridge and, not wanting to waste time scouting the area for a more serviceable crossing, attempted to ford the rain-swollen river. Midway across, the deepening water stalled the runabout's engine. Edsel and his friend would have been left stranded midstream had Henry Ford not been committed to building lightweight vehicles. As it was, they managed to push the Model N to the other side. When the engine dried out, the pair continued on their way. On the return trip they made better time, but only because they did without meals and rest stops along the way. The trials of that trip left Edsel with a sense of the very real challenges he and his companions now had to look forward to—but it had also given him a taste of the thrill of the open road.

Edsel's traveling companions for this new adventure came from the circle he had fallen in with at the Detroit University School, a private preparatory academy on Elmwood Avenue that was favored by the city's upper crust. Most had graduated three years earlier in the 1912 class. Tom Whitehead had been the business manager on the yearbook staff, where Edsel was an assistant editor; he had recently completed his junior year at Cornell. His father's company fabricated steel used in the construction of buildings and bridges throughout the Midwest. Horace Caulkins had been Whitehead's assistant business manager on the yearbook staff. His father ran a ceramics company that fired Arts and Crafts–style pottery in a special type of kiln that the elder Caulkins had invented. Herb Book had been elected class president in the boys' senior year. He went on to study at the universities of Paris and Munich, but he had been home on a visit when the outbreak of the war stranded him in the United States. Bob Gray, the son of a prominent Detroit attorney, rounded out the group.

Edsel himself had decided to forgo college, as might have been expected, given the dim view Henry Ford was known to take of higher education. The elder Ford saw college as just another form of experience. Its value depended entirely on the quality of thought put into it. "If a young man comes out of college uneducated it is his own fault," as he put it on one occasion; "the same would be true if he came out of a canning factory uneducated, or a boiler shop, or anywhere else." A young man had to seize his education wherever he found it, Ford believed: "It is not something that can be handed to him."

The choice had ultimately been Edsel's own. If he wanted to go into business, he told himself, there was no reason "to waste time at college." Weighing the costs and benefits of a college degree, he had come down in favor of travel and the practical education to be found in the offices and assembly rooms at the Ford Motor Company. But Edsel soon came to regret his choice. He saw his college friends enjoying their free-ranging new lives, and he envied their independence. The road trip now looked like a way to grab his share of their youthful abandon.

Parked on the grassy lawn in front of the Fair Lane barn this June morning sat a 1915 Model T touring car, its optional wire wheels bright in the morning sun, and a new eight-cylinder Cadillac, looking solid next to the featherweight Ford. Both cars had toolboxes mounted to the running boards, and the tops were down. Edsel had secured two spare tires to the driver's-side running board of the Ford. The Cadillac had two of its heavier tires strapped between the rear fenders. These were the two automobiles that Edsel and his friends intended to drive from Dearborn west across half the continent as far as Los Angeles before turning north toward their final destination. They were bound, like so many travelers that summer, for San Francisco. The Panama–Pacific International Exposition was in full swing, and it seemed that

the entire country was flocking to the city by the bay. A good number of the visitors would make a beeline for the Ford Motor Company
exhibit, which had been all but overrun by onlookers since the day the
fair opened. Most fairgoers would arrive by train, but Edsel and his
friends had decided to turn getting there into an adventure in itself.

The plan for the first day was to cover the 270-odd miles to Indianapolis, where the party would be joined by Herb Book's brother Frank
and another friend from Detroit, William Russell. The two had traveled ahead by train to pick up a new Stutz touring car that Russell had
ordered from the Stutz Motor Car Company factory. Stutz cars were
in great demand that summer, and Russell had been lucky to get his
in time for the trip. Selling at nearly ten times the cost of a Model T,
the Stutz promised to be a much more capable vehicle than either the
Ford or the Cadillac. But the real test of that would come on the road.

By 7:30 a.m. the temperature had climbed into the low sixties, and
Henry and Clara Ford came out to see the party off. The young travelers clambered into their vehicles. Edsel slotted a leather gun case
between the two spare tires on the Ford's running board, giving him
quick access to a lever-action rifle. He waved his cap, pedaled the
Model T into gear, pulled down the throttle stalk to give it some gas,
and led the Cadillac toward the road.


If his father's recent experience offered any indication, Edsel Ford,
as he embarked on what promised to be a monumental road trip,
could expect the journey to cement the bond he had already established with his traveling companions. In the months following Ford
and Burroughs's trip to New England, the friendship between the two
men had deepened, even as it widened to include Edison. Although
Ford and Edison were longtime friends, Burroughs seemed to cata-
lyze their relationship, adding new interests and a spark of intimacy
to the basic amicability they already shared. It was on a trip to Edi-

son's Florida house, Seminole Lodge, that this camaraderie began to develop, and the three launched into an exploration of nature that would bind them together for the rest of their lives.

Ford had come home from Concord that autumn still more deeply nostalgic for the rural past than he had been previously. And it was not just his own past that interested him. He seemed particularly affected by the reverential way Emerson's house had been preserved just as the philosopher left it, and he became more and more fixated on preserving Burroughs's old family farm in Roxbury and protecting the beech grove where his friend had first become acquainted with the birdlife he now knew so well. Ford stepped up his negotiations with Burroughs's nephew to buy the farmstead.

Burroughs, who had his own attachments to the Roxbury farm, had written to say that he imagined the purchase bringing the new friends still closer together. But he also made it clear that he did not want to see his childhood home turned into a public exhibition. In his mind it would remain a working farm.

"If the place were to come into my possession as you propose, I should want its privacy and seclusion preserved," he told Ford. "I should like to see you have a bungalow here and spend a part of each season here, if that could be, and a few others like you." Burroughs went on to say that Edison had recently paid a visit to the farm, along with his family, and that the inventor had enjoyed his time there.

Like Ford, Edison—born in Ohio and raised, from the age of seven, in Port Huron, Michigan, fifty miles northeast of Detroit—had imbibed in his youth the rural values of the Midwest. His childhood home sat on ten acres of pine-fringed land on a knoll near the point where the St. Clair River flowed out of Lake Huron. The windows of the family's sitting room looked out on both bodies of water, and the back porch opened onto a vegetable garden, behind which stretched an orchard where pear and apple trees flourished. A sickly child, whose hearing troubles began at an early age perhaps as a result of a bout of

scarlet fever, young Edison did not fare well in school, and his teach-
ers dismissed him as either "dreamy" or "addled." His mother reacted
to this judgment by removing the boy from school and educating him
at home, adopting the free rein of his youthful imagination as her
highest pedagogical value. In splendid isolation Edison read widely,
devouring books of history—from Gibbon's *Decline and Fall of the
Roman Empire* to Hume's *History of England*—as well as natural history, physics, and chemistry. In the cellar he tinkered with drugstore
chemicals and built a primitive electrical generator, making room for
the work among bins and baskets of root vegetables and fruits stored
against the winter. By the time he was in his teenage years, the railroad line had reached Port Huron, and he found work on the Grand
Trunk Junction Railway that linked Chicago and Detroit to points
in Canada. Starting as a general factotum, helping to organize and
label freight, he soon transformed himself into a "news butch," selling newspapers and snacks—apples, figs, rock candy, maple sugar—
onboard the trains. By the time he was fifteen, he had taught himself
Morse code, using speeches from Shakespeare as material to practice
on; this new skill opened the way to work in the burgeoning field of
telegraphy and to the world beyond Port Huron and the Midwest.

In many respects Edison was a more natural companion than
Ford for a literary man like Burroughs. For all his drive and
accomplishments—the incandescent lamp, the phonograph, a motion
picture apparatus, to name just a few of the devices described in more
than a thousand patent filings—Edison had a contemplative streak
that Ford lacked; he set aside hours each morning just for thinking.
Even now, he read far more widely than Ford, and not just in the sciences; he still read Tennyson and the Old Testament alongside the
several newspapers he pored over each day. And while Ford still spent
much of his time on his farm, Edison carried the rural world inside
him wherever he went: "Broadway is as quiet to me as a country village is to a person with normal hearing," he liked to say.

Nonetheless, it took Ford to bring the inventor and the naturalist together, although their paths had crossed decades earlier when Burroughs visited the 1876 Centennial Exhibition in Philadelphia, where Edison demonstrated the quadruplex telegraph apparatus he had recently sold to Burroughs's old classmate Jay Gould (who had by that time built a railroad and financial empire on the back of unscrupulous practices that neither Burroughs nor Edison could endorse). Now it was clear the inventor and the naturalist would become friends.

"Maybe he would have a bungalow here," Burroughs's letter to Ford said of Edison. The enthusiasm these two men of industry had shown for his farm gave a new vigor to the naturalist's own appreciation for the agrarian life he almost took for granted. "I should take pleasure in improving the farm and in making several spears of grass grow where only reeds and rushes grow now."

Through the fall and winter Burroughs spent time with Ford whenever the automaker came east, and letters went back and forth regularly between Detroit and West Park. By the beginning of 1914, Ford and Edison had hatched a plan to bring the three men together at Edison's winter house in Fort Myers, Florida. In February the inventor, having just celebrated his sixty-seventh birthday, was buttonholed by a reporter from the *New York Times* who asked about his plans for the trip. The idea, Edison responded, was "to go down to the Everglades and revert back to nature."

"We will get away from fictitious civilization," he went on, "and we expect to be happy and learn much." Even so, Edison could not quite cut himself off from his work. "If I get an idea I will leave my companions temporarily and go to my laboratory and work it out," he admitted.

At 11:00 on the morning of February 21, Edison and Mina drove with their children from their house in West Orange, New Jersey, to the Pennsylvania Railroad station on Market Street in Newark, where they met Ford and Clara and together climbed aboard Ford's private railcar to make the trip south to Florida. Edison, for all his talk of escaping civilization, had not torn himself away from his laboratory until 2:30 the previous morning. But now he and the others were at last on their way to what he told reporters he hoped would be "an ideal vacation."

"I will do a little fishing in Florida," he said, "and we will study the birds and the flowers and the plants."

The following morning Burroughs joined the party in Georgia, where he had spent the previous few weeks with his friend Robert DeLoach, a fellow naturalist and director of the University of Georgia's Agricultural Experiment Station. The next day the Ford railcar was transferred to an Atlantic Coast Line train that, running half an hour behind schedule, rolled into Fort Myers just before 1:00 in the afternoon.

Although Fort Myers was a quiet community with a population of just over three thousand, you would not have known that as Edison and his party stepped down from the train. Some two thousand citizens had turned out to welcome the inventor and his friends. The grounds of the courthouse, adjacent to the train station, were full of onlookers, as were the sidewalks lining Monroe Street. The mayor and a party of civic potentates had boarded the train at an earlier stop to extend the official welcome, and they now ushered the celebrity party to a meeting with a hundred other leading citizens before giving the signal for the start of what turned out to be a parade of Ford automobiles. Leading the caravan were three new Model T touring cars that Ford had wired ahead to purchase for the use of the three friends while they were in Florida. In all there were thirty-one cars, a large part of the rolling stock of Fort Myers and surrounding Lee County. Each was filled with well-wishers. Burroughs and Edison climbed aboard one of the new Fords, while Ford and Clara mounted another, and the parade then made its way up Monroe Street to First Street, turned onto Fowler, and progressed through town to McGregor Boulevard, which carried the party to Edison's house, on the east bank of the Caloosahatchee River. From there Edison, Ford, and Burroughs watched the rest of the parade pass by.

Ford and Burroughs were the real attractions for the crowd that turned out at the station that day; Fort Myers had had a long time to get used to Edison's presence there. He had first visited the area nearly thirty years earlier. In the winter of 1885, initially seeking warm weather and relaxation, Edison had made his way to Florida at a time when transportation in the state was still a haphazard affair. He had taken a train from New Orleans to St. Augustine on the northeast coast, then backtracked fifty miles north to Fernandina, where he caught a Florida Railroad train headed southwest across the neck of the state to Cedar Key. The narrow-gauge Florida Railroad was a Civil War–era train service then limping along on a network of rotting ties and scrap-iron rails. Its trains were so prone to derailments that Western Union had set its telegraph poles unusually far back from the tracks to avoid having them continually knocked over. On the 130-mile trip from St. Augustine to Cedar Key, Edison's train had suffered three derailments. One of these accidents delayed the passengers for more than a day.

"At another place," Edison later recalled, "we ran off the track where there was no operator at the station. I happened to have with me a pocket telegraph instrument. I cut into this station wire and got in touch with Jacksonville. They sent another little train to help us on our way."

From Cedar Key, Edison had traveled by yacht south to Punta Rassa, at the mouth of the Caloosahatchee River. It was there, while enjoying a cigar on the veranda of his rooming house, that he noticed a family embarking upriver aboard a small sloop. Edison asked where they were going. "Up the Caloosahatchee," came the reply, to a rural outpost located not twenty miles upriver. Edison must have liked what he heard about the town. A day or two later the young inventor was aboard a glorified fishing sloop making his way upriver to Fort Myers, where, among other enticements, rumored groves of bamboo promised new fibers for the lamp filament research he was then engaged in.

What Edison found at the other end of his voyage upriver was a sleepy frontier town with a dirt road for its main street. "It was a small cattle village consisting of not more than 40 houses," he recalled. He liked everything about it—its climate, its remoteness, its rustic charm. Before he had been in Fort Myers a full day, he began making arrangements to buy thirteen acres of scrub grass and palmetto thicket on the edge of town. Thirty years later it had been transformed into his Florida bower.

Seminole Lodge, as Edison had dubbed his Fort Myers house, had two matching wings, the main house and a guesthouse, linked by a pergola. This arrangement was a relic of the days when Edison first bought the property, splitting the expenses and the grounds with a business partner. He had then designed a house and had two built, one for his family and one for the partner. After the partner sold his share some years later, Edison eventually acquired that property and connected the two houses.

The original structures had been fabricated by a framing company in Fairfield, Maine, and shipped to Fort Myers by steamer. Each clapboard house was of a simple hip-roofed design with deep, shaded verandas. They were now painted gray with green shutters, and the wooden roof shingles were brick red. On the wall of one porch two large tarpon were mounted, one twice the size of the other. This display was a family joke recalling the day ten years earlier when Edison, after years of fishing for them, had caught his first tarpon, a forty pounder. He had returned home proudly, only to find that his young son Charles, fishing on his own from a small rowboat, had landed a hundred pounder. Adjacent to the house was Edison's winter laboratory, which he referred to as his "playhouse."

The grounds of the estate were lushly cultivated, with flower beds interspersed among plantings of palm and giant bamboo. Flowering vines engulfed the pergola between the two houses. The landscaped gardens were flanked by what the local newspaper referred to as "a large and beautiful park, where deer and other wild life may be seen disporting in the close proximity to civilization." The picturesque surroundings immediately reminded Burroughs of tropical landscapes he had seen in Hawaii and Jamaica. "Pretty nearly an earthly paradise here," he wrote in his journal. "A cocoanut tree loaded with fruit out of my window." He felt healthy and invigorated by the new surroundings.

*Thomas Edison at his Florida estate with John Burroughs and Henry Ford.*

In this environment the three friends soon fell into a comfortable routine. Burroughs wrote in the morning, while Edison slept late and Ford entertained himself. In the afternoons they fished and took walks or drives in Edison's car.

They made "good play-fellows," Burroughs thought. He was coming to like Edison as thoroughly as he already liked Ford. "Edison's is a great mind," he felt. "A great philosopher—loves jokes and good stories. A remarkable man."

Edison liked to build philosophical conjectures on his observations of the unusual flora and fauna he discovered in Florida. He was particularly captivated by a kind of coral that looked like a bush growing in the ocean. "Really," Edison was fond of pointing out, "it is animal matter built into a bush form by the efforts of thousands of insects; it is the work of highly organized individuals massed in a crowd for the purpose of the building."

Edison was coming to think that human life was similarly composed. "What I believe is that our bodies are made up of myriads of units of life," he would later explain. "Our body is not itself *the* unit of life or *a* unit of life. It is the tiny entities which may be the cells that are the units of life." When a person died, as Edison saw it, the community of entities ceased working together as an aggregate. But it was not right to say that the person ceased to exist. "The life-units which have formed that man do not die. They merely pass out of the unimportant mechanism which they have been inhabiting, which has been called a man and has been mistaken for an individual, and select some other habitat or habitats. Perhaps they become the animating force of something else or many other things."

Edison imagined that these basic units of life must be unthinkably small, far smaller than anything visible under the microscope. "I believe the ultimate life-particle could go through glass with the greatest ease, and that not the highest or lowest temperature known to human science could harm it. Such units of life could have come, and possibly are still coming, without injury through the cold of space." As evidence he pointed to microbes, already known to science, that were capable of surviving at temperatures approaching absolute zero. Such microbes, although larger than the entities Edison had in mind, were nonetheless small enough to slip through the matrix of something as apparently nonporous as porcelain.

He also believed that these entities had a memory, and he felt certain that the units themselves lived forever. But he wondered whether, driven by memory, they remained associated with each other in any meaningful way. "If they break up and no longer remain as an ensemble, then it looks to me that our personality does not survive death; that is, we do not survive death as individuals."

By comparison Ford was no philosopher, but the two men did have certain habits of mind in common. On a practical level they shared a willingness to work toward a seemingly receding goal. Their method was to try, fail, and try again. Like Edison searching for the right filament material for his light bulb, Ford was willing to scrap dozens, or hundreds, of ideas as not quite right before settling on the solution to an automotive engineering problem. To Ford, however, it made no sense to speculate about an afterlife, not because he believed that death ended things but because for him the present moment was the essence of life. "Life is always life, and the fuller it is the more present the present is," he would say in later years. "We talk about this present life as if we understood it, and having disposed of it, we are ready to pronounce on another. Well, there is no other, there is only this, going on, going on, and coming to itself more and more. Life cannot die."

The root of Ford's cheerfulness lay in this conviction that experience was valuable in itself. "I have never been discouraged," he liked to say. "I know I am here for experience, and nothing else matters." Even negative experiences held their own value. "What we call evil, it seems to me, is simply ignorance bumping its head in the dark; and every bump is an experience, though the price may seem at times very heavy."

Emerson had held a similar view of the value of experience, but Ford couched all his opinions in his own tone of homespun common sense. Indeed, it was Ford's modesty, unexpected in a man of his wealth and success, that now appealed to Burroughs more and more. "He is not puffed up," was Burroughs's judgment. Ford's concern for humankind, like his love of birds, struck the naturalist as sincere, and he would have an opportunity to observe both during their stay at Seminole Lodge.

The first intrusion on the group's Florida idyll appeared the day after the party's arrival in Fort Myers, when the front page of the local newspaper featured a story about the Leo Frank case, the verdict of which was then under appeal. Frank, the young superintendent of the National Pencil Company's manufacturing plant in Atlanta, had been convicted the previous autumn of the murder of a thirteen-year-old employee named Mary Phagan, whose body had been discovered in the basement of the pencil factory.

Suspicion in the murder had first fallen on the black night watchman who discovered Mary Phagan's body, then on the plant's janitor, also black, and finally on Frank, himself a Jew who had grown up in Brooklyn, New York. The Atlanta *Georgian*, a newspaper that had been acquired by Randolph Hearst a year earlier, had quickly latched onto the story, which its editor saw as a sure route to higher sales. The paper ran banner headlines offering rewards for information, along with pages of photographs of Phagan and her family, intermingled with lurid details about the murder itself. One headline, which ran three days after the murder, read, "Body Dragged by Deadly Cord after Terrific Fight," while another proclaimed, "Girl's Grandfather Vows Vengeance." The following day the ordinarily staid Atlanta *Constitution* joined in the journalistic frenzy, printing an article under the headline "Every Woman and Girl Should See Body of Victim and Learn Perils." Within days the mayor of Atlanta was warning that the inflammatory coverage had fanned hysteria that "might possibly result in grave damage."

During Frank's subsequent trial his defense attorneys, as well as the judge hearing the case, received death threats, and chants of "Hang the Jew" were heard from the throng that gathered outside the courthouse each day. The *Georgian* continued to milk the story, printing a steady stream of rumor and innuendo about Frank, often of a sexual nature, whether it surfaced in the trial itself or outside the courtroom. After Frank's conviction on August 26, 1913, however, the story was picked up by papers outside Atlanta, many of which took a different view of the case. When the judge handed down a death sentence the following day, the Macon *Daily Telegraph* reported that many believed that the jury had been swayed by racial prejudice. "They are convinced that Frank was not prosecuted but persecuted." The verdict against Frank, some argued later, was in another sense an indictment of industrialism itself, a form of protest against the intrusion of the factory system into the agrarian South. Because the region remained, as one observer of the Frank case noted, "distinctive in its attachment to tradition, its relative isolation from the stream of late nineteenth-century immigration, and its esteem for rural values," it "proved more resistant to industrialism than other sections of the country." Going into the trial, Frank already had two strikes, his religion and his occupation, against him.

When hearings began in October to determine if a new trial was warranted in the case, one of Frank's attorneys called his conviction "the most horrible persecution of a Jew since the death of Christ."

The story that ran in the Fort Myers *Daily Press* on February 24 reported that Frank's lawyers, in pressing for a second appeal of the guilty verdict—the request for a new trial had been denied—were searching for one of the witnesses who had given testimony against

Frank in the original trial, a man named Albert McKnight, who had since recanted his testimony and disappeared. An attached story reported that the prosecution's other key witness, Jim Conley, the man who had worked as a janitor at the factory and who had been standing trial for complicity in the murder, had been convicted the previous day.

Burroughs, for one, had strong views on the case. He felt that Frank's trial had been influenced by prejudice and what he called "public passion" and that the man deserved a fair hearing. "Justice should be done," he believed, "the whole thing cleared up, and the guilty man hanged."

He, Ford, and Edison found themselves discussing the case at length. Edison even had a link to the affair: his friend William J. Burns, a private investigator who was becoming known as "America's greatest detective," had been hired to investigate Mary Phagan's murder and, if possible, deliver proof of Frank's innocence.

As it happened, Burns was scheduled to give a lecture in Fort Myers that week for the Chautauqua series sponsored by the local Board of Trade. Edison and his guests decided they would make time to talk with him.

Aside from the Chautauqua lectures, the big attraction in Fort Myers that week was the Boosters' Club carnival, a fundraising event that brought the Wise United Shows circus and carnival to town. On Tuesday evening, February 24, Edison took Ford and Burroughs to see the spectacle. They went first to the Motordrome to watch motorcycles chase one other around a large wooden bowl, the roaring machines rising onto the nearly vertical walls of the structure as the speeds grew faster and faster. There were three riders roaring around the 76-degree walls of the track, which was billed as the largest ever built.

After the motordrome show they made their way to the big top, where a sizable crowd had assembled to watch aerialist Edward Millette run through a daring routine on the trapeze. The performance reached its climax with Millette executing a no-hands headstand on the swinging trapeze bar. Millette's son Ira then performed a routine that involved "juggling and drinking while standing on his head on a trapeze." This was followed by a clown baseball game and a performance by trained dogs "that can do everything but talk."

Before calling it an evening, Edison's party strolled through the midway, where a vaudeville troupe was performing alongside a freak show—"seven shows in one: a collection of freaks from all parts of the country"—and a re-creation of life on an antebellum plantation, in which the harsh reality of slavery was obscured by a false image of a simpler past.

Alongside the traditional features of the carnival—like the trapeze artists and the jugglers—the roaring motorcycles and the idealized plantation on display that evening seemed to illustrate the friction Ford himself had recently felt between the promise of an industrial future and the longing for an agricultural past. It had been his need to connect these two sides of himself that once inspired him to send a Model T to Burroughs.

Ford himself may have played a big part in bringing this industrial future to Fort Myers, but he was not immune from the accompanying bureaucracy. On Wednesday, Ford went with Edison's son Charles to the courthouse, to meet with H. A. Blake, the county tax collector. Blake issued Ford a license to operate his automobile in Fort Myers and surrounding Lee County. Ford, the man who had made the automobile available to more Americans than any other manufacturer of his time, had had to apply, like anyone else, for a driver's license—at a time so early in the history of the automobile that it was only the hundred-and-fifth license granted in that county.

Detective William Burns arrived in Fort Myers at noon on Thursday, and that evening the three friends went into town to hear him speak. Burns lectured on the subject of "American Citizenship," but he interlaced his comments on women's suffrage and political responsibility with allusions to his work as a detective. "Every criminal leaves a track without exception," Burns declared. "This track can be followed, and if there is any mystery about the case it is because it has not been properly investigated."

Burroughs was not favorably impressed by the lecture Burns delivered. "He was too much like a religious exhorter" for the naturalist's liking. But when the detective accompanied the party back to Seminole Lodge, he seemed to become a different man, speaking more candidly than he had in public. Everyone, including Burroughs, found him both likable and interesting. What's more, Burroughs, Ford, and Edison all came away from the evening with a confirmed sense that Leo Frank had been denied a fair hearing. On March 7 another front-page article in the *Daily Press* announced that Frank had again been sentenced to death and that his execution was set for April 17.

When Burroughs passed through Atlanta on his way home a few days later, he told a reporter who asked about his stay in Florida that the Frank case had been much on his mind. "I discussed it frequently with Edison and Ford," Burroughs said, "and we all were of the opinion that the man should have another trial." Within a matter of days both Ford and Edison lent their names to a campaign calling for a new trial for Frank.

The accord that the three men shared in their view of Frank's case, however, was not to extend to other similar matters. Already Ford was beginning to rail against banks and bankers. "I never heard anyone else abuse capitalists the way he does," Burroughs told Clifton Johnson later. "He howls against them as bad as any anarchist. Yes, he pitches into the whole banking fraternity."

The trouble was that the image Ford was beginning to associate with that fraternity looked a lot like Leo Frank, a well-off Jew from New York. In time Ford's sentiments would erupt into full-blown antisemitism.

The day after Burns's Chautauqua lecture, a new visitor arrived at

Seminole Lodge. Edison's friend John Harvey Kellogg, who manufactured a well-liked breakfast cereal, was a health reformer who served
as director of the Battle Creek Sanitarium in Battle Creek, Michigan. He had made a name for himself preaching a religion of well-
ness that viewed the body as a temple. In a popular book published a
few years earlier, he proclaimed that "food and the act of eating are
divinely appointed means of supplying the body temple with living
substance." Vegetarianism was a central tenet of his dietary faith,
both because of Kellogg's interpretation of biblical dictums involving
food and because he viewed meat as the cause of a range of illnesses,
from gout to cancer. He favored fruit sugars and malt sugar in place
of cane sugar. He also recommended the avoidance of "grease in all
forms, vinegar, baking powder, mustard, pepper, and other irritat-
ing condiments," because he believed these led to cirrhosis, which he
called "gin liver." The list of dietary injunctions was seemingly end-
less, and Kellogg was similarly opposed to a good many behaviors,
most notably "self abuse," a health-wrecking compulsion for which he
believed his diet offered a cure.

Edison espoused many of Kellogg's views, but true to character
he took the ideas he liked and ignored the rest. And he did not fear
inconsistency. He was often heard to inveigh against cane sugar,
while reaching for a second helping of pie. Unlike her father, Edison's daughter Madeleine found Kellogg's visit "a bore." But Burroughs, who had always paid close attention to matters involving his
own health and diet, was intrigued. Kellogg caught Ford's attention,
too. Both men would seek out the doctor's guidance in the coming
years, as would Edison. For Madeleine the tedium of the health cru-
sader's visit did not end when he left Seminole Lodge. A month later
she wrote to her fiancé to complain that Kellogg had sent the family
"pounds and pounds of some sort of medicated chocolates which we
shall never get rid of."

Burroughs had already adopted a largely Kellogg-approved diet during his stay at Seminole Lodge, eating many oranges and coconuts from the trees that grew just outside his room. And the diet agreed with him. One of Edison's guests commented that the now seventy-seven-year-old naturalist rambled eagerly around Edison's parklike grounds "just like the rest of the children." A reporter who stopped by on Friday noted that Burroughs had taken to Florida life with gusto. "He delights in watching the exquisite Florida sunsets from a vantage point on the long pier extending from the grounds into the Caloosahatchee," he wrote later. "He has made friends with every bird on the place." When the reporter asked Burroughs about his investigation of the birdlife in Florida, the naturalist scoffed at the formality of the idea. "I never 'investigate' birds," he replied. "I just stand around and watch them, and absorb."

The reporter had more luck engaging Ford on the subject of birds. When he mentioned a local effort to protect endangered egret rookeries, Ford leapt into the conversation, asking where the rookeries were located and how they were to be protected. He learned that there had been four hundred nests the previous year on a pair of small islands located in Alligator Bay, a hundred miles south of Fort Myers in the Everglades, a vast expanse of swampland a hundred miles long and half that wide that was only beginning to be converted to agricultural use along its outer fringes and served as one of the last remaining egret nesting areas in the United States. As Ford knew, the gravest threat to egrets came in the form of hunters seeking the birds' plumage, which was used as ornamentation in the manufacture of fashionable women's hats. Plume hunters targeted egrets at breeding time because the so-called nuptial plumes that developed in that season were the most sought after by the millinery trade, where the plumes were known as aigrettes. "The aigrettes sell for $144 the ounce," Ford was told, "and it requires the slaughter of six or seven birds, both male and female, to secure one ounce of feather." The plume hunters waited until the egret colony became "ripe," meaning that the eggs had hatched, ensuring that the mature birds would remain close to the nests and fledglings. At that time it was easy to kill the older birds and take the plumes. It was a practice of which Ford was well aware and already deplored.

During the previous nesting season, Sam Williams, a native of the town of Marco on the edge of the Everglades and now a deputy sheriff in Lee and Monroe Counties, had been appointed to serve as warden at Alligator Bay. The task, which he undertook without pay, was to protect the egrets until June, when they dropped their plumage and were no longer of interest to poachers. It was a job Burroughs's old friend Teddy Roosevelt had provided the model for in 1903 when he appointed the first bird warden for the newly designated Pelican Island bird sanctuary, the earliest to be created under the National Wildlife Refuge system. Even outside of Pelican Island, migratory birds were now ostensibly protected by the Weeks-McLean migratory bird act that had passed the previous year with help from Ford, Burroughs, and Edison. (While Edison lobbied friends for support of the bill, Ford had gone so far as to instruct the heads of his dealerships—some six thousand strong—to wire their congressional representatives, urging them to vote for the legislation. When Burroughs traveled to Washington, D.C., with fellow nature writer Ernest Thompson Seton to rally support for the bill, Ford had arranged to have a car and driver meet them.) But there was little funding to support the protection effort, and plumage poaching had remained rampant.

Under Williams's watch Alligator Bay had been raided by a group of hunters who fired on Williams's boatman and the assistant warden, Charlie Allen. The poachers killed several birds before Allen managed to maneuver his way through the densely tangled swampland to a position from which he could return fire and drive them away. "Suffice it to say, that, owing to Allen's nerve and determination and good shooting, the Alligator Bay rookery was saved this season," one observer commented at the time.

Now Williams was seeking funding to hire more wardens and

build a small cabin on one of the Alligator Bay islands to serve as a base for guarding the rookeries there and at Mud Island, to the south. With the nesting season about to begin, Ford quickly offered to contribute to the fund.

As it happened, Ford and the others were about to make their own foray into the Everglades. Edison had planned to take Ford and Burroughs on a camping trip to Rocky Lake, some fifty-five miles to the southeast through the swampland. Burroughs, for one, was eager to see what was to him a new landscape, and he hoped "to hear a panther growl." Ford was willing. But Mina Edison did not like the plan. She wanted to go, too. "I never can see why they think we never want to do some of the interesting things too," she complained to a friend.

It was finally decided that everyone who wanted to would go along. In addition to Edison, Ford, and Burroughs, the party eventually grew to include Clara and Edsel Ford, Mina and the three Edison children—Theodore, Charles, and Madeleine—plus two of their young friends, as well as three local men who would serve as guides.

The following morning they all got up early and put on what Madeleine would later recall as "their oldest and toughest looking clothes," packed their toothbrushes, and piled into a caravan made up of the three Model T cars Ford had provided, as well as a pair of Cadillacs. They struck out to the east, along the Caloosahatchee, and drove thirty miles to the small town of LaBelle, just beyond which they turned south. The road, such as it was, took them through pine woods and then wound its way into the Big Cypress swamp, which encompassed seven hundred thousand acres of cypress, palmetto, and mangrove thickets populated by a frightening range of wildlife: black bears, coyotes, alligators, and crocodiles, as well as a variety of snakes—rattlesnakes, cottonmouths, and coral snakes—not to mention the cougar whose roar Burroughs hoped to hear.

Soon there was nothing to show them the way but a pair of ruts tracing a faint trail through brush, often straying into deep sand that bogged the cars down. From time to time the road disappeared entirely when it plunged into one of the many ponds that dotted the swampland. Bouncing through these ponds on a nearly out-of-control automobile reminded Madeleine Edison of a ride she had taken on the "Tickler" at Coney Island.

When they came to a pond the size of a small lake, the caravan of autos had to inch along for a good quarter of a mile, the drivers feeling their way across a lake bottom that could well drop away at any instant. Charles Edison, who was driving the car in which Edison and Madeleine were passengers, worried that they would not make it across. "The water was almost up to the floorboards. You just had to steer by a sense of feeling the wheel." Finally, after snaking through pine brakes and "lovely groves of delicate gray cypress trees," they reached the lake.

Rocky Lake was an all but bottomless sinkhole covering several acres and ringed by palmettos and reeds. Its water was fresh at the surface, but the depths were said to be salt water. Dense clumps of live oaks grew on the few areas of higher land.

While the guides set up camp, Ford and Charles went exploring and quickly found a flat-bottomed boat that had been abandoned on the shore. When they took it out onto the lake, Ford noticed a number of snakes in the grass along the shore and squeezed off a few potshots with his .22 pistol. Charles was impressed with his marksmanship. From a distance of twenty or twenty-five feet, Ford killed three of the snakes, shooting each through the head.

Ford was not the only one shooting that afternoon. One of the guides managed to get close enough to shoot a wild turkey, which became that night's supper.

After the guides had set up tents, they made pallets of palmetto leaves to serve as beds. There was one tent for the women and a smaller one for the men. Edison and Mina were to spend the night in a third, "a dressy tent with mosquito netting and all the comforts of home," but the inventor, seeing the two smaller tents, insisted that Ford and Clara take more comfortable shelter.

As the party prepared for bed that night, a violent storm broke over the lake. In their dash for shelter the campers wound up jammed into what was meant to be the ladies' tent, "huddled together in wildest confusion." With the rain pelting the walls and water rising all around them, the ridge pole suddenly gave way and one side of the shelter flapped loose from the lines that had held it. Edison and Mina plopped themselves onto the loose canvas to hold it down, while Charles hoisted the ridge pole back into position. Everyone was soaked, as were the blankets—"but we were all very merry," Madeleine recalled later, "and whiled away the hours quoting epitaphs to each other—and singing songs of sunshine and green fields." When the storm let up for a moment, Ford and Clara dashed for their tent, where they found Theodore Edison, rolled into a mosquito net, trying to sleep in a quickly deepening puddle of water.

Meanwhile, Burroughs and Edison were taking the deluge in stride. Each had rolled himself into a wet blanket and gone to sleep. Edsel scurried out to one of the Model Ts and brought back a seat cushion to serve as a bed. Sometime in the middle of the night the tent sprang another leak and the water splattering onto the seat cushion sounded like a rattlesnake to Charles, who thrashed around for a while trying to evade it.

When morning finally came, a waterlogged group of campers emerged from the battered tents. Ford strung a clothesline between two palm trees, and the guides kindled a fire. A few wiseacres "remarked how well they had slept and what a lovely thing it is to live in the open." After breakfast the group assembled to consider the best course of action. It was decided that a secret vote would be taken to decide whether to go home or stick it out in camp.

*In Fort Myers, Burroughs and Ford demonstrate the use of a two-man buck-saw, as Edison, Mina Edison, Clara Ford, and others look on.*

"Everybody except Burroughs and my father and I had had enough," Charles recalled. "They all wanted to go home." Camping had lost its appeal in the face of storms and snakes. In the end Edison's resistance to the negative tide collapsed, and the party began to break camp.

Before they left for home, one of the guides killed a deer, greatly upsetting Theodore, who may have absorbed more of Dr. Kellogg's vegetarian philosophy than anyone had realized. The *News-Press* reporter whose account of the story ran the following day either missed that detail or covered it up. "Numerous deer and turkey were seen," the article stated, "but no hunting was done as the season was closed."

On the rainy afternoon of Thursday, March 5, Edison, Ford, and Burroughs went to hear a lecture given by Charles Cottingham, a visiting civil engineer based in Danville, Illinois, who had spent time in

Panama studying "the work and life along the great ocean-to-ocean route." Cottingham's well-rehearsed talk on the Panama Canal was illustrated by more than a hundred lantern slides. Edison was particularly taken by the subject, and Ford and Burroughs both "expressed their delight with the talk and the accompanying pictures."

On March 6, Edison took the group out on a boating excursion to Four Mile Island, a mangrove-covered point on the opposite shore of the Caloosahatchee, a few miles downriver from the Seminole Lodge dock. There they spent the day fishing. The party enjoyed the trip so much that Edison decided to charter the local mail boat, the *Ada May*, for a longer outing over the weekend.

On Saturday they set out upriver and made their way as far as LaBelle, a tidy village set in a fertile valley some thirty miles from Fort Myers on the edge of the Everglades, which they had passed through on the way to Rocky Lake. What they saw of the area that day stuck in Ford's mind; he was charmed, as the others were, by its natural beauty, but, characteristically, he also saw the utility that lay behind the lush vistas. Ten years later he would buy eight thousand acres of land in and around LaBelle with the intention of developing a rubber-growing industry in partnership with his friend Harvey Firestone and Edison, who felt "confident that rubber trees can be grown in certain sections of Florida very successfully."

The party returned to Fort Myers aboard the *Ada May* on Monday evening. The next morning Ford accompanied Burroughs on a visit to the Andrew D. Gwynne Institute, the local school that had opened not quite three years earlier in a new brick building at the corner of Second and Jackson Streets, where Edison had made arrangements for Burroughs to speak to each class. Burroughs talked about his book *Afoot and Afloat*, a volume that combined several pieces he believed would "appeal especially to the large number of boys and girls that enjoy stories of boating, camping and tramping," including accounts of a summer boating trip Burroughs had taken on the Pepacton branch of the Delaware River and a trout-fishing expedition in the Catskills. His favorite of the pieces was the story of the camping trip he had taken to Yellowstone Park with President Roosevelt in 1903. It had been an outing, as Burroughs put it, with "the most vital man on the continent," on which Burroughs, the bird expert, had seen his first elk in the wild and Roosevelt, the nation's foremost hunter, spotted his first pygmy owl. "I think the President was as pleased as if he had bagged some big game."

While Burroughs regaled the students with anecdotes of his outdoor adventures, Ford took the time to speak to a reporter about his visit to Fort Myers, his first. "Mr. Edison always told me that this was the best part of the state," Ford said, "and now I know from my own observation and experience that his estimate is correct. Your fruit is the finest I ever tasted, and your mild climate is something I do not believe can be surpassed anywhere." The mildness of the climate was especially notable: in the previous two weeks the Northeast and Midwest had been struck by a series of devastating snowstorms, and much of the country was still recovering from a record cold snap. Not even sunny Southern California had been spared the spate of bad weather. Torrential rains there had caused severe flooding that had swept away houses and bridges and inundated thousands of acres of orange and lemon groves, while Fort Myers had enjoyed daytime temperatures in the seventies, with not so much as a nip of frost at night.

The last two weeks at Seminole Lodge had been a great success— but the idyll had come to an end. That afternoon Edison's guests caught the late train headed north. Burroughs would return to New York by way of Atlanta, where he left the Fords to continue on to Detroit.

Burroughs felt reinvigorated. "I am sure we shall all go back to our serious tasks with a clearer brain and more deeply grateful for life and this beautiful world in which we live," he announced.

If the trip Ford and Burroughs made to New England had laid the foundation of their friendship, the time they spent together at Seminole Lodge had cemented the bond. From that time forward, the two got together whenever Ford's schedule permitted. That June, Burroughs traveled to Albany to meet Ford and his wife, who were making their way home from the wedding of Edison's daughter Madeleine. Together they continued on to Detroit and then to the Fords' bungalow on the bird sanctuary he had created in Dearborn. Burroughs spent a rainy few days with them, picking wild strawberries and, when the weather cleared, sailing on Lake St. Clair.

The naturalist was captivated by the "strange far-off, elemental look" of the lake. Although smaller than the Great Lakes he had visited, Lake St. Clair seemed to concentrate the qualities he associated with them. "The vast expanse of the blue sky above them seems to have colored them; the heavenly blue is contagious and affects the water. There is a hint of the sea in the look of the Great Lakes."

Not long after Burroughs returned to Riverby, a tremendous explosion startled him out of bed one night. A terrific burst of lightning had struck below his house and torn its way along a helter-skelter path of destruction some twenty feet long and nearly eight feet wide. Burroughs was left scratching his head at the nature of the damage he found the next morning. The electrical force seemed to have leapt this way and that, jumping from the ground to the fence wire that ran alongside his vineyard and then, skittering out of its course, concentrated its efforts on a pair of bird boxes attached to a free-standing post. "It acted like some blind, crazy material body," he thought. "A sheaf of electrons rooting around like a pig." What made electricity behave that way? It was a question to put to Edison.

The lightning strike might well have been an omen of the days to come; the bonds of friendship that had been so readily bolstered in Fort Myers would soon be tested, as the war and, with it, greater work pressures and differing political views pulled Burroughs, Ford, and Edison in other directions. By the beginning of 1915 the news from abroad was growing steadily more alarming. After a brief Christmas truce, combat had quickly resumed, with Germany in February launching a submarine assault on British shipping. By April a second battle was underway at Ypres, where fighting in the fall had claimed nearly a quarter of a million lives; this time Germany was using poisonous chlorine gas against French and British troops. Although the United States remained officially neutral, Americans, who had largely viewed the war as a European problem, were increasingly split on the question of how the nation ought to respond to German aggression. As the weeks wore on, Ford in particular found himself drawn into the debate.

Most mornings that spring and summer Ford left his Dearborn farm shortly after 8:00 and drove the fifteen miles to the Ford factory in Highland Park in a Model T coupelet, a snappy new body style—half coupe, half cabriolet—introduced only the previous fall. After dropping the car off at the plant garage, he checked in at the administration building, where meetings with his managers kept him occupied for an hour or two. By 10:00, Ford had usually made his escape from the office and could be found wandering through the factory itself, a smile on his face as he greeted workers and chatted with them about the work underway. By this time he had come to know a good many of the men by name and would often ask after their families. Nodding to a mechanic wiping grease from his hands in order to return the boss's handshake, Ford was as likely to ask how a sick child was recovering at home as he was to inquire about a new shipment of parts.

But while he was happiest getting his hands dirty on the factory floor, Ford certainly did not shy away from more sweeping attempts to manage his employees. And in these efforts the line between concern and control sometimes blurred. Now, for instance, he was preparing to launch a new department of dietetics at Ford General Hospital in the hope of convincing workers to eat less and thereby promote efficiency. Recalling his stay at Seminole Lodge, Ford pointed to his old friend from West Orange, New Jersey, as a model. "Thomas Edison eats less and does more than any other man I know," Ford told reporters. "I myself have tried out the theory that less eating is beneficial and I'm thoroughly convinced that it is reliable." Along the same lines, he had recently established a program to teach English to his foreign-born workers. The first class, of some 1,600 men, was scheduled to graduate near the end of July.

Inspired by a comment Edison had made in Florida about the dangers of smoking, Ford also redoubled his campaign against cigarettes, bringing out a new edition of his antitobacco pamphlet, "The Case Against the Little White Slaver." It was aimed at improving the health, and the productivity, of young people by steering them away from cigarettes. The problem for workers was that Ford's plans to help often turned into requirements for remaining employed. "If you smoked, you had to steal a smoke," one worker grumbled. "Mr. Ford would fire them quicker than lightning for smoking." For better or worse, the impulse behind these schemes was deeply rooted in Ford's nature. Where he saw a problem, whether for others or for himself, he looked for a solution. The trouble came when he assumed his solution would work for everyone.

A similar pattern was emerging with respect to the war. Ford's concern over what was happening in Europe and what it could mean for the United States now began to blur into the belief that he, Henry Ford, might take control of the situation.


At John Burroughs's farm in West Park, the month of May had come in like the proverbial lamb. The apple, pear, cherry, and plum trees all sprang into bloom at once. Peas in the kitchen garden shot up two inches practically overnight. Burroughs, a few weeks past his seventy-eighth birthday, observed the coming of the new season with a naturalist's keen attention but without the "snap" he had felt in previous years. He was able to see more of the world in bloom than he once could, thanks to the Model T his friend Ford had sent him two years earlier. Even taking into account the occasional flat tire, Burroughs appreciated the ease with which he could now scout the countryside from the driver's seat of a Ford. At the same time, he felt the outside world intruding into his country life in a way it never had before.

Burroughs had been outspoken about what he saw as America's moral obligation to put a stop to the German kaiser's war. As a result, his mail, once a steady stream of appreciative letters from admirers of his many books on birding and the natural world, now brought unexpected salvos of animosity from readers with isolationist or pro-German leanings. One anonymous correspondent had recently proposed having him "shot from the end of a torpedo." When the war and his mail led him into "long sad thoughts," he took the course most familiar to him. He turned his attention back to the sights and sounds of the spring days that even now, despite the times, buoyed his spirits "like music." On May 5, as a light rain fell, Burroughs was surprised to spot a young bluebird, still being fed by its parents but already flying on its own. Nature continued to take care of its own. That at least was some consolation.

The following morning the old naturalist rose with the sun and caught the early train to New York. By noon he was knocking on the door of the house in West Orange, New Jersey, where Thomas Edison lived. The two spent the afternoon together, taking a long drive in Edison's Simplex touring car. That evening, in the company of Mrs. Edison, they motored into New York to meet Henry Ford at Carnegie Hall, where Edison was to receive the medal of honor from the Civic Forum of New York City. An accolade bestowed annually in recognition of a lifetime of distinguished public service, the forum medal was previously awarded to George Washington Goethals, the chief engineer of the Panama Canal. On this evening the presentation of the award to Edison had brought an astonishing group of luminaries to Carnegie Hall. Others who were not able to be there sent messages, including Alexander Graham Bell and former presidents Theodore Roosevelt and William Howard Taft. Woodrow Wilson sent a letter from the White House expressing his admiration for Edison's "distinguished services and achievements."

Edison, Burroughs, and Ford sat side by side on the platform that night, overlooking a fully packed house, while one speaker after another eulogized the inventor as the nation's foremost "seer, wizard, and master of the forces of nature," as Nicholas Murray Butler, president of Columbia University, put it when he presented the medal. Radio pioneer Guglielmo Marconi hailed Edison as the friend and benefactor of all mankind. Former New Jersey governor John Franklin Fort called him "the most modest great man of the present time," while the newspaperman and former Manhattan borough president George McAneny credited Edison with helping to create the modern city. For all the praise of his inventive genius, however, Edison seemed most pleased when Charles A. Coffin, the first president of General Electric, rose to pay tribute to his "charming human qualities." It was left to President Butler to inject a note that reminded everyone present of the challenges that very likely lay ahead. "If the European war represents the triumph of brute force over the better nature of man," he proclaimed, "this award represents the triumph of man's better nature over brute force."

Through it all, Edison remained perched on the stage like an avuncular sphinx, his feelings hidden behind a cheerful smile, and he spoke not a word. Watching his old friend on the platform that night, John Burroughs felt as if he could read the inventor's thoughts. "Edison hates all the talk and palaver," Burroughs imagined. It only made sense. Such trivialities could mean nothing to a mind like his.

When it was all over, Ford and Burroughs saw Edison and Mina off to West Orange and then made their way a dozen blocks downtown to the Hotel Belmont, a massive new thousand-room structure soaring above Grand Central Terminal, where they spent the night.

It was fair and cool the next morning, May 7, when Burroughs and Ford stepped out of the colonnaded lobby of the Belmont after breakfast. The plan for the day called for Ford to visit Burroughs's doctor for a checkup. Ford claimed never before to have consulted a physician, but he had recently begun to complain of some minor ailments. Burroughs, accustomed to keeping a hawkish eye on his own health, had great confidence in his doctor and had taken the initiative to arrange for an appointment with Dr. Johannes Von Tiling, a forty-year-old German-born physician who had served as the house doctor for Vassar College since his arrival in the United States some ten years earlier.

A little before lunchtime, Ford and Burroughs arrived at Von Tiling's office at 278 Mill Street in Poughkeepsie. Burroughs introduced Ford to the doctor, and Von Tiling soon got down to business, putting his new patient through a battery of tests. Once he had completed his examination, the doctor pronounced Ford "sound." The only hint of trouble he could find was "a little sluggishness in the liver."

As he was explaining his findings to Ford and Burroughs, Von Tiling was called to the phone and excused himself. When he returned a few minutes later, the doctor had shocking news to relay. Around noon word had reached the United States that the British ocean liner *Lusitania*, bound for Liverpool from New York with nearly 2,000 people on board, including more than 150 American travelers, had been torpedoed by a German submarine off the promontory known as the Old Head of Kinsale, in St. George's Channel, between Ireland and Wales. It was not yet clear whether anyone had survived the attack.

Burroughs, already feeling oppressed by the "horrible war," was "terribly upset." But the news pushed Ford in a different direction altogether. "Well, they were fools to go on that boat," Von Tiling was surprised to hear his new patient exclaim. "They were warned."

The following day a reporter from the *New York Times* made his way into Thomas Edison's laboratory in West Orange and found the inventor sitting at his desk poring over newspaper accounts of the catastrophe. When the reporter caught his eye, Edison waved the man away. "I am too shocked by the news of the sinking of the *Lusitania* to comment on it now," he said. "I had friends aboard, and I mourn their loss."

Edison's immediate reaction to the tragedy was characteristic: he shut himself off from outside distractions and plunged back into his work. The *Lusitania* news had come while he was in the middle of rebuilding his entire West Orange operation in the wake of a fire that had swept through the laboratory complex on the evening of December 9 after an explosion in the film department. That night Edison and his son had joined firefighters in battling the flames, while the plant's telephone operators stayed at their posts in order to alert any employees who might not be aware of what was going on outside their respective departments. Before it was over, twenty-five buildings had been destroyed, along with much of the company's scientific equipment and fabrication machinery. Thousands of Edison phonograph recordings and miles of movie film were also lost. Edison had vowed to rebuild— and Henry Ford had quickly stepped in to provide the resources his friend would need to begin putting his operation back together.

Now the reconstruction campaign provided a welcome diversion from news of the war. By the middle of May news wires were reporting that the famous inventor had not seen his family in weeks and was working twenty-four-hour days.

Another week would pass before Edison was ready to talk publicly about the war. Near the end of May he sat down with veteran newspaperman Edward Marshall in the library of his West Orange laboratory for an interview that would run in both the *Detroit Free Press* and the *New York Times*, and he laid out his plan to prepare the United States to defend itself against an attack from abroad. Even with the threat of war looming, Edison believed that a small standing army was sufficient, provided that these regular soldiers were trained not just to fight but also to teach military skills to a much larger force of volunteers who would be called upon as needed. Edison imagined an army of a hundred thousand men, forty thousand of whom were drill instructors. What would make his plan work, he argued, was the stockpiling of a large reserve of munitions and the building of massive industrial capability that could be turned to war production at a moment's notice. "Modern warfare is more a matter of machines than of men," Edison told Marshall. "Most of the machines are simple matters, if we compare them to the machines of industry."

He also recommended the establishment of a research facility dedicated to the development of munitions and other war matériel. "At this great laboratory we should keep abreast with every advanced thought in armament, in sanitation, in transportation, in communication," he said. To illustrate the point Edison alluded to recent advances in telephone and telegraph technology, as well as to the boom in automobile production. No doubt with his friend Ford in mind, Edison proposed that automobiles might serve better than railways to provide rapid transportation for a modernized military force. "It would be easy to commandeer 200,000 automobiles," he suggested, "and 1,000,000 men could be moved 100 miles in a night." Warming to this line of thinking, Edison went on to suggest that the army and navy could profitably learn from the very techniques Ford had used to revolutionize automobile production. "Business, in a sense, is warfare," Edison concluded.

Although Edison's comments on preparedness made it all too clear that industry and warfare had become inextricably linked, the celebration of industrial progress on display at the Panama–Pacific Exposition nonetheless offered, on its face, a distraction from the reports of death and destruction that came crackling across the news wires from Europe each day. Americans in great numbers were by now thronging westward—not insignificantly away from Europe—to visit the fair in San Francisco.

In July, not quite a month after Edsel Ford's departure for the Pacific coast, Edison's seventeen-year-old son Theodore turned up in Dearborn. Like Edsel, he was motoring his way across the country in a Ford car, bound for the world's fair. Traveling with a young friend, he had driven from New Jersey in a 1915 Model T that Henry Ford himself had sent him some months earlier, the first car of that model year to come rolling off the assembly line. After a stop in Akron, Theodore turned north, driving some 170 miles out of his way to pay Mr. Ford a visit. He was eager to show Ford how he had outfitted his Model T for the cross-country journey. It now sported four large Edison batteries, four headlights, two electric sidelights where the basic model had only kerosene lamps, a pedestal-mounted searchlight, an inclinometer that measured the precise grade of the road while he was underway, and a silver-plated horn engraved "To Theodore from mother and father." Pleased by Theodore's efforts to improve on the car's basic features, Ford took young Edison on a tour of the Highland Park assembly plant and showed him around his model farm, then put him up at his Dearborn house for the night.

The newspapers were still abuzz with the story that the secretary of the navy, Josephus Daniels, would name Thomas Edison the first member of a new Naval Consulting Board. Now the latest reports were suggesting that Daniels would also tap Ford—along with Orville Wright and Simon Lake, the inventor of the submarine. With these rumors in the air, Ford and Theodore spent much of the evening talking about the prospects for war and the role economics and industry had to play in the crisis. In Ford's mind industrialists like himself held the key to bringing about a lasting peace.

Like Theodore, Edsel Ford and his friends were discovering both the thrills and the hardships of long-distance automobile travel. At the beginning of their trip that summer, all had gone well. The first day out of Dearborn they had covered nearly three hundred miles—an impressive day's run that had augured well for the rest of the journey. Except for one muddy stretch, the roads had been, although dusty, perfect for motoring. Two days later, however, as they made their way westward across Illinois, the party began to encounter difficulties.

Eighteen miles shy of St. Louis, the Ford became bogged down in mud. Edsel and his friends attempted to pull the little Model T free with a block and tackle but with no luck. Finally, they flagged down a passing wagon and watched while the driver hitched his team to the car and hauled it onto solid ground. Meanwhile, the expensive Stutz roadster was proving finicky: the morning after Edsel's friend picked the new car up in Indianapolis, it refused to start until every speck of dirt had been cleaned from the vacuum pump.

Over the next few days the number and severity of the mishaps mounted. Approaching the Mississippi River crossing, the Ford went into a skid on wet pavement and damaged spokes on one rear wheel. The following afternoon the party was stalled in mud for two hours. Two days later, leaving Kansas City, the Ford was navigating a clay road in heavy rain when it careened into a ditch, cracked a rear wheel, and was stuck for five hours. It took Edsel until noon the next morning to clean the mud out of the car and make the tools and equipment usable again. The Cadillac and Stutz were even more frequently delayed by breakdowns.

By June 29 the party had reached Denver, where they made the acquaintance of Gretchen Wood, the former Countess Stoeffel, who invited the travelers to visit her ranch. Wood was an Austrian by birth, who had studied medicine in Vienna and opera in Milan before moving to Colorado, where she now lived on a 360-acre estate, Wigwam Ranch, in the mountains southwest of Denver. Around a quarter past five that evening, Edsel's party assembled near Mount Morrison, outside Denver, and began the sixty-odd-mile climb up to the ranch. Very quickly the terrain grew rugged, and the road pitched skyward. As night fell, the Stutz strayed onto a rocky outcrop and punctured its crankcase, putting it out of commission for the time being. While the Stutz crew set up a bivouac for the night, Edsel and the rest of the group pressed on in the Ford and Cadillac. On the final steep approach to the ranch, Edsel was forced to nurse the Ford along, making constant adjustments to the carburetor. When his party reached the ranch at last, it was 1:30 in the morning. Altogether they had covered seventy-four miles that day.

The next morning the Cadillac crew retraced the route down the mountain to assist the Stutz gang, while Edsel busied himself patching holes in inner tubes for the Model T's tires. When the group reassembled later, there was time to explore Wigwam Ranch and to have some fun with the western gear Wood had on hand. Edsel suited himself up in full cowboy regalia—hat, neckerchief, chaps, and all—and posed for a photo with a rifle held casually in his left hand. Later he had his photo taken standing atop a cooperative horse, waving his hat in what looked like triumph at pulling off the stunt. The group visited the Cheesman Dam—the world's tallest when it had been built eight years earlier—and marveled at the force of water cascading from its lip. Tom Whitehead ventured down the boulder-strewn cataract below the dam with Wood, who was attractively, if inappropriately, arrayed for the adventure in a white lace dress and hat. The man in charge of the operation of the dam then guided the party through a tunnel that ran underneath the structure. It was an encounter with sheer hydraulic force that Edsel's father and his friend Edison would have relished.

After a day of rest they were on the move again, motoring along the Ute Pass as the road climbed toward the Continental Divide. On July 2, having reached an altitude of 10,482 feet above sea level, they found themselves driving through the Garden of the Gods, winding their way among massive red sandstone formations, some standing and others toppled, that looked like a great geological explosion frozen in time. They spent the night in Colorado Springs at the Hidden Inn, a pueblo-style waystation put up by the parks department to house visitors to the area. Edsel took the opportunity to phone home.

The following morning, July 4, the Stutz was again lagging behind. Rather than wait, Edsel in the Model T left Colorado Springs with the Cadillac crew. After lunch in Pueblo, they drove slowly through the afternoon, hoping the Stutz would catch up, but it never appeared. That night, in a bivouac the party set up near Walsenburg, Colorado, Edsel camped out for the first time on the trip. He was not prepared for the experience, and the nagging alarm of a sore back woke him the next morning. But after a smooth, fast day's run of 176 miles, he was again sleeping in luxury, at the Harvey Hotel in Las Vegas.

The coming days followed a similar pattern. As they traveled westward, the population thinned out; one morning they drove for forty miles without spotting a single dwelling. That evening, July 8, pitching camp on the edge of a petrified forest west of the town of St. John, Arizona, they managed to set up their tent atop a nest of tarantulas. When the spiders made their presence known, at least one member of the party decided to spend the night in the relative safety of his car.

On the morning of July 12, having arrived at the Grand Canyon the evening before, the party rose early and set off along the trail that descended in a series of switchbacks toward the canyon floor. They had arranged to be accompanied by a guide and had hired horses and a pack mule, but since there were only four horses for the party, Edsel and his friends traded off walking and riding. The heat was oppressive, and the nine-hour, fourteen-mile round trip down to the Colorado River and back up to the canyon rim turned out to be, although the shortest day's run of the entire journey, by far the most grueling. That evening they set up the Edison phonograph they had brought with them and listened to music on the rim of the canyon, marveling as the recorded sound echoed back again and again.

Leaving the Grand Canyon two days later, the Model T broke an axle, and the party was forced to flag down a passing hotel chauffeur and send him back for replacement parts. After waiting all day to get hold of all the parts he needed, Edsel found that, night having fallen by then, he had come to know the Model T well enough to put the car back together in the dark. It was yet another tribute to the simplicity of the vehicle his father had designed. A day later the party was in Kingman, Arizona, and soon after that they reached Los Angeles, where they turned north toward San Francisco and the great exposition.

Altogether they had covered 4,202 miles. The Model T had burned through 15 gallons of oil along the way, and Edsel had bought 420 gallons of gasoline—the most expensive tankful ringing up at 20 cents a gallon—for an average of 17.5 miles to the gallon.

While Edsel made his way across the country, Ford, at home in Michigan, found himself increasingly preoccupied by the war, but he was keeping busy on other fronts too. With sales of the Model T booming, he was looking for a location for a new plant, and he believed he had found the right spot along the Rouge River; he spent the summer buying up acreage. Above all, though, he was beginning to catch some of Edsel's enthusiasm for the exposition in San Francisco. His son's reports from the road and eventually from the fairgrounds had Ford itching to make the trip himself. The Ford Motor Company exhibit was proving to be one of the fair's most popular attractions, and he was as eager as the average American to see the scaled-down assembly line that was turning out some twenty Model T cars a day while fairgoers watched in amazement. Like other Americans, Ford was attracted to the utopian mood of the fair, and more than most he wanted to believe that innovation and industry could provide a solution to the problems the war in Europe represented. Once the wheels of his mind began turning in that direction, it was not long before Ford was planning an expedition to visit the fair that fall.

On July 30 he paused long enough to celebrate his fifty-second birthday. He took the morning off and spent the day puttering around his farm on a Fordson tractor before drinking "his own health," as a local newspaper reported, "in iced tea."

# 4

# THE PALACE OF INDUSTRY AND THE GARDEN OF EARTHLY TREASURES

Organizers of the Panama–Pacific Exposition had first con-tacted Thomas Edison with an invitation to the fair in the summer of 1912, just months after then-president William Howard Taft cut the ribbon on construction of the fairgrounds and some two-and-a-half years before the fair opened in February 1915. Edison politely declined the overture on grounds that were the usual basis of his demurrals: he was too busy. By the time Henry Ford began trying to persuade his friend to make a visit to the fair, Edison was in fact busier than he could have imagined.

In August 1915, Edison's company launched a series of "tone tests" in which audiences seated before a darkened stage were challenged to distinguish between live performances and recordings made using the "Diamond Disc" format Edison had recently released. In the early rounds of the tests, which would continue for several years, American contralto Christine Miller sang duets with the Edison phonograph, switching between the high and low parts as audiences strained to determine which sound was a live human voice and which the record-ing. The ear, Edison advertisements maintained, could not tell the difference. But while the tone tests attracted media attention, Edison himself was focused on other work altogether, listening for subma-rines rather than opera singers, and he remained uninterested in the exposition taking place on the West Coast.

Henry Ford took a different view. He had ties to San Francisco: the first Ford dealership in the nation had opened in the city in 1903 under the stewardship of a local bicycle salesman, William Hughson, who had met Ford at a bicycle show in Chicago a year earlier and immedi-ately recognized the sales potential of automobiles. In 1911 Ford had set up a small assembly plant at the corner of Van Ness Avenue and Fell Street, just a few miles from the area that had now become the fair site, to supply vehicles to the entire region. Now Ford's company had three separate exhibits at the fair, and he was already making plans to see them in action. Those plans took on a new dimension on September 15, when Ford arrived at the office to find a telegram from a man named Frank Fagan waiting for him on his desk.

A bespectacled California native who ran the lamp division of the General Electric Company's Pacific Coast operation, Fagan had sprung into action when he learned that Edison was not expected to attend the exposition. Soon he was making plans to celebrate an Edi-son Day at the fair. Fagan now wanted Ford's help in getting Edison himself to San Francisco.

A few days later Ford received a telegram from J. M. Hill, a com-missioner for the exposition, proposing a Ford Day to follow Edison Day. A letter from Hill arrived later that week, clarifying that little would be asked of the two honorees beyond the acceptance of ceremo-nial medals that were to be struck in their honor. No speech would be required, but, if they were amenable, each would be asked to plant a tree by the marina. This, as Hill put it in a letter to the exposition board, was one "of but very few requests made to the greatest living

Americans to plant such memorial trees." Ford and Edison would be joining a company that included Presidents Roosevelt and Taft.

Ford had his secretary write to Edison saying that he would go if Edison would. Edison replied that he would be delighted to make the trip with Ford, but he was at the moment working under pressure to manufacture certain chemicals he had contracted to supply to a rubber tire company. He could not yet say whether he would be free to travel or not. Edison remained undecided until the morning of October 9, when he finally had his secretary send a telegram to Ford saying he would go.

At 7:00 on Thursday evening, October 14, Edison arrived at the home of Miller Reese Hutchinson, his neighbor in the Llewellyn Park neighborhood of West Orange. An Alabaman who had invented the klaxon "ahh-ooga" alarm used, among other things, to signal that a submarine was about to dive, Hutchinson was now the chief engineer at Edison's laboratory. He had invited his boss to attend a farewell dinner before his departure for San Francisco.

Among the guests milling around Hutchinson's living room that evening, Edison recognized Secretary of the Navy Josephus Daniels, with whom he had been in frequent communication since the summer.

The son of a North Carolina shipbuilder, Daniels was a lawyer by training but had spent most of his life in the newspaper business, buying control of his first paper at the age of eighteen. As majority owner of the Raleigh *News and Observer*, he had also made himself one of the most influential men in Democratic party politics. In 1912 he had thrown his support behind Woodrow Wilson's campaign for the presidency, not only endorsing the candidate in the *News and Observer* and orchestrating support for him inside the party but also lending Wilson his Washington correspondent to serve as press secretary before taking up that job himself. With Daniels's aid Wilson had secured both the Democratic nomination and the presidency. The day after his inauguration, the new president, who had taken a liking to

Daniels over and above the political debt he owed the man, returned the favor, naming Daniels to serve as secretary of the navy. Whether his appointment to the post was a stroke of good luck or bad, Daniels had not yet decided.

Early in his tenure as secretary, Daniels had steered himself into conflict with navy tradition. In one of his first acts after taking office, he ruffled feathers among the officers' corps when he departed from the navy's class-bound hierarchy and addressed a group of incoming enlisted men as "young gentlemen." Not long after, he signed an order replacing the nautical terms "port" and "starboard" with "left" and "right," inviting ridicule not just inside the service but also in the press. But the crowning achievement of his first two years in office had come in the form of a general order he issued in June 1914, banning the consumption of alcohol on navy ships and installations. The press again had a field day, lampooning Daniels as a teetotaling landlubber not fit to lead the navy. It was not long before men aboard ship began to refer to the coffee now served in place of wine or beer as "a cup of Josephus Daniels."

In recent months Daniels had become the subject of more serious public debate. In a speech delivered at the Biltmore Hotel in New York in mid-May, President Wilson had indicated that he was relying on Daniels to guide the nation's efforts to prepare for a war that it might have no choice but to enter. At the same time, critics in the press were wagging their fingers at the secretary, blaming him for the diminished state of the navy's fleet, which some maintained was little more than a mothball flotilla of rusting, out-of-date vessels, further handicapped by a shortage of trained sailors to man them. A similar sentiment had taken hold inside the navy itself. As one officer put it, "The fleet is deteriorating like an eagle in a cage."

At the end of June, Daniels had taken the bull by the horns and announced a plan to restructure the navy. His proposal would alter what he saw as an antiquated command hierarchy, impose governmental control over naval supply lines, and make the fleet, as he put it, "self supporting." Meanwhile, behind the scenes he had begun to craft a still more radical strategy for dragging the navy into the modern world. At 3:00 on the afternoon of July 15, Daniels had caught a train from Washington to Newark, New Jersey, and reached West Orange by dinnertime. That evening, shortly after 9:30, he met with Edison at the inventor's house in Llewellyn Park, where the two men talked in private until well after midnight.

Daniels sketched out a plan to put his new navy on a scientific footing by bringing the nation's best minds to bear on the technical challenges of modern warfare. For one thing, he explained, the navy must develop new devices and strategies to confront the threat posed by German submarines. The government could not do it alone, however. The job called for "the natural inventive genius" of men like Edison. The secretary did not hold back on flattery, telling Edison, "You are recognized as the one man above all others who can turn dreams into realities." At the same time, Daniels was candid about the lack of funds for such research. "I unfortunately have nothing to offer you but the thanks of the Navy and I think of the country at large." Undeterred by the difficulties, Edison took to the idea quickly, but he urged Daniels to look beyond the handful of well-known inventors the secretary had mentioned.

"You will need more than a few men to undertake this gigantic task," Edison told Daniels. He advised the secretary to contact the top engineering societies in the country—he named eleven in all— and ask each of them to nominate two of their members to serve on the board. Daniels concurred, and he pledged to follow this course of action. By the time the evening drew to a close, Edison had agreed to head a board of scientists, engineers, inventors, and industrialists who would tackle the problems that had plagued the fleet in recent years—among them the buildup of toxic gases during the operation of submarines under battery power—while also working to develop new defensive and offensive technology that would give an advantage to the navy's ships at sea. Satisfied that he now had a powerful ally in his corner, Daniels caught the 3:00 a.m. train back to Washington to begin putting the plan into action at the earliest possible moment.

By the time of Hutchinson's party three months later, Edison and Daniels had become firm friends. Daniels had himself supervised the installation of the navy's exhibit at the exposition and knew there would be much for Edison to see and be inspired by. He wished the inventor a good trip.

After the party Edison and his wife picked up Theodore and Charles and made their way to the railway station in West Orange. When they arrived, they found a crowd waiting to bid them farewell. As soon as Edison was recognized, he was rushed by a group of young women who wished to kiss him on the cheek. It took him a moment to realize what was happening, but he soon broke into a smile.

"I feel like a prince," the inventor told the crowd, demonstrating his pleasure with a boyish two-step before explaining that he would be traveling in a private railcar his friend Ford had dispatched to transport him to the fair. "I'm going to San Francisco like a prima donna."

Edison had brought a small library on board with him, which included a selection of books on applied chemistry, volumes on education and art—and the latest from his friend John Burroughs. In *The Breath of Life*, Burroughs had collected his recent meditations on what he called "the mystery" of life, "its nature and origin." In his humble way Burroughs compared his effort to understand this vast subject to the explorations of an ant whose measuring of a garden walk is as close as it will come to understanding the geography of a continent. "But the ant was occupied," Burroughs supposed, "and she must have learned something about a small fraction of that part of the earth's surface." It was a suitably vast subject for Edison as he set off across the country.

On Saturday, October 16, the two major newspapers in Akron, Ohio, ran stories about the warm send-off Edison had received at the railway station in New Jersey. Harvey Firestone, at home in Akron, was surprised to read the news that his friend Edison was on his way west to attend the exposition. At forty-six Firestone was the head of the largest tire manufacturing concern in the country. His had been one of the first tire and rubber companies to begin manufacturing tires specifically for automotive use. He was also a close friend to both Edison and Ford. Since Firestone had himself been planning for some time to make a visit to the fair, he now made up his mind to join the Edison party. Soon after he received the news, Firestone sent a telegram to his brother Elmer, the manager of the Firestone company's branch in San Francisco, directing him to set up a commemorative display at the store to mark the fair's Edison Day. Other business, he told Elmer, could wait. Edison was top priority. Firestone had a reservation made for himself and his son Harvey at the Inside Inn, where Ford and Edison were staying. That evening, as rain clouds gathered over Akron, he and Harvey left the city by train, bound for the West Coast.

Henry Ford's own railcar, a new steel model named the "Washington," carrying Mr. and Mrs. Ford and Edsel, had departed Chicago ahead of Edison's train, and reached Omaha at 10:15 on Friday morning. After chasing away some reporters who approached the car, Ford clambered down and walked into town on his own to take a look at the Ford facility at the corner of Twentieth and Harney. He shook hands with the surprised mechanics working there and took time to inspect a plant he had under construction nearby. During the delay the "Washington" was switched from the Northwestern line to a faster Union Pacific train. Ford was back aboard and underway again at 2:00 that afternoon.

On Monday morning, October 18, Ford arrived in Oakland and

caught an early ferry to San Francisco. As soon as he stepped ashore, he set out for the Chronicle Building, eager to see his old friend Joseph Rycraft, who was chief engineer there. The two friends were soon reunited in the building's mechanical room, deep in a subbasement.

Rycraft had grown up on the farm adjacent to Ford's family homestead in Dearborn, and as boys, the two had shared a fascination with all things mechanical. They had started out building models together—including a working model of a threshing machine—and wound up building a water-driven mill that they used to grind sand. But not all their enterprises turned out as expected. Once, while experimenting with a magnifying lens that they used to concentrate the rays of the sun, they had started a fire that burned up a considerable amount of property before it was extinguished. "We did not tell of our part until thirty years after," admitted Ford. "But it was only one of many pranks we played together."

What Rycraft recalled was Ford's extraordinary mechanical ability. "I never saw a man who could see through a piece of machinery like he could. He has a brain like a butcher knife. When he was 16 he could set a jewel or put a mainspring in a watch as good as any watchmaker." Except for the incident with the magnifying lens, Ford's flair for engineering kept him out of trouble. "He never smoked, drank or chewed. As a boy he was studious and industrious. His keen brain was always concerned with mechanical problems."

When the young Ford had begun experimenting with automobiles, Rycraft thought he had taken a wrong turn. "I respected his mechanical ability, of course, and knew he was a hard-working, level-headed fellow, but I didn't think so much of his automobile ideas." When Ford, just getting his start in the business, invited Rycraft to join in with him, Rycraft declined, choosing to move to California instead. If he had regrets about that decision, they did not show through his good humor this morning, and the two old friends parted amiably.

That same morning Edison rose at 5:30, as his train snaked its way through the Sierra Nevada. Gazing at the passing scenery with the enthusiasm of a child, he began to explain to Mina how geological forces had shaped the mountain landscape. Some of the landmarks were familiar to him from the trip he had made on the same rail line forty years earlier. But at one stop, near where he had once gone on a hunting trip, he was puzzled by the lay of the land. "The roadbed is changed," he remarked, and at the next stop a railroad worker confirmed his hunch; the railbed had in fact been altered some years earlier. By 8:00 a.m. the train had reached Colfax, California, where what looked like the entire town had turned out to greet the famous inventor. A line of schoolchildren came aboard Edison's car, the "Superb," and deposited a mound of flowers for the inventor. At Sacramento, the next stop, the botanical wizard Luther Burbank was waiting to pay his respects to the electrical wizard Thomas Edison. Burbank climbed onto the platform of the "Superb," and the two men, who had corresponded but had never before met, shook hands. Edison had long admired Burbank's work in crossbreeding and the selection of new varieties of plants for agricultural and industrial uses. Now, standing before a crowd of onlookers, Burbank praised Edison for his work with electricity and went on, to the surprise of some in the crowd, to predict an unusual outgrowth of his research.

"I believe that in time either through the work of Edison directly or indirectly, communication will be had with other planets," Burbank declared. "There is not so much to be overcome even at this early date, and I expect to see the time when there is transplanet communication."

When the train pulled away from the platform, Burbank stayed aboard. He and Edison were soon involved in an animated discussion of "the dawn of vitality," with Burbank leaning close to be heard and Edison nodding and chuckling. Vitalism, the idea that some special element or spark distinguished living things from inanimate nature, was the focus of Burroughs's latest book. It was as congenial an idea to Burbank as it was to Edison, and it generated a conversation that tumbled on from topic to topic.

"Science is greater than any fairy tale," Burbank eventually said. "You have made the impossible possible."

When Edison's attention turned to the trees and fields passing by beyond the window, Burbank told him the names of the plants. This spurred Edison to ask how Burbank's gardens were faring. "They are not blooming well this year," he replied, "but I want you to come and see them before you return."

Soon they were discussing the nature of water. "A thousand years we have been trying to find out what water is," Edison said.

"And we know nothing of it—that is true," Burbank answered back.

"Only roughly," said Edison, "nothing of its minutiae."

Leaning in, Burbank offered, "I begin to believe with Franklin that it is a fluid form of matter something like electricity."

Before long Edison began singing the praises of a microscope he had recently acquired.

Later that afternoon they arrived in San Francisco. Edison and Burbank had not interrupted their conversation since Sacramento.

Henry Ford was waiting to meet Edison on October 18 when his train arrived at the Oakland Mole, the long railroad wharf that served as the gateway to San Francisco. "I see you are traveling like a prima donna," Ford quipped when his friend emerged from his private railcar.

Together, Ford, Edison, Burbank, and the rest of the party made their way onto a ferry for the short voyage across San Francisco Bay. The weather had been cloudy and foggy in the morning, but it was beginning to clear. Light winds were blowing out of the west. As the ferry rode the choppy water, the three men stood arm in arm, observing the scenery and joking with one other. "They all have gray hair and the eyes of boys," one observer noted.

A lean and distinguished-looking naval officer with close-cropped gray hair approached the group and was introduced as Admiral William F. Fullam, the commander of the Pacific reserve fleet. Fullam, who had graduated first in his naval academy class in 1877, had commanded everything from sailing ships to the latest battle cruisers. "I go on the retired list in two years," he announced, "and I leave it to you men to prevent all war in the future." Edison laughed. "We will do it," he said.

When they reached the ferry terminal in San Francisco, a large crowd had already assembled in the hope of getting a look at the famous inventor. A police escort cleared a path for the party to pass. The itinerary called for them to have the rest of the day to themselves.

Edison rose early the next morning, as he often did, and went out for a walk around the hotel grounds. He and Ford and the others had spent the night at the Inside Inn, the only hotel within the fairgrounds. Perched on a plateau overlooking the Palace of Fine Arts and its artificial lagoon, the 638-room inn was a three-story structure modeled on an Italian Renaissance villa. To the north Edison could see the bay and beyond it in the distance Mount Tamalpais. Abutting the western edge of the plateau was a Japanese garden, where a winding man-made stream flowed through a naturalistic landscape of dwarf trees and shrubs intermingled with pagodas and stone teahouses. To the east the morning sun glinted off the glass dome of the Palace of Horticulture, a massive architectural confection loosely modeled on the Blue Mosque in Istanbul.

It was a little before 8:30 when Edison returned from his morning jaunt and, with a freshly plucked gladiolus in his buttonhole, met Ford for breakfast. Half an hour later they were strolling out into the fairgrounds, headed east along the Avenue of Palms. As they passed through the 435-foot Tower of Jewels that served as a gateway to the central complex of exhibition palaces, Edison gazed up with interest at the spire that loomed over the exposition grounds like a colossal wedding cake sprinkled with candy gems. They were making their way to the Palace of Machinery. When they reached the building, the inventor and the engineer found a paradise of mechanical wonders inside. Edison was enthralled. "He peered into the pumps," one onlooker noted, "tapped cylinder boxes, stood with rapt attention before a Diesel engine and kept up a running fire of comments and exclamations."

When the two men came across an exhibition that conferred an award of merit on the storage battery Edison had himself designed, the inventor pulled Ford aside to deliver an ebullient account of its development. They inspected every inch of a unique million-volt transformer and stood watching a color press rolling out copies of the *San Francisco Examiner* at an unthinkable rate.

When Ford, whose antiwar sentiments were deepening, came across a display of field artillery guns, he first let out a grunt of dis-

*Thomas Edison and Henry Ford at the Panama–Pacific Exposition.*

pleasure, then brushed it off. "Well," he said, "they are where all such things belong—on exhibit."

From the Machinery Building they wandered through the Palace of Mines and found their way into the Palace of Transportation. The Ford Motor Company maintained three exhibits at the fair. In the Mines Building was a sociological exhibit that touted the company's profit-sharing plan, while in the Education Building the company offered a series of lectures and motion-picture presentations on Ford's education program for immigrant workers and the operation of the Ford plant in Detroit. But it was the exhibit in the Transportation Building that drew the attention of the public.

If you wanted to locate a woman at the exposition, the saying went, look in the Palace of Food Products. If you were looking for a man, he would be at Ford's exhibit. More than just a display of Ford automobiles, the exhibit was a working assembly line that churned out more than twenty cars a day.

The operation was supervised by thirty-year-old San Francisco native Frank Vivian. Vivian had done steamfitting work as a young man and attributed his luck in getting hired by Ford to a rainstorm that washed out a construction job he had been working at the time. On the way home he had ducked out of the rain into a building that was under construction on the corner of 21st and Harrison Streets. This turned out to be the future home of Ford's West Coast operation. When Vivian asked for a job, the man in charge said, "How about running some pipe?" And, like that, Vivian was in the automobile business. Before long, he had a hand in every aspect of the Ford operation, from upholstery to the assembly of the Model T bodies, and in 1914 he was put in charge of preparations for the Ford exhibit at the exposition.

The exhibit was an immediate sensation. On opening day so many enthusiastic fairgoers crowded around the assembly line that they knocked down the retaining rails and spilled onto the conveyor. "They were holloing and shoving," Vivian recalled. He had been forced to shut down the line that day and spent the night sinking supports through the floor of the building to bolster the retaining wall, which now held a jostling crowd of eager observers at a safe distance from the assembly area.

As he and Edison watched cars rolling through the line, Ford observed, "They are coming out faster than that at the factory, now, since we improved it." "Yes, I suppose so," Edison replied. "I dare say they will begin to spawn before long."

Ford led Edison onto the assembly floor for a closer view of the operation. Edison climbed into one of the nearly complete cars and made a show of taking the wheel before signaling for Ford to climb into the passenger seat. The reporters on hand were delighted, and for a moment the clicking of camera shutters nearly drowned out the crowd and factory noises.

Next, the two friends visited the Palace of Manufactures and the Horticulture Building. At the California Building, they saw a garden exhibit devoted to Luther Burbank's contributions to plant science, which included varieties of flowering plants—Shasta daisies, roses, and amaryllises—in addition to his signature crop plants, such as rainbow corn and beardless barley, as well as the famous spineless cactus.

If Ford's assembly line represented the fulfillment of the American dream of industrial progress, the Burbank exhibit showed a competing vision: the scientist working in harmony with nature to cultivate and improve the natural resources in which the nation was so rich. In the wake of his conversation with Burbank on the train, Edison was primed to admire these products of the botanist's patient dance with nature. The garden display also fed Ford's agrarian nostalgia—and his obsession with discovering cheap native substitutes for materials, like rubber, that went into the manufacture of his automobiles. Both men were transfixed by the exhibit.

Around 2:00 in the afternoon, Edison suddenly stopped short. "Great Scott, Ford," he exclaimed. "We were to meet our wives at 1 o'clock." They dashed toward the tea garden near the Inside Inn, but it was too late. Clara and Mina had already given up on them and gone back to the hotel. Edison, however, was not ready to call it a day. "I want to see the Panama Canal reproduction," he told Ford.

Among the most popular exhibits at the fair, the reproduction he referred to was a five-acre model of the Panama Canal on which scaled-down ships and barges moved through locks and waterways that represented a significant stretch of the recently completed canal, while trompe l'oeil murals on the surrounding walls gave the impression of thousands of square miles of lush tropical terrain. Visitors were transported through this simulated world on a 1,440-foot-long electric conveyor made up of 144 sections of box seating. As they enjoyed the sights, guests could pick up telephone receivers mounted next to their seats and listen in on a lecture about the canal that was synchronized to correspond with their progress through the exhibit.

Edison's laboratory had designed the audio system that made this possible. It employed an array of forty-five phonograph machines playing new Edison Diamond Discs—and remained in such continuous operation at the fair that summer that it burned through a set of discs every six weeks.

When the two friends found the exhibit, Edison made a detailed inspection of the phonograph system. Then they climbed aboard the conveyor for a ride through the simulated canal zone. Ford, a conveyor expert in his own right, became fixated on calculating the speed at which this one moved. At the end of the ride he compared his estimate with the engineering notes for the exhibit and was pleased to see he was correct.

Around 5:00, after a swing through the "Joy Zone," which housed a bewildering variety of concessions and shows, they turned back along the Avenue of Palms toward the Inside Inn. It had been a long, interest-filled day. Ford and Edison had covered a good many miles in the day's walking. "But both gray-haired men appeared to be as fresh as striplings," one observer noted, "and they had so much to talk about the things they had seen that physical fatigue appeared to have no place in their scheme of life."

When a bespectacled automotive editor from the San Francisco *Chronicle* later dropped by the Inside Inn to interview him, Ford let it be known that the exhibit that most captured his interest was his own assembly line.

That evening Edison and Mina went to the headquarters of the Commercial Club in the Merchants Exchange Building at 465 California Street to attend a banquet held in his honor by the city's telegraph operators. Edison had learned telegraphy as a boy working on the Grand Trunk Junction Railway, and he had taken to it right away. "From the start I found that deafness was an advantage to a telegraph operator," he recalled. "While I could unerringly hear the loud ticking of the instrument, I could not hear other and perhaps distracting sounds." He found that even the clacking of the telegraph of an operator sitting next to him was conveniently muffled by his deafness.

Learning telegraphy had allowed Edison to rise in the world, transforming him overnight from a mere newsboy into a "key man," as telegraph operators were called. But it had given him more than a vocational leg up. Even after he had made a name for himself as an inventor, he found unexpected uses for the Morse code he had learned as a telegrapher. Soon after he met Mina, he had taught her how to make sense of the dots and dashes that made up the code. During their courtship the ability to tap out messages on their hands had given the two a secret language, completely inaudible to anyone else. On one trip through the White Mountains they had grown closer because they were able to exchange private sentiments and address each other with pet names, all with no fear that their fellow travelers would overhear. In the end Edison had even tapped out his marriage proposal in Morse code. "The word 'Yes' is an easy one to send by telegraphic signals," he recalled, "and she sent it." Edison still wondered what she might have said if she had had to speak her reply aloud.

Now, as a married couple, they still used Morse to communicate privately. When they went to a play, Mina sat with her hand on Edison's knee so she could tap out the dialogue that would otherwise be lost on him. At the first meeting of the Naval Consulting Board, Edison made use of the same tactic. He had been appointed chairman, and his chief engineer, Miller Reese Hutchinson, was named assistant chairman. That had proved fortunate when the board met in Washington early in October.

Edison had worried that his deafness, now worsened by age, would prove an embarrassment at the conference. He was able to take part in a one-on-one conversation with some difficulty, but the rapid-fire back-and-forth exchanges of a group discussion turned all the voices into a wash of noise. Yet he managed to preside over the meeting without difficulty. Neither Daniels nor the other members of the board or indeed President Wilson, who was also present, had any idea of the cunning Edison had employed. When the inventor took his seat at the table, Hutchinson quickly claimed a spot to his right and telegraphed notes to his boss to help him keep up with the conversation.

The banquet organized by the telegraph operators of San Francisco might well have made it necessary to employ the same technique when the invited speakers rose after dinner to celebrate Edison as guest of honor. Tonight was different, though. Throughout the dinner Edison sat smiling genially, but he did not so much as taste the food that was put before him. When it was time for dessert, however, his hosts showed Edison how well they knew him. The waiter brought him a large slice of apple pie and a glass of milk—the combination Edison had preferred for lunch when he was a young key man. At this his smile widened, and he dug into the pie with relish.

The master of ceremonies then opened the evening's celebration, not with the usual spoken introduction of the guest of honor, but with a dash-dot-dash-dot-dash. It was the Morse signal to clear the line for the start of a new message. It turned out that the miniature telegraph poles that decorated each table were working models. All the speeches that evening were presented in code. After each extended burst of clicking and clattering, the otherwise silent room would erupt in laughter and applause. Edison, leaning close to the clacking receiver on his table, was able to take in every witticism and "hear" all the praise heaped upon him. Normally shy about public speaking, he even clacked back a message of his own.

The only man to deliver his speech aloud that night was a representative of the Commonwealth Edison company, who said that he had accompanied Edison to banquets for more than three decades, and this was the first time he had seen him engaged by what was going on—"the first time he had ever made a speech and the first time he ever had really enjoyed himself at such a function."

The banquet was scheduled to end at 9:00, but the enthusiastic transmissions clicked on until nearly 10:00. Edison, already late for his next appointment, finally delivered his code 73—best wishes—to sign off for the evening.

He and Mina then rushed down to the street level, where a car was waiting to take them to Nob Hill. In the back seat Mina stroked Edison's hand, which had been battered by the numerous handshakes delivered by his fellow telegraphers in farewell. As they rolled up Market Street, there were tens of thousands of onlookers lining the sidewalks. An hour earlier, when Edison had been expected, the crowds were even larger. When the car let them out at a granite-walled apartment building at Stanford Court, once the home of industrialist Leland Stanford, Edison and Mina were escorted by San Francisco mayor James Rolph upstairs to a rooftop garden, from which a vast expanse of the city was visible stretched out beneath them.

Mayor Rolph had asked all San Franciscans to turn on their lights to welcome the man who had illuminated the city and the world. Market Street shone below "like a jeweled bracelet of light." A high fog had rolled in off the bay, obliterating the night sky, so that only Edison lamps could be seen. They sparkled everywhere. Nearly every building was aglow. Bright beams had been trained on the dome of city hall, while along Market Street gleaming letters spelled out a welcome to the inventor. On the waterfront the exposition grounds blazed with light. Even the boats in the harbor flashed out a welcome. In the distance the luminous sign flashed out its message: "Long Live Edison—the Greatest Man on Earth!" Edison gave what one of those present took to be a "whimsical" shake of his head and smiled.

After lunch the next day the entire Edison party met up with Admiral Fullam, who had been enlisted by Secretary Daniels to give the inventor a closer view of some of the naval technology that would occupy his attention in the coming months. At the marina they piled into the admiral's launch for a trip out to the USS *South Dakota*, the armored cruiser that served as Fullam's flagship, the pearl of the Pacific fleet then at anchor in the bay.

Once aboard the *South Dakota*, Edison, true to form, embarked on an inspection of all the ship's electrical devices. Mina trailed along with him, dodging cameramen and laughing as she listened to her husband musing about the equipment. Edison paid particular attention to a new model of generator that the navy hoped he might help to improve.

Soon the party was shuttled to the nearby USS *Oregon*. An aging battleship that had seen action in the Spanish-American War, the *Oregon* provided Edison and Mina with further opportunity to nose around gun turrets and machinery as the vessel took the party on an excursion around the fog-enveloped bay. When they returned to the *South Dakota*, Admiral Fullam served tea, and the party toasted

*Thomas Edison and Admiral William Fullam aboard the USS* Oregon *in San Francisco Bay.*

his health on his birthday, which his shipmates were celebrating that day. To mark the occasion, Ford told Fullam and three of the other naval officers present that if they would come by his exhibit in the Transportation Hall he would give them each a new Model T car.

When the party returned to the Inside Inn and nudged their way through the throng of visitors in the lobby, they found that their friend Harvey Firestone had arrived in San Francisco and checked into the same hotel. He had made the hasty trip from Akron to the coast, he told a reporter, "in order to pay his respects to the inventive genius." It was important to Firestone to be in Edison's company "at a time when all of California was doing him homage."

Thursday was Edison Day at the exposition, the day the organizers had set apart to commemorate the thirty-sixth anniversary of the birth of the incandescent lamp. That morning, before the festivities got underway, Ford walked to the Palace of Transportation, where he met Admiral Fullam and three of his officers at the Ford Motor Company exhibit. He intended to make good on his promise to give the men cars—but the machines first had to be assembled. So, with Fullam and the other uniformed officers watching, Ford pulled on a pair of overalls, picked up a wrench, and joined his mechanics on the assembly line. Soon a Model T began to materialize from the parts arrayed around the exhibit. "This first one," Ford called out as he worked, "is for Admiral Fullam. Step over here admiral and see how your car is made."

The admiral, his white service cap in his hand, stepped forward with a smile to watch as Ford worked at the car with a large, open-end wrench. As he went about his work, Ford explained the function of each component of the vehicle. When the car was fully assembled, Ford stopped short for a moment.

"Just a minute," he said. "We have a rule that everybody who takes a car out of here must first learn to put a tire on." He turned to the wire-rimmed wheel and rubber tire. "Here you go, Admiral."

One of the bystanders observing the proceedings was William McAdoo, President Wilson's secretary of the treasury, who was visiting the fair and had just then found his way to the Transportation Hall. He and his wife "watched with amusement while the admiral, with sailor-like deftness, wrestled the tire onto the wheel."

Once the other three officers had passed Ford's tire test, each man slipped behind the wheel of his new car. Ford climbed in next to Admiral Fullam, and they paraded out onto the fairgrounds.

At 3:00 that afternoon, in an overcrowded four-thousand-seat auditorium in the Festival Hall, Edison sat looking sheepish next to Mina, as the chairman of the Edison Day committee kicked off the day's formal ceremonies, declaring, "Mr. Edison is the man of the century." The president of the exposition board, Charles Moore, then rose to present the exposition's commemorative medal to the inventor. "From the day that he first made an incandescent lamp glow his name has been stamped on history's pages in a plane by himself," Moore said. "It is fitting that we should come here and that we should burn incense to him." He went on to speak of Edison's genius and of his humanity. At one point during the address Edison turned to Mina and whispered, "I'm glad I can't hear him. I'd feel so foolish."

Moore then turned to make the presentation of a simple bronze medal. Edison rose and started toward the lectern as Mina plucked at stray threads on his jacket. He accepted the award from Moore, gave a deep bow, and returned to his seat, handing the medal to Mina with a smile. Moore explained to the assembled audience that their honoree had agreed to attend the ceremony only if he was not required to give a speech. The crowd joined Moore in giving three boisterous cheers for the medal recipient.

As the ceremony concluded, hundreds of attendees rushed onto the stage and crowded around Edison, hoping to speak to him and shake his hand. When he stepped out through the door of the Festival Hall, a crowd of ten thousand who had not been able to enter the auditorium and had waited more than two hours to catch sight of the inventor burst into cheers and applause.

Moore led Edison through the throng to the Palace of Liberal Arts, where the American Telephone and Telegraph Company had arranged for him to make a transcontinental telephone call from the equipment in their exhibit. At 5:08 p.m. a voice erupted from the line.

"Hello! Mr. Edison?" It was Edison's chief engineer, Miller Reese Hutchinson, speaking from the laboratory in West Orange.

"That's me! Is that you, Hutch?" Edison shouted into the mouthpiece. It was the first time the inventor and telegrapher had ever spoken into a telephone. For almost an hour the line was kept open as Edison talked to Hutchinson and others in the lab. He listened to some new recordings that had been made there and remarked at how clearly the sound was transmitted across the 3,400 miles separating the two telephone devices. It was a vivid demonstration of the way technological advances like those for which Edison and Ford were celebrated had begun to shrink the world.

A half-hour later the Edisons and Fords were seated for a dinner given by Central Electric Company at the "Home Electrical" exhibit, where all the food was cooked electrically in view of the diners. After dinner the party was escorted to the marina, where a colossal screen had been erected overnight. Edison sat with Mina and watched a screening of motion pictures that had been made of his visit so far. The images unfurled like a time-lapse rehearsal of all that had happened since his arrival in San Francisco. He saw himself enjoying the breezy ferry ride across the bay from the Oakland Mole. Edison and Ford were again seen striding through the exhibits in the Palace of Machinery and the Transportation Hall. The city on the screen was again illuminated in his honor as the on-screen Edison watched. There again were Edison and Mina visiting the *South Dakota* and taking a voyage around the bay on the *Oregon*.

When the motion-picture show was over, a tremendous burst in the sky announced the beginning of the fireworks display that would end the evening. Edison sat with Ford on the steps of the Transportation Building and gazed upward as half a ton of explosives lit up the night sky in colorful bursts that resounded over the marina. In the harbor a fireboat cast streams of water into a pillar of colored lights projected into the sky by huge electrical "scintillators" specially built for the exposition.

By the end of the evening some 96,000 people had made an Edison Day visit to the fair, more than on any other day commemorating a distinguished American. Edison's numbers had eclipsed those of

Presidents Taft and Roosevelt, as well as George Goethals, the engineer who oversaw the construction of the Panama Canal. Through it all Edison had said almost nothing. But now he stood, smiled, and doffed his cap to the crowd of 50,000 that had gathered to watch the fireworks.

Later that evening, as the celebration was winding down, a man appeared on Market Street carrying a large can labeled "guaranteed to exterminate insects." Whenever he saw a Ford automobile coming along the street he stepped out, held up his hand, and signaled it to stop. He then scooped a handful of powder out of the can, sprinkled it on the car, and uttered the word "Die." When the police arrived, they found that the can contained Buhach, an insecticide commonly used to eradicate fleas. After dusting the automobiles, the man announced, "They'll die before they jump far." He was then arrested and taken to the Detention Hospital for the Insane, on Gough Street, for psychiatric evaluation. When he arrived there, he handed the steward a letter addressed to the patent office. Its contents were not disclosed.

For all the fanfare celebrating Ford and Edison, the Market Street incident hinted at a substrate of resistance to the technological transformations they had introduced. The fair was undoubtedly an impressive monument to America's utopian faith in progress. But in light of the war news from Europe—each day cataloguing the devastating effects of such technological advancements as submarines, high explosives, poison gas, and machine guns—industrial progress looked increasingly less like the unalloyed boon the fair made it out to be.

In a letter published in the *New York Times* a few months earlier, no less a prognosticator than the futurist and science-fiction writer H. G. Wells had warned that "scientific warfare" had now placed "civilization at the breaking point." Wells predicted a bleak future if advances in governance were not quickly enacted to rein in the advances in death-dealing machinery: "The course of human history is downward and very dark indeed unless our race can give mind and will . . . to the stern necessities that follow logically from the aircraft bomb and poison gas and that silent, invisible, unattainable murderer, the submarine."

Following Wells's logic, the world's fair, in its uncritical celebration of industry, risked falling out of step with this dire historical moment. But its enthusiasm for agriculture offered a worthwhile counterbalance. Ford and Edison, both farm boys who had grown up to change the world through their industrial innovations, remained themselves poised between the mindsets of the farm and the factory. Between the exposition's Palace of Industry and Palace of Agriculture, they could map the terrain that lay before them.

In the coming years the U.S. entry into the war would place new demands on both men's innovative capacities, calling upon them to combat the horror of "scientific warfare" not with statecraft, as Wells had imagined, but with still more effective technology. At the same time, the rural travels they would undertake in the company of their naturalist friend Burroughs would nudge them back toward the agrarian mode, leading both to work in closer harmony with the natural environment. Camping under the stars and exploring the nation's still-wild mountains and rivers would nourish Ford's interest in waterpower and small-scale village industries, as well as Edison's growing obsession with finding domestic plant sources for industrial materials.

While they remained in California, however, it was Luther Burbank who assumed the naturalist role.

A little after 10:00 Friday morning, Edison, Ford, and the others were aboard a ferry crossing the bay to begin a fifty-mile train trip north to Santa Rosa. Burbank had invited his new friends to visit his gardens and experimental farm, something both Edison and Ford, for their own reasons, had long wanted to see. Ford, still nostalgic for the farm of his youth, even while recalling the back-breaking labor farm life entailed, was always interested in improvements to farming practices. Burbank's improved crops fit the bill. Edison was particularly interested in new varieties of plants for the novel materials and chemicals they contained. Both men had an interest in advances in plant science that might provide an alternative supply of rubber. This was a concern they shared with their friend Harvey Firestone, who, with his wife, Idabelle, joined them for the day.

In Santa Rosa, Burbank met the party at the train station and gave them a tour of the city before taking them to his house on Tupper Street, at the corner of Sonoma and Santa Rosa Avenues, where his sister and his secretary were waiting to welcome the visitors. While Ford's party looked around the house, Burbank spun out tales of his latest efforts to coax more beneficial plants from a nature that did not always cooperate with his ambitions. But everyone was eager to see the real attraction—the gardens and the elegantly arched brick-and-glass greenhouse, which looked, appropriately enough, like a cross between a laboratory and a chapel. For the next hour Burbank led his visitors through the gardens. Although it was autumn and the growing season was all but over, there was still much to see. He showed them a new tomato that ripened months earlier than other varieties and was capable of bearing several flushes of fruit in a single season. They sampled an improved variety of strawberry, which Edison particularly liked. "Isn't that delicious," he said, smacking his lips.

When they sampled the spineless cactus Burbank had developed, it was Ford who took a liking to the flavor. "Let's take some and have it prepared on the car as we go back," he proposed, with what an observer said was "a schoolboy's glee." Edison was more interested in how the spineless wonder was cultivated. "Will that grow anywhere?" he asked Burbank. "Grow?" Burbank responded. "Why it will grow on a stove if you don't light a fire underneath it."

*Thomas Edison, Luther Burbank, and Henry Ford in Santa Rosa.*

   In the seed house Burbank showed them how he stored thousands
of seeds for future experiments. They also saw a new kind of pea that
could be grown in particular sizes to accommodate machine harvesting, an idea that appealed to Ford. He had long wished to shift more
of the farmer's workload onto machinery. When a reporter covering
the visit that afternoon asked him about this, Ford announced that
he was developing a tractor he hoped to place on sale the following fall
at a price of two hundred dollars. "I intend to get at work manufacturing them just as soon as the Lord will let me," Ford said.
   Outside, a group of schoolchildren had assembled in the hope of
catching a glimpse of the great inventor. Edison waved to them but
was as usual reticent. Burbank stepped forward to introduce his

guest. "This is Mr. Edison, children, the man who gave you the electric light." The children broke into a cheer.

As the afternoon wore on, the four men made their way deeper into the gardens, talking warmly as they inspected stands of white blackberries or stooped to take in the aroma of a calla lily that had been bred to bear the scent of violets. With Burbank's terrier gamboling around their heels, they marveled at hybrids like the plumcot—a plum crossed with apricot—a tomato made to grow on a potato vine, and an otherworldly plant that was half petunia, half tobacco.

When conversation turned to the war, Ford put forward his usual argument that the United States should remain neutral; entanglement in the conflict would cost lives. This time Firestone chimed in with a more material concern: expansion of the war might further threaten supplies of rubber from Malaysia and Ceylon.

Burbank's sentiment was with Ford—he regretted any loss of life—but Firestone's argument also caught his attention. This war, whatever happened, would not be the last, he said, and in any case dependence on distant sources of crucial materials was dangerous. Such thinking had led Burbank to develop his spineless cactus: why transport cattle feed to arid regions when it was possible, given enough ingenuity and patience, to grow it where it was needed? The same thing, he believed, could be accomplished in this case.

"Who will be the one," he had long wondered, "to produce a plant which shall yield us rubber—a plant growing, perhaps, in the deserts, which shall make the cost of motor car tires seem only an insignificant item in upkeep?" This way of thinking was music to Ford's ears, and Burbank pushed the idea a step further. Why stop at rubber? It was entirely feasible to cultivate other plants, perhaps "side by side" with rubber-yielding crops, which could be made into cheap alcohol to serve as fuel for the automobiles that rode on native-grown tires.

Before Edison and his companions left, Burbank asked his new friends to sign his guest book. The page they signed was divided into three columns—one for the signature, one for the visitor's home address, and a third labeled "Interested in." Ford watched as Edison signed his name and then filled in the interest column. The inventor's response came as no surprise to Ford. He had written simply, "Everything."

As much as Edison relished the work he carried out at his laboratory in New Jersey, Burbank's garden, along with the expanse of open country he had observed on the trip across the country, had him churning with ideas for experiments he might be able to conduct in nature's laboratory. What Burbank had managed to do with fruits, vegetables, flowering plants, and succulents made Edison's dream of developing a native rubber source look more and more feasible.

Rubber was not the only natural resource Edison was coming to see in a new light thanks to his experiences in California. The next day, Saturday, October 23, while Ford tinkered with his Model T exhibit and Firestone visited his brother Elmer at the Firestone offices on Van Ness Avenue, Edison and Mina took the train to Palo Alto, where they were met by Edison's former associate Dr. Thomas Addison, now the head of General Electric's West Coast operations. After a stop at Stanford University, Addison drove the Edisons to his house in Los Altos before escorting them to the Lick Observatory at the summit of Mount Hamilton in the range east of San Jose, where the party spent the night. Their host for the evening was the astronomer William Wallace Campbell, an old friend of Edison's—they had met on a ship crossing the Atlantic in 1911—who was now involved in an effort to confirm Einstein's theory of relativity by measuring the deflection of light from stars that become visible during a solar eclipse.

The mountaintop observatory where Campbell worked had been completed in 1887. It was so remote that although the observatory had its own post office, mail was delivered infrequently. Edison had himself donated the electrical generator that powered the station for many years. Around the turn of the century the observatory's great thirty-six-inch refractor telescope had been the first instrument to register all the moons of Jupiter. For the last few years astronomers there had been occupied with photographing nebulae, the colorful deep-space clouds that some were beginning to believe might be distant galaxies. Once thought to be rare phenomena, hundreds of nebulae had been recorded from Mount Hamilton.

When darkness fell that evening, Campbell took Edison to the telescope. The inventor spent the next hour looking at the heavens as Campbell helped identify the distant objects, observing Vega, the bright star in the constellation Lyra, and the nearby ring nebula. Then Campbell turned the telescope toward Jupiter. "This is what I like to see," Edison exclaimed. Like Burbank, Campbell had given Edison a glimpse behind the veil of nature's laboratory. After dinner they returned to look at the full moon that had risen.

That evening as Edison and Campbell discussed the optics of the telescope at the heart of the observatory, it came out that optical glass was a material, like rubber, that the United States acquired almost entirely from overseas suppliers. If the country were to become entangled in the war in Europe, Edison came to realize, that fact could be of strategic importance. Homogeneous glass, as it was called, was used to make lenses and prisms for artillery range finders, submarine periscopes, binoculars, and gun sights. The two men would later take up the issue in their correspondence and work to find a domestic source for the glass. More and more it was the products of what he called nature's laboratory that interested the inventor.

On Monday morning, October 25, around 11:00, Frank Vivian looked up from his work at the Ford exhibit to see his boss, Henry Ford, standing over him, with Edison at his side. For a moment Vivian was apprehensive. He did have some reason to be nervous about questions that might arise during Mr. Ford's visit. Although he had always been a model employee, he sometimes let his initiative run away with him when it came to serving the Ford interests.

One afternoon in July, when the exposition was in full swing, Vivian had been busy supervising the assembly line at the exhibit when he noticed a young man dressed in khaki pants and a worn-out cap who seemed to be signaling to him from the back of the crowd. Vivian had his hands full keeping the assembly line running smoothly while fielding questions from fairgoers, so at first he paid little attention to the fellow. But after he had caught Vivian's eye and waved several more times, Vivian finally slipped under the rail that kept the crowd at a safe distance from the assembly line and made his way through the throng to find out what the young man wanted. When he reached him, the slender man held out his hand and introduced himself. It was Edsel Ford. The two talked for a while as the assembly line hummed along and finally agreed to meet that evening.

Fresh from his cross-country drive, Edsel Ford was eager to continue the adventure. He wanted to see Chinatown, he told Vivian. Always eager to please, Vivian agreed. He led Edsel to a bar called Purcell's in the red-light district near the shipping docks known as the Barbary Coast. Although the main attraction at Purcell's was the house band, just as many people crowded into the bar for the taxi dancers and to watch the fights that inevitably broke out on busy nights. "When the fights started in there, they used to be throwing these big beer mugs and chairs," Vivian remembered. "It was a hard place." While he and Edsel were in Purcell's that night, a fight did break out, and Vivian, who was a big man, did what he could to protect his young guest, covering Edsel with his body and rushing him toward the door. Just as they reached the exit, two policemen in helmets came barreling through the swinging doors brandishing billy clubs. Vivian kept Edsel's head down, and the two managed to slip out before the scene erupted.

"Boy that was an instance," Vivian recalled. If Henry Ford had heard the story, Vivian might have trouble on his hands. But Ford had other things on his mind the next morning. He took Vivian aside. "Have you had lunch yet?" Ford asked. When Vivian said that he usually ate later in the day, Ford went on, "Well, you know the good places around here. We're going up to have a bite to eat."

Vivian noticed that Edison, standing quietly next to Ford, wore a grin on his face. He was perplexed for a moment, not quite sure what the boss and his friend were driving at. But then Ford said, "You better come along, Vivian. You better come with us."

Vivian scrambled back along the assembly line, giving instructions to the men, then caught up with Ford and Edison and strolled out onto the fairgrounds, which were almost deserted at that time of day. They zigzagged their way through the Court of the Universe, past the Tower of Jewels, then turned up the main road and headed for the area known as the Amusement Zone. A Bohemian village was set up at the far end of the zone, and Vivian thought it might be a good place for lunch. Before they had gone far, though, a white-hatted hot dog vendor caught their attention. He was calling out, "Coney Island hot dogs!" Ford had heard all he needed. "There's the place we'll go and eat," he said.

Vivian could do nothing but agree and soon found himself sitting at a lunch counter, drinking coffee and eating Coney Island dogs with Henry Ford and Thomas Edison. While he ate, he watched Ford carefully peel the casing from his hot dog before beginning to eat it.

When the vendor put the check on the counter, Vivian made a grab for it. Ford tried to stop him, but Vivian stood his ground. "No, sir, not on your life," he said. "This is the chance of my life to treat you two gentlemen to a banquet." The bill came to 45 cents.

Dinner that evening could not have been more different, and the contrast highlighted the distance the inventor and the automaker had

traversed between their rural beginnings and their public celebration
at the fair. The Firestones held a dinner party at the Fairmont Hotel
for the Edisons and Fords and many of the friends they had made
during their stay. Among the guests were Luther Burbank, Admiral
Fullam and his wife, and the exposition president, Charles Moore.
Firestone had hired the orchestra from the Hawaii exhibit, and the
dinner party took place against the sinuous strains of island music.
Ford was so pleased by the performance that at the end of the evening
he hired the entire orchestra and began making arrangements for
them to travel to Detroit.

Edison, against his own expectations, had enjoyed his time at
the exposition. "It has really been a wonderful vacation for me," he
announced. "Really the first one I have ever had. I shall take back home
with me wonderful recollections." But he was already thinking of work
he wanted to get back to. He had told reporters that afternoon that he
was developing a new system for recording musical performances. It
involved a forty-foot concrete bowl in which musicians would perform,
while wiring set up around the mouth of the bowl captured the sound
waves. "I don't know yet whether it will work," Edison admitted. "I am
up against the devilish perversity of inanimate matter."

The next evening, October 26, the Fords and Edisons were back
aboard the private railcars Ford had provided. They were scheduled
to appear three days later in San Diego, where the smaller California Exposition would also put on an Edison Day. When the Sunset
Express for Los Angeles pulled out of Oakland at 9:00 that night, the
party bade farewell to San Francisco, its exposition illumination still
visible across the bay.

By the time the train reached Riverside the next morning, Harvey
Firestone had convinced the party that they should leave the railcars and travel into Los Angeles by automobile, giving them a chance
to observe the landscape of hills and farmland at close range. "That
suited Mr. Edison exactly," Firestone recalled, "for he likes to ride in

a motor—as long as he can ride in the front seat. He has no use for any other part of a motor car!"

In the orchards outside Riverside, figs and persimmons were ripe for harvest, while other trees hung heavy with oranges; fields of tomatoes remained, though most had been picked earlier in the season. Much of the land here had once been given over to wheat production, until soil depletion caused the yields to drop, just as imported wheat began to drive prices down. The thriving orchards and vegetable operations showed how smart husbandry could turn a crisis into an opportunity for renewal.

In Los Angeles, Edison and the others watched a moving picture being developed, and Edison laid the cornerstone for a new movie studio. As the party motored on toward San Diego, Ford and Edison became more and more focused on the "water-power potentialities of California." Every river and stream they crossed was viewed as a potential power plant. They traded ideas about how to channel streams and how much power a given flow might produce. "It was Mr. Edison's thought that, if only we had enough cheap power, we should be able to reduce manufacturing costs to a minimum and bring on widespread prosperity," Firestone noted.

In San Diego many of the encounters they had experienced in San Francisco were repeated on a smaller scale. Crowds greeted Edison, and schoolchildren tossed flowers. Ford and Edison inspected displays of tractors and other farm machinery. When the party drove past a gargantuan plow train pulled by a string of sixteen horses, Ford predicted that such work would soon be done by machine. Edison agreed, sparking a discussion of whether this would be achieved using gasoline engines, as Ford believed, or electric power, which Edison preferred.

The group spent a week in Los Angeles and San Diego. On Friday, November 5, they were due to leave for home on the 9:00 train departing on the Santa Fe line. They would be traveling, as Edsel had on the way out, by a route that would take them to the Grand Canyon, where they would spend two days, followed by two more in Colorado Springs. It would be a long trip home, but already Ford, Edison, and Firestone were feeling wistful about the travels that were about to come to an end.

As railway workers scrambled to make the train cars ready for departure that morning, Edison gave voice to their shared sentiment. The trip had been a great success. They should all travel together again soon. And taking a cue from Edsel and Theodore, perhaps they would travel by car and—if they could put the sodden experience in the Big Cypress swamp behind them—sleep out at night.

Luther Burbank, whose botanical knowledge and enthusiasm for the natural world had helped make their visit to California such a success, was tied to his gardens and would no doubt be unable to join future excursions. But their friend Burroughs might capably resume his role as chief naturalist.

⚬━━━━⚬

# 5

# SEPARATE WAYS

On Monday, February 21, 1916, Henry Ford made his way to the sanitarium run by Dr. Ludwig Kast at 777 Park Avenue, on Manhattan's Upper East Side. A physician and adjunct professor at the New York Post-Graduate Medical School and Hospital, Kast was engaged in pioneering work on arteriosclerosis and other diseases of aging. He had developed new ways of analyzing the cholesterol and urea contents of blood and had written on disturbances of sugar metabolism. He was also the expert on whom the editors of *Nelson's Loose-Leaf Medical Encyclopedia* had called to write its lengthy chapter on the origin, diagnosis, and treatment of constipation.

Ford was not there for his health, however. He had come to Dr. Kast's clinic to see his friend John Burroughs, who had been under the doctor's care since the beginning of the month. Burroughs had been visiting his friend Robert DeLoach in Georgia when he and his wife had both become ill—Ursula with the grippe and Burroughs with the digestive problems he referred to as "my old trouble." He had treated himself for a time with calomel—a powerful purgative formulation of mercuric chloride—but after a few weeks without improvement, he had traveled north in DeLoach's care and admitted himself to Kast's clinic.

Although Ford's own health was sound, as always, the preceding weeks had proven challenging for him as well. On December 4, the same day that the Panama–Pacific Exposition had closed its gates for the final time, Ford had embarked on a voyage to Europe with the intention of brokering a peace settlement among the nations currently at war. Like other rich men before him, he assumed that his material success was evidence of a special ability that was as applicable to world affairs as to his own field.

The voyage of what became known as the Peace Ship was the culmination of a string of events that had been set in motion some months earlier. Late in August, as Ford watched the nation drew closer to war with Germany, he had made a public declaration of his intention to work toward peace. "I will do everything in my power to prevent murderous, wasteful war in America and in the whole world," he had vowed in an interview published in the *Detroit Free Press*. Ford went on to argue that preparedness, far from preventing war, precipitated it more surely.

From the masses he believed he heard a call for peace rather than preparation for war: "We do not want war. We will not have war. We will not have amongst us the breeders of war, be they men who cry out that the enemy seeks us, and we must prepare for him, or be they only those who would dazzle with the false glory that has been the cloak of murder for centuries." Ford admitted that he did not know how to turn the United States back from the brink of war, not to mention bring peace to Europe. "I realize it is a vast undertaking." But he felt the answer lay in education—"I would teach the child at his mother's knee what a horrible, wasteful and unavailing thing war is"—and in "fair and just conditions" for workers, both of which could be brought about only through the cultivation of a philosophy that valued "equitable prices and commercial unselfishness."

"I could today make vast sums from warfare if I so chose," Ford claimed, "but it would be better to die a pauper than that anything I have helped to make or any thought, word or act of mine should be used for the furtherance of this slaughter." At the same time, he argued that war preparation and war profiteering were in the long run simply bad business. "Aside from the burning fact that war is murder, the waster of lives and homes and lands, and that 'preparedness' has never prevented war but has ever brought war to the world—aside from all this," he said, warming to his theme, "is the utter futility (from a cold, hard business view alone) of the equipment of an army today with weapons that are obsolete tomorrow."

Ford had anticipated resistance to his ideas, and he fully expected to be sneered at. But some of the criticism took forms he could not have predicted. Within days newspapers around the country were falsely reporting that Ford had applied and been accepted to join the businessmen's army training program at Fort Sheridan, outside Chicago. On August 31, Ford was back in the pages of the *Free Press* dismissing the claim as "a deliberate, malicious lie." Apparently some prankster had latched onto a comment Ford had made in his interview—"It's a good joke to see these big-business men, now in the newspapers, spending a few weeks' vacation, learning the art of soldiering"—and turned it into a joke on Ford himself.

Criticism of a more serious nature was soon to come. The editor of the *Army and Navy Journal*, William J. Hicks, dismissed Ford's view of the United States as a peace-loving nation, pointing to its recent military involvement in Haiti, San Domingo, and Vera Cruz. "Ford is a victim of the optimism of great wealth," Hicks maintained. "He believes that the expenditure of millions can change the qualities of human nature that have produced wars for centuries."

Apparently in reaction to Ford's declaration for peace, the Naval

Advisory Board headed by Edison announced that it would bar pacifists from membership. The board also let it be known that Ford, whose
name had been mentioned while the group was being assembled, had
never been seriously considered. "While due honor is granted him as a
business organizer," a report on the matter stated, "he is not believed
to be an inventive genius of the type required." Secretary Daniels
eventually denied that Ford's pacifism had kept him off the board.

Meanwhile, a *Wall Street Journal* article suggested that Ford had
come out for peace because he lost money when the suppliers of parts
and material to his factories had turned their own production to
munitions. This was a notion that would be repeated often in publications across the country.

An editorial in one Washington, D.C., newspaper took issue with
Ford's suggestion that the current agitation for preparedness was
fueled by the "false glory" that attached itself to the idea of war, asking if the towering figures of the nation's military history had been
duped by a false notion. "Should the statues of Washington, Jackson,
Grant, Sherman, Sheridan, Lee and Stonewall Jackson be tumbled
over because they recall the fighting spirit in America aroused by
situations which those men considered a warrant for war?" the editors asked.

Over the following weeks Ford, undeterred by his critics, pledged
first one million and then ten million dollars to further the peace
effort. At one point he said he would be willing to spend half of his
fortune to shorten the war by a day. He was becoming ever more
singularly focused on the issue. In October, when he arrived in San
Francisco to visit the exposition with Edison, his first utterance to
reporters came in the form of a diatribe. "The European war is being
carried on by Wall Street," Ford pronounced. "If the right men were
shot the war would be over in a week."

Ford's urgent public declarations for peace soon attracted others who wished to help him achieve his goal or at least have him spend his money to help them achieve theirs. On November 19 one of these peace activists managed to bypass the circle of employees who normally shielded Ford from public intrusions and met with him at his house in Dearborn.

Rosika Schwimmer was a thirty-eight-year-old Hungarian pacifist who had been fighting for progressive political causes much of her life. In her own country she had founded both a feminist organization and a peace society. When the war broke out, she had been working with the International Women's Suffrage Alliance in London. Unable to return home, she had spent much of the past year campaigning for peace in the United States, where she helped form the Women's Peace Party. One acquaintance noted there was "something of the cloak-and-dagger tradition of international politics" about Schwimmer, while at the same time she came across "as a cosy, hausfrau type, homey as a crock of pfeffernusse." For all the contradictions in her presentation, however, her aims appeared selfless; it was rumored that she had pawned her jewelry to pay her way to the United States.

Her experience as the Hungarian delegate to the International Congress of Women had led her to Ford. In the spring she had traveled to The Hague to put forward a proposal for the formation of a neutral commission to promote negotiations between the warring countries, but though the proposal had been adopted, it had not yet been put into action. Schwimmer claimed that she had received communications from the various belligerent parties indicating their willingness to participate in such an undertaking. Now she believed that Ford could help make her vision a reality.

Ford, still wearing his farming boots and interrupting the conversation with his customary rants about the detrimental effects of smoking and drinking, made little pretense of giving his visitor his attention. At one point he mentioned he had already discerned the force behind the war. It was, he said, "International Jews." Nothing in Ford's casual delivery indicated that he saw anything untoward in the assertion. "I have the facts," he added.

Schwimmer—a Jewish woman born in Budapest, who had spent much of her adult life campaigning throughout Europe and America—was perhaps as close to an "International Jew" as Henry Ford was ever likely to meet. But if she was offended by his remark, she kept it to herself. As the virulence of Ford's antisemitism grew in the coming years, his outbursts would not be so readily overlooked.

While an astute politician might put forward a public face of probity as a cover for darker motives—greed, nationalism, or a lust for power—Ford, whether from naivete or sheer hayseed cussedness, wore the darkness on the surface when it came to blaming Jews for the world's ills. Beneath this repugnant obsession, however, he remained dedicated to stopping a war that he believed put the interests of the rich above the well-being of the masses. The fact that Schwimmer was herself Jewish ultimately had no bearing on his assessment of her plan, and although he had not appeared to pay proper attention to the discussion, he had in fact taken in enough to persuade him.

Before the afternoon was over, Ford was asking what it would cost to carry out Schwimmer's plan. Two days later, at a meeting held at the McAlpin Hotel in New York, Ford and Schwimmer presented her proposal to a group of pacifists that included Columbia University dean George Kirchwey, social reformer Jane Addams, and Louis Lochner, a representative of the Carnegie Peace Endowment. The group saw promise in the general premise and urged Ford to meet with President Wilson and try to engage the participation, or at least the encouragement, of the government. In the course of the conversation, Lochner, perhaps in jest, alluded to the need for a ship to put a scheme like Schwimmer's into action. At that, Ford was off and running. Over the objections of Addams, who viewed the idea as unnecessarily and unwisely ostentatious, Ford began to look for a ship.

Barely a week later, newspapers were reporting that Ford had engaged all the first- and second-class rooms aboard the Scandinavian-American Line steamship *Oscar II*. This would provide space for some two hundred "peace pilgrims," as Ford's group was now being called. Ford quickly issued invitations to a broad array of peace advocates and other luminaries and politicians, including state governors and Secretary of State William Jennings Bryan.

Bryan was known to be sympathetic to the idea of negotiations, and it was initially reported that he would join the Ford party. One wag from Worcester, Massachusetts, wired Ford to caution that during a transatlantic voyage with Bryan, who was a somewhat long-winded speaker, "time is apt to hang heavy on your hands." He offered to provide a vaudeville troupe to keep Ford and his companions entertained on the trip. "Can give you German acrobats, English jugglers, French dancers, Austrian sword swallowers, Turkish magicians and Italian musicians. With these on board *Oscar II* peace is assured and neutrality of United States safe."

In the end Bryan was not among the pilgrims who joined Ford on the voyage. Many of the other high-profile invitees also rebuffed Ford's overtures. The explanation Ford received from David Starr Jordan, renowned ichthyologist and president of Stanford University, typified the concerns about the effort. Ford's campaign, Jordan believed, had two contradictory aims: a peace demonstration, which the voyage itself constituted, and the formation of a commission for mediation. The latter aim, Jordan argued, was more important, and it would be undermined by the ballyhoo surrounding the demonstration. The job would most effectively be carried out quietly, by delegates who were "thoroughly versed in European affairs, devoted to the cause of peace, tactful and influential" and not, the implication was, by an automaker and a quickly thrown-together mob of publicity seekers.

Ford had also invited both Burroughs and Edison to accompany him on the trip, though neither was by inclination likely to involve himself in what amounted to a high-profile act of protest. The situation was further complicated for Edison by the fact that he had already taken up his post as head of the Naval Consulting Board when Ford gave his original *Free Press* interview. "They have called in Thomas Edison to help their war plans," Ford said at the time. "Let me say that Thomas Edison never has, and in my opinion, never will use his great brain to make anything which will destroy human life or human property. He could destroy nothing. His mind is a constructive mechanism that abhors destruction, and war is destruction." The fact was, however, that Edison had already handed the operation of his own laboratory to his assistants and was himself engaged full-time in work for the navy. He politely declined Ford's invitation.

Burroughs, for his part, had thought the enterprise wrongheaded from the start. A few days before the set departure date he wrote to Ford to decline the invitation. "It was very good of you to think of me in connection with your peace trip. I wish I had the courage to go and

*Thomas Edison at the Brooklyn Navy Yard in 1915.*

could be of real service to you." His health, he went on to say, would
not permit him to make a voyage of the kind Ford envisioned. More
than that, there was Ursula's fragile state to consider. As the letter
went on, however, it became clear that these were not the real imped-
iments to his accompanying Ford. Burroughs in fact held a starkly
different view of the situation than his friend. He spelled out his sentiments delicately, like a man picking his way through a minefield.

"I have such affection for you and admiration for your life and
work that I hesitate to speak any discouraging word about any wor-
thy scheme you undertake," he continued. "God knows we all want
peace—a real enduring peace and not a mere truce." Ford, Burroughs
knew, was spending a good deal of money in his effort to achieve that
goal, and he himself, he told Ford, would gladly give all of his own
meager wealth if he thought it could help. In his view, however, no
solution could be bought, and a premature peace could well be worse
than war. "To stop the war now would be like stopping surgical operation before it was finished. The malignant tumor of German militarism must be cut out and destroyed before the world can have a
permanent peace." As Burroughs saw it, that would take time, perhaps another year of fighting.

In the end Burroughs wanted to believe the best of Ford, and he
held open the possibility that his friend might indeed manage to bro-
ker a meaningful settlement to the hostilities. "Here," he offered, "is a
prayer from a man who never prays, that you may succeed."

Despite his misgivings, Burroughs accompanied Ford and Clara
to the docks in Hoboken when the day of departure rolled around.
Ford, carrying a walking stick and wearing a derby hat and a sable-
collared overcoat, appeared to be in his element. As they made their
way through a great crowd and boarded the steamer, Burroughs was
struck by his friend's demeanor. "Ford is sanguine and happy," he
thought, but that was because his "heart is bigger than his head." For
Burroughs it was a delicate situation. He had to balance his affection

for Ford as a man against his own sense of what was best for the nation and, indeed, the world. He also had what he felt was a more realistic view of the forces driving the war. In the end he told Ford that "he might as well try to hasten spring as to hasten peace now."

Under a threatening, leaden early December sky, some three thousand well-wishers and other observers gathered on the pier to see Ford off on his peace mission. Secretary of State Bryan, despite declining to travel aboard the *Oscar II* himself and recently comparing Ford's ship to Noah's ark, was among those present, and was seen lifting his hat in repeated gestures of goodwill to the peace party. As the celebration got underway, a shipboard band traded off songs with another assembled on the pier, with the recently composed antiwar anthem "I Didn't Raise My Boy to Be a Soldier" giving way to "Ain't

*Henry Ford departs for Europe aboard the "Peace Ship" Oscar II on December 4, 1915.*

You Coming Back to Old New Hampshire Molly." At a greater distance a group that had stumbled out of a German-style beer hall near
the waterfront could be heard intoning "Deutschland über Alles."

Edison came aboard to wish his friend well, but he was evidently
in no mood to linger amid the crowd and quickly departed. As one
reporter noted, "He seemed to have a fear that the peace craft might
back out into the river before he had a chance to disembark." One
observer on board believed he heard Ford making a last-minute
appeal to Edison to join him on the voyage.

"Tom, will you take a million dollars to come along?" the man
thought he heard Ford say.

Edison, perhaps falling back on his hearing difficulties as a crutch,
replied, "It sure is, Henry."

Raising his voice, Ford repeated the appeal. "I say, will you come
with me for a million dollars!" Edison gave his friend what looked like
an affectionate smile and ambled down the gangway.


At sea that evening Ford spoke to reporters who had remained on
board to cover the journey. He told them that the send-off in New York
had been "a good beginning" to his mission, and he was pleased to see
the show of support. It was clear to him that, as he put it, all classes
of people "from Edison up" were behind him. To the reporter for the
*New York Tribune* he added, "I know Edison well enough to say that."

Soon, however, the peace mission began to show signs of trouble.
On December 8 a wireless transmission from a reporter aboard the
*Oscar II* detailed rifts that had opened among different factions in
the party. One group had demanded that they be shown the evidence
Schwimmer claimed to have proving that the warring nations were
amenable to working toward a peace settlement. Another group was
calling for the delegation to issue a rebuke to President Wilson, in
the wake of the State of the Union address he had delivered the day

before, in which he called for "the thorough preparation of the nation to care for its own security."

As the voyage continued, so did the fracturing of the party. In some cases the arguments became heated, with one of the peace delegates reportedly leaping onto a table and shouting. Within days Ford himself had come down with a severe cold and taken to his bed. When the divisions among the pilgrims on board deepened, the sickroom became a place of refuge, and Ford was little seen on deck for the remainder of the voyage.

The *Oscar II* reached Kristiansand, on the southern tip of Norway, at 3:00 on the afternoon of December 18, then proceeded to Christiania, the Norwegian capital, where Ford's peace ship slid into dock at 5:00 the following morning. It quickly became clear that Schwimmer had overstated her clout among European diplomats. Representatives of the government in Christiania revealed that Schwimmer's overtures had been rebuffed on her earlier visit there. Peace negotiations at this time, she had been told, "were inappropriate." The Ford party would receive no official recognition. From Denmark word came that the pilgrims would not be welcomed at all. After an initial barrage of negative press, Norwegian reporters quickly warmed to Ford himself. On December 22 an article appeared in the Christiania *Orebladet* praising the automaker's "philosophy of life, his great idealism, and his warm noble heart." But the mission itself was dead in the water.

Ford, looking wan and frail, had had enough. "Guess I had better go home to mother," he said to Louis Lochner. "I told her I'll be back soon. You've got this thing started now and can get along without me." For the time being at least, the fractious squabbling he had witnessed on the voyage had shaken his confidence that he could tinker his way to peace as he had tinkered the Model T into existence. The political classes were proving less readily tuned than an internal combustion engine.

Members of the delegation began working on Ford to convince him to stay, but his mind had already turned back toward home. When a group of Norwegian reporters cornered him that evening, Ford talked to them about the tractor he was developing, which would "cost the price of one horse and do the work of six."

Sometime between 3:00 and 4:00 in the morning on Christmas Eve, Ford had his baggage removed from his Christiania hotel. The following morning he sailed for home aboard a Norwegian liner departing from Bergen. Before he left, Ford spoke one last time to a group of Norwegian reporters. "Norway is like every other country," he said. "The people are all right."


Despite the failure of his Peace Ship voyage, Ford did not give up his struggle against the war; instead he tried a different tack. When he paid his visit to Burroughs at Kast's sanitarium in February, Ford had just arrived in New York from Detroit, and he intended to keep his presence in the city a secret. He was, as only a few close associates knew, on something of a mission. The man he had left in charge of the peace expedition, his New York branch manager Gaston Plantiff, was expected back from Europe the following day, and Ford had arranged to meet with him in private.

He had checked into the Waldorf Astoria under an assumed name, lest "Henry Ford" be noticed in the hotel's registry. But he was quickly recognized by the hotel staff, and word of his arrival soon spread. The following day the New York Times ran a story headlined "Ford Here for New Fight," reporting that the automaker had "slipped into town" to meet with Plantiff; it went on to reveal Ford's plan to launch an advertising campaign "against preparedness." A day after that, a full-page advertisement appeared in the Times and other newspapers in which Ford addressed "the American people." He quoted President Wilson's recent assertion that "nobody seriously supposes that the United States need fear an invasion of its own territory" and went on to say that the real threat to American security was an internal one. "We are confronted by the danger of militarism," Ford argued. He pointed to a series of speeches delivered by Illinois representative Clyde Tavener, in which, as Ford described the matter, the congressman had claimed that the "agitation" for what had come to be called preparedness was financed "by a group made up largely of war traffickers" who stood to profit substantially from the effort to put the nation on a war footing. After several paragraphs detailing what he took to be proof of the profiteering behind the impulse toward preparedness, Ford ended with a call for all Americans who wanted peace to write to their representatives in Congress and to the president. "A sentence or two will do," he concluded. "But make your meaning plain."

The day the initial *Times* story broke, Ford had returned to Kast's sanitarium to find Burroughs preparing to move to the house of a prominent family in Lakewood, New Jersey, where he was to spend the next fortnight recovering and reading "war books," along with "3 daily morning papers, and two evening papers." By the end of his stay in Lakewood, Burroughs was again eating well and gaining weight— up to 131¼ from the low of 125¼ he had reached at the depth of his malady. Try as he might, however, he could not satisfy his appetite for news of the war.

By March 20 Burroughs was back at home at Riverby. The weather was cold, with two feet of snow covering both the ground and the still-frozen Hudson River. Burroughs received a letter that day from DeLoach in Georgia, where Ursula continued to convalesce. Earlier in the month she had begun to experience back pain, in addition to her other symptoms, and now the discomfort had moved to her chest. DeLoach, no doctor but still a careful scientist, suspected angina pectoris. On March 28 another letter from DeLoach broke the news that Mrs. Burroughs's condition was not likely to improve. "I am well these days," Burroughs wrote in his journal, "while she, poor woman, suffers more or less every day." A sense of desolation overcame him when he thought of the time they had spent together in that house, and it seemed to extend to the natural world around him. All he saw about him looked barren, and Burroughs wondered if spring would ever arrive.

As the vernal thaw came on at the end of March, Burroughs distracted himself with the maple harvest. Tapping trees and boiling off the sap remained his favorite farm chore. Now it became a kind of meditation. "How the old days, when I helped boil sap in the home sugar bush and looked off over the fields through the lucid air, come back to me!" he wrote in his journal. "I was happy then. I am happy now—except when thoughts of my poor suffering wife cross my mind."

The rituals of sugaring returned the past to him. He recalled the experience of boiling sap at night as a boy and gazing across the valley toward a distant farm on the slopes of Batavia Mountain, two or three miles away. He could just see the twinkling of the fire that indicated that the same sugaring operation was underway there. Back then, the sight of that distant fire had given the young Burroughs a sense of community and connection; now the memory helped to dispel the solitude that had engulfed him.

Early in April, walking again in the woods above his farm, he saw a world repopulated by nature. "Do not remember so many birds in the spring as now," he wrote. "Robins, bluebirds, juncos, song sparrows— probably 3 or 4 times as many as usual." He heard wood frogs croaking and watched the activity of chipmunks and ground mice. "Never before saw signs of so many meadow mice. Their little settlements and villages on the surface of the ground under the snow are seen everywhere." But above all he welcomed the return of the birds— "birds, birds everywhere."

A week later Ursula returned from Georgia, thin and frail, but stronger than Burroughs had expected. Taking his arm, she was able to walk upstairs, and she was in little pain. With his wife home Burroughs's thoughts quickly turned back to the war. "Looks as if we might break with Germany over the submarine issue," he noted in his journal little more than a week later. "Hope we will and that war will follow. It might be our good luck to share in the honor and glory of helping the Allies crush this pirate of the seas and desperado of the land." Then he added, "Two eggs in the robin's nest in my summer house."

As the April afternoons grew milder, he began to take Ursula out for drives in the Ford. But the turn his thoughts had lately taken toward the past inclined him more and more to his old habit of walking. "An hour's walk," he noted after one outing, "hand in hand with April."

Near the end of the month he received a telegram from Detroit, forwarded to West Park from Roxbury, for which service Burroughs was charged forty cents. Ford wished to report that he had seen two bobolinks. Nearly two weeks later Burroughs spotted his own first bobolink of the season.

Though the spring revived the country around Burroughs's farm, Ursula remained weak. Near the end of May, Burroughs noted his growing concern for her health—"fear she is not really mending."

On Monday, June 5, a warm, rather cloudy day with rain in the forecast, Burroughs found himself thinking about the fragility of the lives of songbirds. Over the foregoing weeks he had been reading news of the staggering scope of casualties at Verdun. And now, with the newspapers full of rumors of a large-scale naval battle in the Baltic, he worried that Britain, the once great power, was on the verge of losing not just its empire but its homeland as well. As Burroughs assimilated these concerns, he began to fret about the sparrow whose call he had once debated with President Roosevelt. "The tree nesting bird that most often comes to grief is the chippy," he wrote in his journal.

Burroughs resolved to put these worries aside that evening as he set out for Detroit to visit Ford, who was anxious for his friend to see his latest project. Burroughs caught the 8:10 train in Albany, and the next morning Ford met him at the station. The two drove straight to

Dearborn, where the Fords had recently finished construction of a palatial new house.

Situated on a rise partly surrounded by woods and overlooking the River Rouge, the house was impressive without actually being attractive. Built of gray limestone, in no discernible architectural style, it seemed to have been constructed with comfort in mind. The bathrooms had taps that supplied both well water and rainwater, as well as warm air for drying. There were elements that were familiar to Burroughs, like the screened sleeping porches overlooking the river. Others, like the heated swimming pool—even the benches around it were heated—and bowling alley, were oddities to him. On the whole he judged the house "fine—a house one could live in."

None of the opulence seemed to interest Ford, however. The one feature of the house he appeared proud of was the power station, which he had designed himself. It was a marble-lined chamber with a vaulted ceiling, linked to the rest of the house by an underground tunnel. A waterwheel, turned by a channel rerouted from the Rouge, ran a series of turbines that provided electricity. The design of the room blended the elements present in Ford himself. On the one hand there was the mechanical beauty of the turbines and the brass piping that fed them; on the other was the decorative motif of birdlife outlined in the brass grillwork that ran around the walls. The whirring turbines and the robins were equally a part of the Ford whom Burroughs had come to know.

Only one other room bore Ford's unmistakable imprint. Named the "Field Room," it had walls faced with rough timber "to give the impression one had entered a log cabin out in the Michigan woods." Carved into the oak mantel above the fireplace was a quotation from Emerson's friend and neighbor Henry Thoreau: "Chop your own wood and it will warm you twice."

Burroughs was given a room facing the River Rouge, where he was lulled by the murmur of the current. Rain kept the party inside on

Wednesday, but by Thursday the weather had begun to clear. Ford took Burroughs on a tour of the property, which had changed a great deal since he had first seen it nearly three years earlier. Ford had built a hydroelectric dam and had it disguised as a natural waterfall. Work was underway all around, both to develop new farm methods and to preserve the estate's natural environment.

As always, Ford and Burroughs paid particular attention to the birdlife. There were some five hundred birdbaths on the property, and Ford had tapped into his power system to keep them from freezing in the wintertime. To augment the local bird population, he had imported six hundred pairs of English songbirds, among them warblers, thrushes, and larks. The previous summer Ford had ordered a halt to all work in one of the farm fields when he saw a tractor about to drive over a nest. As Ford told the story, he had been walking into the field with Burroughs's latest volume under his arm when he saw the danger. "Don't you see that you were going right over that lark's nest?" he had shouted at the man on the tractor. "It has three eggs in it!" Ford had left the tractor sitting in the field for ten days, until the eggs had hatched and the fledglings had left the nest.

In the afternoon Ford and Burroughs drove through the four-hundred-acre meadow Ford had been developing as a sanctuary for lowland species. "Grass and clover knee-high," Burroughs noted. "Plenty of bobolinks."

This time Ford's bobolinks had not cost Burroughs a cent.

**6**

◁━━━▷

# SUNBURNED AND
# FULL OF VIM

By the end of June, Burroughs had returned to Riverby, and
Edison was growing impatient to make good on the travel
plan he had hatched with Ford and Firestone as they were
leaving California. The San Francisco excursion and the comically
disastrous camping trip in Florida had whetted his appetite for more
adventure, and he was eager to immerse himself in a rustic setting
where he could put aside the pressures of work and really think. The
inventor roped Firestone into the scheme first. Throughout the month
of July letters and telegrams went back and forth between Akron and
West Orange as the two men worked out the details of scheduling and
supplies. Ford meanwhile remained noncommittal, pointing to a trip
he was expected to make to the West as an impediment to his joining
what was shaping up to be a camping excursion somewhere in the
Northeast. Edison had invited Burroughs, who agreed to go but was
having second thoughts. Undeterred by the reluctance he encountered
in Ford and Burroughs, Edison barreled ahead with his preparations.

He secured a complete set of camping gear and designed a battery-powered electrical system to illuminate the camp. Meanwhile, Firestone slipped into the role of "chief of the commissary" and began stockpiling provisions for the trip. He even managed to recruit the chef from the Clubhouse Restaurant, an eatery that had opened the previous year on the grounds of the Firestone manufacturing plant in Akron, to serve as camp cook.

On August 28, Firestone, although he still had no idea where Edison intended to travel, was in New York with his son Harvey, on his way to meet the inventor at his laboratory in West Orange. It was a dreary morning, with rain hammering the streets outside the hotel. Firestone lingered inside long enough to send a telegram to Ford in Detroit. He told Ford that Edison was especially eager for him to join the expedition. "Hope you will not disappoint him if only for a day or two." He promised to wire again as soon as he knew more of Edison's plans for the trip.

When Firestone and Harvey reached West Orange they found Robert DeLoach, Burroughs's agronomist friend from Georgia, already there with Edison. Together they waited out the weather for a while before deciding, a little before 10:00, to set out through the rain toward Roxbury, where they would rendezvous with Burroughs.

Traveling in Edison's Simplex touring car, followed by a Ford car and a White truck, the party motored north along Pompton Turnpike and by afternoon began climbing into the eastern foothills of the Catskills. Toward evening the rain let up, and the sky began to clear. With Edison navigating, they made their way to a farm field situated alongside a creek some eight miles south of the village of Ellenville. Here they began to set up camp for the night. The tents were hardly up, however, before the landowner appeared and told them they had to leave. Firestone stepped in to introduce Edison, thinking the presence of the figure San Francisco had recently crowned Man of the Century would placate the farmer. But the man was not having it.

He did not abide tramps, "even if one of them is named Edison." Firestone recalled, "We settled it after giving him $5, which is what he was after."

The next evening around 5:00 the Edison party rolled into the orchard at Woodchuck Lodge. They had covered nearly a hundred miles that day, winding on a northwesterly route over the crest of the Catskills before turning north at Arkville, New York, for the final straight shot into Roxbury.

They found Burroughs preoccupied with events in Europe. "I lived from day to day on the War news as usual," he said in recounting his experiences over the last few weeks. "When the paper comes, I want to run away to some secluded spot and read it undisturbed, as I would a love letter." Burroughs seemed pleased to see Edison and Firestone, but his enthusiasm for travel was at a low ebb. He did not wish to join the expedition. "He said he was too old and that he was through with journeys," Firestone recalled.

Nevertheless, Burroughs watched with mounting interest as his guests set up their camp in his orchard. In no time, he saw, they had established "a campers' extemporaneous village under my old apple trees—4 tents, a large dining tent and, at night, electric lights, and the man, Edison, the center around which it all revolved." That evening, Firestone instructed his cook to prepare something special. The effect of the meal on Burroughs was remarkable. "There was no convincing Burroughs that he should come along—that is before dinner," observed Firestone. "But the cook did himself extremely well that night and when we were through Mr. Burroughs suddenly announced that he would join us in the morning."

After the sumptuous supper Burroughs sat with Edison, Firestone, and DeLoach by the campfire as the conversation drifted toward the topics they shared an interest in. They spoke of matters well known to Edison—chemistry and physics—but also of things Edison enjoyed learning from Burroughs, the characteristics of the flora and fauna around his Catskills farm. Before long the talk turned to the war. Edison was pleased with the news that Romania, which had remained neutral thus far, had two days earlier joined forces with the Allies. Burroughs hoped to live long enough to see Germany taught a lesson.

There was a chill in the air that evening, but the campers slept outdoors. Burroughs noted with a touch of admiration that while Firestone came into the house to use the bathroom, Edison, once he had reverted to the natural state, would not allow himself even that concession to civilization.

The next morning, before breakfast, Burroughs led Edison up the hill from Woodchuck Lodge to get a view of the surrounding countryside and to point out the old farmstead where Burroughs had been born nearly eighty years before. The two men stopped where the roadcut had exposed a large, fractured granite boulder that now jutted from the hillside. Edison saw that Burroughs had chiseled an inscription into the rock—"The Ford Lot"—in a flowing cursive script. Beneath the words were a date—1914—and a line drawing of a pointing hand, of the sort used to draw attention to items in newspaper advertisements, marked with the initials J. B. The pointing index finger led Edison's eye down the hill and across the road to a large field. Burroughs explained that this was the meadow Ford had helped him clear of rocks and turn into one of the most verdant fields on the farm.

Burroughs drew Edison close and pointed out the striations that marked the face of the stone. These, he explained, had been scraped into the granite by the retreat of glaciers after the last ice age. "They've been there thousands of years," Burroughs said. "Mine ought to last a hundred or so." "Yes," Edison replied when he had made out what his friend was saying, "five hundred, at least."

After lunch under the apple trees the party began making preparations to leave. It was quite an operation with three vehicles to make ready. Edison's big, high-topped Simplex touring car, a right-hand-drive model with a powerful six-cylinder engine, would lead the way. The Ford touring car was a newer model than Burroughs's own. Finally, the sturdy White truck was outfitted to carry all of the camping and cooking gear.

The man in charge of the truck and gear was fifty-six-year-old Edison employee Fred Ott, who in addition to his other qualifications was the nation's first movie star. When Edison's cinematographer, William Dickson, had been scouting for an actor to appear in a short film he was planning to shoot at the beginning of 1894, he had had little trouble recruiting Ott, an outgoing, mustachioed cutup who had been hired as a mechanic in Edison's West Orange laboratory. Dickson's five-second film depicted Ott taking a pinch of snuff and hesitating for a moment before letting fly a dramatic, handkerchief-flapping sneeze. It would become the world's first copyrighted film. More than twenty years later Ott was Edison's right-hand man in the West Orange laboratory.

The chief cook—and the man who had changed Burroughs's mind about the trip—was a stout, dark-haired Englishman named Humphrey Endicott, who always looked tidy in the close-fitting clothing he favored. Although Endicott was now employed by Firestone, he liked to tell people that he had learned his way around a kitchen in the employ of the Duke of Devonshire. George Williams was Edison's driver, while two others, C. K. Lee and a man named Johns, would serve as camp assistants. They were already busy loading the truck with gear that included a kitchen tent and cooking utensils, four shelter tents, folding camp chairs and sleeping cots, as well as a large-format camera to document the adventure.

At 1:30 Burroughs said goodbye to Ursula and climbed aboard Edison's Simplex. With the older men riding in the Simplex and Harvey driving the Ford, the caravan trundled along a path leading down from the orchard and turned north on the main road that ran along the east branch of the Delaware River. With the late start and roads that twisted and turned through the mountainous Catskill country-side, it proved to be a taxing day. The light truck was having trou-ble keeping up on the steep grades, and the caravan did not reach Albany, the day's destination, until 8:30 that evening. The winding roads had turned a sixty-mile trip, as the crow flies, into ninety-five miles on the odometer of the Simplex. But they were moving.

In Albany that night the group violated the central tenet of Edison's camping philosophy: they slept indoors. Because it was still unclear when Ford might join them, and they needed to secure a replacement truck before leaving Albany, they had stopped at the Ten Eyck Hotel on State Street, near the state capitol building. The Ten Eyck billed itself as one of the "Natural Places to Pass the Night," but that was not likely to assuage Edison. The staff did, however, accede to his desire to keep his presence at the hotel under wraps. Nonetheless there was excitement among the other guests, and anticipation mounted over the possibility that Ford would join the inventor there. When a lean, gray-haired fellow happened into the hotel around 9:00, he was soon accosted by guests wishing to make Ford's acquaintance. The man said he regretted that he could not oblige them, and he admitted it was not the first time he had been mistaken for the automaker.

A stringer for the *New York Times* tried to engage the group in con-versation about the railroad strike then underway and other current affairs, but to no avail. "Mr. Edison," the reporter wrote the next day, "who is looking as brown and healthy as an Indian, refuses to discuss anything which does not pertain to woods, camps, fishing or atmo-spherical conditions." Burroughs was feeling better about his fitness for the expedition. "After the one day of it," he said, "with the hotel bed at the end to break me in, I'm all ready for the next stage, and I'll be enjoying camp as much as I ever did."

Before they left the hotel the following morning, Firestone telephoned Ford in Detroit. They were having a wonderful time of it, he said, and all hoped Ford would join them. Like Burroughs, Ford saw his resistance fade. He agreed to meet them in two or three days.

A little after noon the travelers piled back into the vehicles and left Albany, headed north along the west bank of the Hudson River. Just beyond Cohoes, ten or twelve miles above Albany, Edison spotted what looked like an abandoned house by the roadside and signaled a stop for lunch.

The crew set up a table, and Endicott had soon whipped up a meal. But before Edison and the others could tuck in, two women appeared driving along the road. "They had an air of possession," Firestone noted. He asked them if they had any objection to the party lunching there and was told that they did. The house, it turned out, was not theirs but belonged, or had belonged, to their grandmother. When Firestone offered to pay them for the use of the lawn, they simply drove away. But they were quickly followed by another vehicle hauling a prodigious load of hay. This time it was clear that the lunch party, which had set up on the road that led to the house, was blocking the way. "Hey," Edison called out to the driver, "can't you wait a bit?" The man indicated that the load was heavy, and he needed to be on his way. When Edison proposed waiting half an hour for two dollars, the man agreed. He took the money and then just drove around the table and proceeded along the road. After lunch the men took advantage of their hard-bought proprietorship of the place and sat on the porch reading.

Beyond Cohoes the route parted company with the Hudson for a while and angled toward Saratoga Springs, which they passed through later in the afternoon. When they came to a grove of mature pines growing close to the road, they stopped for the night. Tents were set up in neat rows beneath the pines, and a campfire was soon sending a curl of smoke into the treetops.

As a ground fog drifted into the woods that night, the party gathered around the campfire and spent the evening trading stories. The mood was lighter than it had been at Woodchuck Lodge, and soon the pine woods resounded with laughter. "The doctors think there is great remedial power in mechanical vibration," Burroughs remarked. "But the vibrations set up in the diaphragm by stories told around the campfire beat even that."

The group rose early the next morning, and by 10:30 they had broken camp and started toward Corinth, which lay just a mile to the north. When they entered the town, they could see rows of houses and shops, neatly arranged along a wide main street that cut across a grassy plain ringed by evergreens. In the distance ahead, a series of low, tree-crested ridges climbed up to a rounded peak that overlooked the town, a railway line skirting its base. Along the river there was a long, low-slung building with a brick smokestack at one end spewing a spiral of dark vapor from its tip. From the vicinity of this building, which appeared to be a factory, a deep rumble could be heard. As the cars came to a break in the line of shops near the middle of town, the men could suddenly see that the sound was not coming from the building but from a great waterfall that lay just beyond. Here the Hudson River tumbled through a tight, S-shaped curve, at the middle bend of which the river bottom seemed to simply drop away, leaving a rushing, roaring tumult of whitewater in its place. The cars slowed to a stop as the party took in the vista. From here it was clear that the long building housed a paper mill powered by the falls.

Just six years earlier this had been the site of a millworkers' strike that exploded into violent riots, triggering sympathetic strikes at mills throughout the region and ultimately involving some five thousand men. Strikers had attempted to destroy the town's bridges and railroad trestles with dynamite in order to block the entry of strikebreakers. In the end the National Guard had been deployed, but even then it took more than two months to settle the dispute. This cautionary tale did little to temper Edison's chief interest in the locale: how much electricity the powerful waterfall might be made to generate.

Beyond Corinth the road ran north alongside the river, then made a hard left to follow the Sacandaga River for some distance before curving right to cross the Sacandaga by way of an iron bridge. Just beyond the bridge the route turned left and passed through a railroad underpass. Here the tree cover was denser; pine and spruce ran to the edge of the stream on one side and leaned over narrow, meandering stretches of road. Another hard right carried the party onto a larger iron bridge that crossed over the Hudson. This far north the stately river that flowed past Burroughs's house at West Park was confined to a narrower channel, and the automobiles quickly rattled over the expanse of bridge, leaving the river behind. Another eight miles of mostly macadam road—surfaced, as many improved roads had been since the middle of the nineteenth century, with a matrix of crushed stone and stone dust—brought them into the town of Lake George, a picturesque waterfront village ringed by peaks and ridgelines of the southern Adirondack range into which their route would soon climb. Here they stopped to stretch their legs while the crew took on fuel and supplies.

From the town landing they could see the long, narrow lake stretching away to the northeast. James Fenimore Cooper, in *The Last of the Mohicans*, had given the glimmering body of water the name Horicon, after an Indian tribe he believed had once lived there, and that was also the name emblazoned on the bridge of the massive steamboat docked at the wharf. It was a successor to the elegant side-wheel vessel of that name that had plied the lake's waters at the end of the nineteenth century.

From Lake George it was a straight shot to Elizabethtown, sixty-odd miles to the north. But Edison had other plans. He enjoyed traveling back roads, and he had a landmark in mind to show his friends. So after following a street lined with trolley tracks to the edge of town, the party turned northwest on a paved road, which they followed until it crossed an iron bridge some five miles out of town. There they picked up another set of trolley tracks that led them into the town of Warrensburg, a bustling mill town perched astride the meandering Schroon River. There were several sawmills in operation, and workers could be seen walking homeward for the evening from a woolen mill and a handful of small factories that clustered near the river.

Thanks to Edison's guidebook, the camping party knew to watch for an iron water trough at a four-way intersection near the center of town. When they reached it, they crossed diagonally onto another macadam road that they were to follow until it forked four-and-a-half miles beyond the town. At the fork they bore left onto a winding road that carried them along the shore of Tripp Lake and into Chestertown. The route from Lake George had so far followed an itinerary the Blue Book called "Around the Horn," but at North Creek, five miles beyond Chestertown, Edison led the party off the macadam and onto a dirt and gravel road, which they followed for eight miles until it spilled them onto a bridge that crossed the Indian River and deposited them in the village of Indian Lake.

Just beyond the village the party stopped in an open field and set up camp for the night. The next morning, as the crew heaved boxes of gear into the truck, Edison and Burroughs wandered off to a bare outcrop of rock and sand at the edge of camp. The two men, Burroughs in his Stetson and Edison in a newsboy cap, were soon engaged in a lively conversation about the mineral makeup of the rock. Before long Edison was down on his knees peering at the ground while Burroughs sprawled nearby. The Wizard was excited by what he recognized as feldspar veining the fragments of granite rock he had scooped from the barren ground. Edison had been working on a method to extract valuable potash, which he used in his alkaline storage batteries, from feldspar. His enthusiasm was contagious, and he soon had Burroughs

*Burroughs and Edison discuss the mineral makeup of the landscape at their Indian Lake camp.*

identifying more examples of the mineral. As their geological interest mounted, they edged closer, Burroughs leaning in to shout his discoveries into Edison's cupped ear.

By 10:35 the vehicles were loaded—the crew by now referred to the truck as the "Waldorf" and called the Ford "Astoria"—and the caravan was rolling again. The day's route now took them onto a well-maintained dirt road that crossed the Cedar River over yet another iron bridge. Soon they were winding along the shore of Blue Mountain Lake.

As the Simplex came around a bend along the shore of the lake, Burroughs and Firestone caught their first glimpse of the landmark Edison had been aiming for when he selected this circuitous route over dirt and gravel roads. Prospect House Inn, visible in the distance across a stretch of open water, sat on a promontory extending into the lake, where it commanded panoramic views of the surrounding mountains. When the hotel opened in 1882, it had stood out among the guest houses then beginning to appear in the region. "It is the largest and the most beautiful of all the houses in the Adirondacks," proclaimed

one magazine at the time, "and a perfect marvel in the completeness
of its appointments." It could accommodate up to five hundred guests
in an atmosphere that blended "antique" open fireplaces with modern
furniture and fashionable Brussels carpets. Prospect House was one
of the first hotels to call guests' attention to its up-to-date kitchen,
which was "made one of the exhibits of the house." It also boasted a
steam elevator, bowling alley, shooting gallery, and billiard room, as
well as its own telegraph office. The hotel's signal point of distinction,
however, was one that Edison had himself helped bring about. Every
guest room was illuminated with electric light—a first not just in the
region but in the world. Edison lights also shone in the hallways, dining room, and parlor and on a good part of the grounds. Electric signal
bells connected the guest rooms to the front office.

When Prospect House was under construction in 1881, Edison had
worked with the builder's engineers to design and install the hotel's
electrical system. With the railway some thirty miles away, it was no
easy job transporting materials to the site, and some modifications
to the power plant had been entailed by the demands of the remote
location, where wood rather than coal would be used to fuel the boilers that turned Edison's dynamos. But it had all been made to work,
though the hotel itself had been in operation for a relatively short
time: the construction and maintenance costs had driven the original
proprietor into debt, and the hotel had finally closed in 1903.

By now much of the hotel building had been demolished, but from
across the lake Edison and his friends managed to get a photograph
of what remained, one wing of the original building standing alongside the windmill that once pumped gallons of Adirondack water to
its guests.


From Blue Mountain Lake the caravan drove on toward Long Lake,
where they picked up a macadam road that carried them eighteen

miles northeast to a fork. Edison directed them left, onto a gravel track that curved through the village of Tahawus, on the slopes of Mount Marcy. The town was a relic of the iron mining industry that had played out at the middle of the previous century. When the mines shut down, the abandoned town had become a waystation for hunters. It was here that Burroughs's old friend Theodore Roosevelt, then vice president, had been encamped when he got the news that President McKinley, who had been shot a few days earlier, had taken a turn for the worse. Roosevelt had set off at midnight for Buffalo, where McKinley lay dying, and he had quickly covered—at night in a buckboard wagon—some of the same rugged ground Burroughs and Edison had just crossed.

Burroughs was struck by the grandeur of the Adirondacks. "They take the conceit out of my native Catskills," he conceded. "Their vast geological age awes one, holding their heads so high after a hundred or more million of years, and their magnitude and primordial look— all stir the imagination."

The gravel road out of Tahawus took Edison's party almost twenty miles farther east, into the village of Schroon River. There they rejoined the road toward Elizabethtown and pushed north for twelve miles. Around 6:00, still a few miles shy of the town, they found a farmer, a man named Sharow, who agreed to let them camp on his land. The field was flat and closely clipped, an ideal campsite. The crew set up the dining fly in the open and tucked the sleeping tents behind it in the shelter of a copse of balsam and fir trees that flanked the site. By nightfall it was growing colder, and when the talk around the campfire ran out, the entire party knew it was going to be the coldest night they had yet faced. As it happened, the local sheriff was working with a convict crew nearby, and when he learned that Thomas Edison was camped at the Sharow farm, he had his charges chop wood for the campfire. That night as the campers threw log after log onto the fire in an effort to warm themselves, they laughed about spending the night as the guests of the sheriff. But there were no bars on their woodland cell.

Edison had come up with his own method for creating a warm cocoon of his blankets on nights like this: "He made them interlock so-and-so," Burroughs observed, "then got into them, 'made one revolution,' and the thing was done." It was a trick that would be put to good use that night. In the morning the campers woke to find their tents enveloped in frost, and over breakfast all agreed that it had been a wintry night's sleep.

Moving slowly in the chilly air that morning—it was Sunday, September 3—they did not leave camp until after 11:00. From Elizabethtown they drove east to Essex, on the western shore of Lake Champlain, where the Ausable River emptied into the lake. There they turned north toward Keeseville.

Routines were beginning to emerge as the campers grew accustomed to traveling together. Edison would rise at dawn or before and feed the campfire. Burroughs was also an early riser. Sometimes when he awoke in the middle of the night, he would tumble from his tent and sit by the embers of the fire thinking what he called long thoughts. At midday the caravan would stop for an hour, and lunch would be served, often by the roadside. After lunch the travelers would relax for a while before getting back on the road. Firestone often read the newspaper, Burroughs a book. Edison liked to read sitting in the front seat of the Simplex. Just as often, though, he would carry a blanket to the shade of a tree and take a nap. When they stopped on this afternoon outside Keeseville, Firestone sat on the running board of the Model T reading a newspaper in the sun. There was more news to please Edison: the Romanians, whose entry into the war on the Allied side he had so recently applauded, had taken the port of Orsova on the Danube, a choke point for river transport of Austrian and German war materiél.

A few miles east of Keeseville the party came to the Ausable

Chasm, "a deep gash in the old Potsdam sandstone," as Burroughs described it. Here the Ausable River, flowing out of the Adirondacks, had cut a two-mile-long gorge through the ancient sandstone bedrock of the region, creating striking rock formations and exposing layers of stratification. The visible layering of the rock recorded the slow-acting processes that had formed the landscape itself. Looking down at the sharply cut walls of the gorge was like looking back through five hundred million years of geological time. It was the kind of view that made Edison throw his hands up like a delighted schoolboy.

The party then turned west, following the river some eleven miles upstream toward Au Sable Forks, where the east and west branches of the Ausable came together. At a bend in the river, two miles from the fork, they stopped and set up camp. As usual Edison chose the campsite, and it was just the kind he preferred: remote, rugged, and close to flowing water. The crew pitched the tents on a sandy beach enclosed by the river bend. Across the water rose a steep, wooded hill.

For all its natural beauty the Ausable campsite had one problem. Its situation in the sandy headland created by the bend in the river left the campers exposed to cold winds breathing across the water. As the sun started to set and the temperature fell, it became evident that they were in for another chilly night. Firestone suggested that sleeping under such conditions might be unhealthy for a man Burroughs's age, particularly after the cold they had weathered the previous evening. After some discussion it was agreed that Firestone would drive Burroughs into the town of Au Sable Forks and install him in a hotel for the night.

When Firestone and Burroughs reached the town, they found a hotel perched next to an iron railroad bridge. Both went in, and when Firestone, who had been reluctantly conducting himself on the trip according to Edison Rules—no sleeping indoors, no bathing, no shaving—found himself in the familiar and comfortable environment of a hotel, he decided that he had better keep Burroughs company for the evening.

The next morning the two hotel guests checked out and started back along the state road leading to the river bend where they had left their friends. Back at camp they found Edison and Harvey Jr. sitting by the campfire. Edison eyed Firestone disapprovingly. "You're a tenderfoot," he chided. "Soon you'll be dressed as a dude." *Dude*—the overdressed city slicker who can't cut it in the wilderness—was a grievous insult in Edison's book. Firestone knew he had it coming to him. "When I saw the hotel bedroom and bath I could stand the strain no longer, and I struck," he admitted. "Not only did I have a shave and a bath, but I also spent the night comfortably in bed."

Once Edison's feathers were smoothed and camp broken, the reunited party set out along the Ausable, following the river upstream some twenty miles to Lake Placid. There they turned left up a steep macadam road for five miles until they saw the Raybrook Sanatorium,

*John Burroughs, Thomas Edison, and Harvey Firestone swap tales in camp along the Ausable River, September 1916.*

a sprawling stone hospital where tuberculosis patients convalesced in the clean Adirondack air. Here they bore left and followed another macadam road until it intersected with the main street of Saranac Lake. As the Simplex drove along the wet streets of Saranac, a large automobile crested the hill in front of them. When the car drew nearer, they saw it was driven by a young woman with another young woman as a passenger. Edison and the others watched as the car suddenly lost its traction. The driver had braked too abruptly on the wet road, and the car, as Burroughs observed, "suddenly changed ends and stopped leaving the amazed girls looking up the street instead of down." Edison was quick to analyze the situation. "Organized matter," he said calmly, "sometimes behaves in a very strange manner."

Leaving Saranac on Broadway, they crossed the railroad tracks near the town depot and followed the road out of town before stopping for lunch and some berry picking. It was an overcast afternoon, and the men wore overcoats as they scoured a scrubby hillside for berries. After lunch Firestone and Edison warmed themselves by the embers of the fire as they discussed the day's political headlines. The Allies had attacked the German front at the Somme, which Edison viewed as a step in the right direction, and President Wilson, to avert a railroad strike, had signed a measure cutting the workday of railroad workers to eight hours. This was folly to Edison, who believed in working a ten-hour day at the very least. When they had digested the news, the party resumed their journey. A few miles and two bridge crossings farther on, they passed through Paul Smiths, New York, a hamlet named for the hotel that stood at the intersection where several roads came together at the center of town. Half a mile from the hotel they turned right onto a winding stone road that took them north toward the town of Malone. They followed this for another dozen miles. Then, after putting in a seventy-three-mile day and still eighteen miles shy of Malone, Edison called a stop for the night.

The next morning, Tuesday, September 5, they drove into Malone, where they rested for an hour at the Hotel Flanagan. Despite Firestone's flouting of the Edison rules for camp conduct, the travelers had by this time achieved the disheveled appearance Edison favored. "Dressed for camping, one would not suspect their identity unless he knew them," a local resident observed.

Around 3:00 that afternoon they reached Plattsburgh, on the western shore of Lake Champlain, and stopped at the Hotel Champlain, where a telegram was waiting for Firestone from Ford's secretary; it reported that Ford and Edsel were leaving for Buffalo by train and would transfer to a car there and motor to meet the camping party. But the message was dated three days earlier. Later in the afternoon, a new message arrived: Ford had obligations in the West and would not be joining the party at all. It was disappointing news, but by now Burroughs, Firestone, and Edison were making the most of their time together, slipping comfortably into roles that would be well established by the time Ford came to join them on future trips: Edison mapped the routes and kept the caravan on course, Firestone handled logistical problems and smoothed the way with the locals they met, and Burroughs catalogued the birds and flowers.

After camping for the evening on a farm owned by the Behan family, just north of the Plattsburgh town line, the party motored back into town on Wednesday to spend the morning at the Clinton County fair in the company of John Myers, the local Firestone tire dealer. Leaving a little after noon, they then drove fifteen miles north to Chazy Landing, where they caught a ferry that would take them in stages across the lake to Vermont.

The party crossed Champlain at one of its widest points. The lake itself lay like a tremendous watery dragon, crouched in a 125-mile-long depression stamped into the Adirondacks. Its head flopped across the Canadian border; the front legs reached for the city of St. Albans,

Vermont; the back ones kicked at Burlington; and its tail trailed away toward Ticonderoga, New York. Because the surface was just a hundred feet above sea level, the mountains in the distance ringed the lake like tall, ancient sentinels.

The twelve-mile distance to the Vermont shore made island hopping the best strategy for the crossing. At Isle LaMotte, the ferry's first stop, Edison, Burroughs, and the others went ashore, and after walking around the island found a sheltered spot on an outcropping of rocks just north of the village. Here they built a fire and cooked a late lunch. They spent about two hours on the island before continuing the trip across the lake, touching at Grand Isle and North Hero before going ashore in Vermont. By 7:00 they had reached Burlington and set up camp outside town on Bellevue Road in a part of the village of Winooski known as the Second Heights. On Thursday morning, September 7, Burroughs rose before the others and made breakfast. He had cooked flapjacks on the camping trip in Florida, and Edison, who came limping to the breakfast table because of a tumble he had taken the day before, was eager to have them again. With a good meal under their belts, the party was underway by 8:30.

They drove into Burlington, where Firestone had arranged to receive mail. While at the post office, he asked to have any further deliveries forwarded to Pittsfield. That afternoon they spent about an hour in Middlebury, Vermont, before driving on to Rutland, where they stopped for lunch.

The longer the camping party lingered in any one area, the more public attention came their way. (This fact, combined with Edison's ambitious itineraries, kept the cars on the move, leading Burroughs to quip that even the inventor's holidays were "strenuous.") By and large the local response was favorable, but when a wit at the *Rutland News* got wind of the Edison party "roughing it" in his state, he could not resist poking fun. "Of the three automobiles one was a Ford," read an article that appeared the day after the group had passed through Rutland, "which perhaps was for roughing it, and into which when the roads became too smooth and comfortable the distinguished men all piled." Even while taking a swipe at the Model T for its uncomfortable ride, however, the report conceded the Ford's other virtues. "Then again, when they wished to ascend a precipitous cliff mayhap they used the Ford, for it is related that it can climb a tree, a church steeple or anything like that."

From Rutland the party drove south, climbing higher into the mountainous terrain of Vermont. As Burroughs said later of this leg of the trip, "We took a great slice off the Green Mountains."

After camping for the night near Arlington on the land of a stocky, gray-haired man named Bronson, the campers got an early start toward Bennington, just fifteen miles to the south. From there they continued south across the Massachusetts line. Reaching Pittsfield at lunchtime, the rest of the party managed to persuade Edison to violate one of his camp precepts: they ate a hot lunch in the restaurant of a hotel in town. It was fortunate that the scruffy vagabonds were allowed into the hotel in the first place. "They were sadly in need of clothes brushes and shaves," one local noted, "but they were too happy to notice it." For Burroughs's friend DeLoach, who was leaving the party at Pittsfield, the hotel lunch served as a celebratory farewell to the men who had been his companions for the last ten days.

After lunch Harvey encountered some difficulty in starting the Ford he was driving. While the others stood by watching him crank the flivver's starter, a bystander commented on the stubble beard Edison was wearing. The inventor had a simple reply. "Burroughs never shaves," he said, "so why should I?"

Once the Ford was running again, the caravan followed the trolley tracks south out of Pittsfield for a mile and a half, then picked up a good macadam road that took them as far as Lenox. Six more miles of winding road brought them to a sign for Great Barrington. Here the road descended steeply, following the slope of Monument Mountain. The panoramic view of the surrounding countryside once again made Edison throw up his hands. When the road leveled out at the foot of the slope, they turned to follow another set of trolley tracks, which led them into Great Barrington.

With it nearing noon, they picked up supplies for lunch and found a spot just beyond town to take a break. Harvey's experience with the Ford that morning stuck in Edison's mind. For several months he had been working to perfect a battery for automotive use, with the plan of creating a convenient electrical starter. It was an idea to mull over after the meal. While the others rested or read, he could be seen scribbling in a notebook.

Once the crew had reloaded the truck, they pushed on southward, crossing into Connecticut and passing through Salisbury and Lakeville. Twelve miles beyond Lakeville the road ended at a cemetery, where they turned right and drove into Amenia, New York. At a stone watering trough they angled onto a road that climbed a steep grade for a mile and a half. At the top they turned left and pushed southward. That afternoon they passed the gates of the Charles Dieterich estate, where a sprawling Queen Anne mansion sat on more than two thousand acres of property the gas tycoon had acquired in the 1880s. Straining toward home now, they reached Poughkeepsie just in time to catch the 6:00 ferry across the Hudson River.

When they reached the western shore, they began looking for a campsite and eventually settled on a farm off Milton Road, four miles south of Highland. "The whole party looked brown and hearty," a local reporter observed. The weather had turned hot again, and the group enjoyed a warm night's sleep after their longest day on the road. Since leaving "Camp Bronson" that morning, they had covered just over 143 miles.

The next morning the owner of the farm came out to meet his

guests. A compact, wiry man with a walrus mustache, Reverend George Allen wore a white, short-sleeved shirt and a tie, black trousers, and a white belt. Allen was accompanied by his two daughters, the younger one on horseback. He and Burroughs stood talking while the crew dismantled the tents.

Burroughs's son, Julian, arrived a little later in the morning, and the old naturalist said goodbye to his traveling companions. Then he and Julian set off on the five-mile drive to West Park. That evening Burroughs continued on to Roxbury, where he was reunited with his wife.

When camp was broken, around 9:30, Edison and Firestone and the crew drove south through Newburgh and Harriman. They stopped for a final lunch—thick slices of bread with tea—and for Edison a final midday nap, stretched out on the grass in the shade of a tree. After lunch they drove on through Pompton and Montclair, reaching West Orange at 3:00. From there Firestone and Harvey would return home by train. Altogether the camping party had driven through more than 1,100 miles of the Adirondacks and the Green Mountains.

As soon as he arrived in West Orange, Edison swapped his traveling clothes for a laboratory coat and went to check on things in the lab. The man his assistants saw coming through the door was "sunburned and full of vim." He was also full of ideas. The inventor had filled a notebook with schemes he wanted to explore and new experiments to try.

When reporters asked the next morning how he had liked his vacation, Edison responded that "a good time was enjoyed by one and all." But he quibbled with the suggestion that the camping excursion had given him a break from work. He had done plenty of work while away, he said, before explaining "that the hard work consisted in trying to find some sort of flower or tree along the way that John Burroughs couldn't name right off the bat."

After the respite offered by the Adirondack trip, the campers settled back into daily routines that still unfolded in the shadow of war. On October 20 Burroughs was walking in the fields above Woodchuck Lodge in Roxbury when he came upon a large garter snake in a newly seeded field. It was all but immobile, its system slowed down by the chilly autumnal temperatures. When Burroughs tried to stir it with his cane, it flattened itself into a tight coil and opened its mouth, but did not strike or try to escape. As the naturalist continued to toy with the snake, it slowly folded its body and twined the lower half tightly around the upper. Burroughs, steeped as he was in the latest war news, interpreted the situation strategically. "If he thought my stick was another snake trying to swallow him, this was good tactics—it would have made the problem much more difficult."

A few days later Burroughs moved from Roxbury back to West Park for the winter, and on the afternoon of October 24, he caught the train to New York to see Ford. From the train station he began to walk toward the Ritz Carlton, where Ford and Clara were staying, but on Madison Avenue, Ford intercepted him. He told Burroughs he saw him coming "a block away," and he was "hitting it up lively." Ford escorted Burroughs back to the hotel where they spent the night.

The next morning Burroughs went along with Ford to the Democratic party headquarters in the city, where the automaker was scheduled to meet with the chairman of the Democratic National Committee, Vance McCormick, and the finance chairman, Henry Morgenthau, to discuss a plan to support President Wilson's reelection campaign. In the wake of the Peace Ship debacle, Ford's interest in political action, far from being defused, had strengthened. The difference was that now he was willing to throw his support behind Wilson as the antiwar candidate. Burroughs, although he believed the United States should join the fray, agreed with Ford's choice on the grounds that Wilson was "a much stronger man" than his Republican

opponent, Charles Evans Hughes; Wilson was, as he put it, "the man
the pro-Germans don't want."

After the meeting Burroughs and Ford had lunch with Clara
before Ford walked Burroughs to the train station, where the naturalist caught the train home. Ford meanwhile boarded a train to
Long Branch, New Jersey, where he met with the president himself. He first told Wilson that, inspired by a discussion the two had
a few weeks earlier about "forward movement among womankind,"
he had put his women employees on the same pay standard as the
men. Ford's Emersonian sense of compensation, one of the earliest
ideas he had imbibed from his friendship with Burroughs, had now
been extended to include both sexes. Ford then revealed the real business of his visit, showing the president the advertisements for his
reelection campaign that the automaker intended to have published
in newspapers around the country. If Ford could not stop the war by
direct action, he intended to make sure that Wilson remained in a
position to do it for him.

⌒——○

# 7

# AT SEA

November 1916 began mildly at West Park. The maples had lost most of their leaves, and light frosts chilled the evenings. The autumn, Burroughs had long felt, was nature at its most easeful. In stark contrast to the season, recent news from Fort Myers was deeply disturbing. As reported in the November issue of *Bird Lore*, the magazine of the Audubon Society, the egret rookery at Alligator Bay, the nesting ground that Ford had helped to protect, had been raided by poachers who had not stopped at killing the birds and stealing their plumage. They had gone on to hack down the brush where the egrets nested and then burned the entire rookery. It was doubtful that any birds would return next season. It was as if the European war had engulfed nature itself.

On November 4, Ursula Burroughs, who had weakened over the summer, was moved to the sanitarium in Middletown. Three days later Burroughs walked into West Park to cast his vote for Wilson, but he harbored no hope, either for the election or for much else. He felt himself weakening as well. It might have been a sympathetic response to his wife's decline—he had been losing weight and was down to 135 pounds—but the deeper effect was one he experienced not so much physically as philosophically. The world was changing in ways that he felt were sealing him off from the increasingly modern sympathies of the masses, despite the fondness he had at times felt for Ford's Model T. As the tempo of American life accelerated, thanks in part to the inventive contributions of Ford and Edison, Burroughs remained largely the same man he had been in the 1880s, when life had moved at a walking pace and he had sauntered through the countryside with Walt Whitman—"the great bard on my right hand and the sea upon my left." That world now seemed a distant planet.

Nature reflected his own solitude back at him. "Woods deserted," he wrote in his journal after a walk on November 8. "The only live thing one chickadee that flew across the road in front of me." The creek he had crossed that afternoon was "choked with brown leaves."

The following day he learned from Ursula's doctors that X-rays had revealed cancer of the colon. She was expected to live no longer than a month or perhaps six weeks. Burroughs went home that night and slept on a cot he placed at the foot of her now-empty bed. Overcome by loneliness and regret, he found that he was experiencing physical symptoms himself. He began to treat himself with a patent elixir called Russell's Emulsion, a clove-scented mixture of beef fat with coconut, peanut, and olive oils. By the beginning of December he felt it had helped him, "as if it oiled all my machinery."

Ursula, although still weakening, held on through the winter, but by February it was evident to the entire family that her death was near. She hardly acknowledged visitors. Burroughs himself was near collapse under the strain of watching his wife's decline.

When Ford contacted Burroughs with an invitation to accompany him on a sea voyage to Cuba, the naturalist's family and friends, sure that an escape from the strain would extend his own life, all encouraged him to go. Burroughs was torn, reluctant to leave his wife but aware that his presence would do nothing to help her. He agreed to go with Ford.

On February 19, a cold and cloudy morning, Burroughs went to tell Ursula goodbye and felt that she hardly knew he was there. "I stood by her bedside some moments," he recalled, "gazing upon her emaciated face, yellow with jaundice, and wondered if I would ever see it again, not believing I would." He pressed his face to hers, his wife of almost sixty years, and said, "Good bye." To his surprise, she was able to reply. "Good bye, dear."

When Ford learned that Ursula Burroughs lay near death, he feared, as did Burroughs's family, that the old naturalist might not have the strength to survive her last days. Suddenly, Ford's already-planned voyage to Cuba took on a second purpose as a rescue mission, to distract his friend from the tragedy unfolding at home.

In the afternoon, following his poignant goodbye to Ursula, Burroughs met Ford at the depot, and by 9:30 that evening their train was leaving New York, headed south. The same day a local newspaper reported that their friend Edison had withdrawn to a concrete building on Eagle Rock at the summit of Orange Mountain in the Watchung range, where he was at work on secret experiments thought to involve submarines. Edison had been seen looking through a telescope at the valley below. Observers trying to guess his purpose on the mountain suggested that the distant prospects visible from Eagle Rock mimicked the conditions involved in observations at sea "and that it would be an ideal place in which to develop some powerful glass."

Ford, too, had innovation on his mind as he pursued this latest venture. He had initially arranged his trip to Cuba in order to meet with Milton S. Hershey, the millionaire chocolate mogul who, in addition to his candy-making operations in Hershey, Pennsylvania, owned three sugar plantations in Cuba, vast tracts of sugarcane that supplied the raw materials to feed America's ever-growing sweet tooth.

Like Ford, Hershey had made a small start in business and expanded through relentless innovation. He opened his first candy shop in Philadelphia in the late 1870s, then built a so-called caramel house in Lancaster, Pennsylvania, where he boiled sugar into a kind of sweet mud that he laced with various flavorings and nuts. Constantly tinkering with both recipes and production methods, by 1900 Hershey had shifted his product line from caramel to chocolate, and he soon had several factories operating around the clock to transform sugar and cocoa into a novel chocolate drop he called a "kiss," utilizing assembly-line production methods that foreshadowed those Ford would adopt in his automobile plant. Hershey had also preceded Ford in raising the pay of his workers; since 1912 he had paid every employee a bonus that matched, in percentage terms, the dividend received by his shareholders.

Hershey's aim in Cuba was not simply to ensure a steady supply of sugar but to streamline its production. Rather than ship jute bags filled with raw sugar that required further refining in the United States, as had been the practice up to that point, he milled the sugar in Cuba, and he was constructing a railroad that would allow him to transport the finished product in massive hopper cars of the kind normally used to move coal. These would then be ferried to a rail terminal in Key West, from which point they could be quickly transported anywhere in the country.

Ford, who avoided sweets, had his own reasons for wanting to inspect Hershey's operation. Under the influence of Burroughs and Luther Burbank, he and Edison had grown ever more focused on using plant-based alternatives to replace scarce resources their businesses depended on. Ford saw the sugarcane that Hershey turned into sugary treats as a potential source of ethanol, an efficient, clean-burning fuel that could free him from the vagaries of oil pricing.

Ford and Burroughs, traveling in Ford's private railcar, reached Charleston, South Carolina, the next evening around midnight. They went aboard Ford's yacht the following morning. The *Sialia* was a luxurious 207-foot-long, steam-driven vessel with a beam of 27 feet. It drew just over 11 feet of water. There was a crew of 30, including the skipper, a young New Englander who looked to Burroughs like "the real thing." Ford showed his guest to a large stateroom adjoining the one he shared with Clara. It was outfitted in the most lavish fashion—"too fine for a Slabsider like me," Burroughs thought.

After they had settled in that afternoon, Ford and Burroughs took the ship's launch to look at a German steamer that had been scuttled in the harbor a few weeks earlier. To Burroughs the derelict vessel looked "German," by which he meant "coarse, dirty, ugly."

The next morning, with Fort Sumter now visible in the distance, the crew of the *Sialia* hoisted anchor and motored slowly out of the harbor. Through the calm, clear afternoon Burroughs sat on deck watching gulls hovering overhead and marveling at the adroitness of their flight. The *Sialia* slipped past Saint Augustine the next day. The sea remained visibly calm, but the boat rolled uncomfortably through the following evening. On February 24, as they passed Palm Beach, Burroughs watched two porpoises frolicking in the vessel's wake. "What jolly, sportive creatures they are—the school boys of the sea!" he thought.

The next day they anchored off Miami and went ashore to visit Firestone and his family at their house in Lemon City, where they were staying for the winter. ("Why is 'Lemon' less dignified as the name of a PO than 'Orange'?" Burroughs wondered.) Firestone's house, a large and elegant structure built of coral rock, sat on the edge of the bay and was surrounded by orange and grapefruit trees, inside a ring of coconut palms. There were children—Firestone had seven—all about the grounds. Ford and Burroughs spotted two robins and a number of red-poll warblers among the orange trees. After dinner Firestone took his guests on an automobile tour of Miami, "a large fine town" of twenty thousand, before the Ford party returned to the *Sialia*.

Their plan was to come back ashore the following day for an excursion into the Everglades, no doubt a more comfortable one than Burroughs and Ford had enjoyed with Edison on the western side of the state. But when the sea grew rough that night, Ford decided to sail on to Key West, where the *Sialia* stayed for two days, taking on oil and supplies, before steaming south through choppy seas on Wednesday morning. That afternoon they entered the harbor at Havana.

The first days of March were pleasantly warm. On March 2, Ford and Burroughs drove with Milton Hershey fifty miles inland to visit a number of large sugar plantations. Burroughs was impressed by the quality of the road, a twenty-mile stretch of which ran smoothly under an arching canopy formed by laurel trees. The surrounding countryside, however, was unkempt, and the dwellings he saw looked to him primitive and ugly. He saw no fruit groves and no crops growing besides the ubiquitous sugarcane. Yet even in this apparently barren terrain, he and Ford spotted an array of birdlife.

"Flocks of boat-tailed grackles here and there, and now and then a kingbird, and a shrike, and a mocking bird. No crows, but buzzards very common, and a few red-poll warblers," Burroughs recorded. "Also I saw one ring-necked plover."

The sugar plantations themselves contrasted with the impoverished country around them. In the afternoon the party visited a 13,000-acre estate managed by a distinguished-looking elderly Spaniard. His house sat in the middle of a lushly cultivated garden, and the milling operation he oversaw was a study in efficiency that might have been modeled on a Ford factory—"the cane coming in by carloads or train-loads, at one end, and going out in big sacks of sugar (325 lbs) at the other—only 2 or 3 hours from the cane to the sugar."

This image of an efficient tropical plantation was one Ford would

carry with him. In his mind it promised a source of ethanol, even as
it hinted at a solution to the problem of rubber supply that he had so
often discussed with Edison and Firestone. As for Hershey, though
Ford admired the efficiency with which he had organized his own sugaring operation on the island, the two men, for all they had in common, could not have differed more in character. Hershey enjoyed fine
cigars and champagne and spoke of the thrill of gambling, whether at
casinos or racetracks. Risk itself seemed to please him. When their
car was flagged down by a man who warned of brigands operating in
the area, Ford naturally assumed they would turn back, but Hershey
blithely argued for going on. "We both need the publicity," he quipped.
"What a headline it would make: Ford and Hershey Captured by Ban-
dits!" Ford was relieved to make it back aboard the *Sialia*.

   The next evening the party went ashore in Havana for dinner.
Standing for fifteen minutes on a street corner, Burroughs counted
fifty automobiles rushing past. They were all Fords. "The paper here
said they hoped Mr. Ford would not be run over during his visit by one
of his own cars," Burroughs noted.


When Ford and Clara left to join Hershey on a tour of plantations
that lay farther inland, Burroughs remained aboard the *Sialia*,
reading a biography of Emerson, loafing on deck, and sometimes
getting lost in his nostalgic long thoughts. On Wednesday he went
ashore in the morning and sent a telegram to his family. At 3:00 that
afternoon he was reading a New York newspaper on deck when a
reply arrived. Ursula had died the day before. Burroughs had known
this day would come soon, but he was nonetheless unprepared for it.
"Here in this peaceful harbor, on this calm summer day, with the big
ships going and coming about me, came this sad news. A long chapter in my life, nearly sixty years ended. I am too much crushed to
write about it now."

*John Burroughs aboard Henry Ford's yacht* Sialia *in 1917.*

The following day he sent a telegram to his son, Julian, asking if he should return home. But it was too late to make any difference. Although it was an especially hot day, he went ashore in the launch and walked in the hills above the harbor. In his pain he subsided into the mode of living he had always relied on. He enumerated the wildlife—"a slim, brown warbler . . . a long, slender, swift-footed salamander . . . buzzards soaring . . . large yellow flower on low shrubs."

On Friday he finished reading the biography of Emerson and sat on deck recalling the times he had met the Concord sage. He remembered one episode from the 1870s when he was living in Washington, D.C., and Emerson gave a lecture in Baltimore. Burroughs and his friend Walt Whitman had gone to hear him. When they talked afterward, Emerson told Burroughs he had his first book, *Wake-Robin*, on his table. "Capital title!" Emerson had said. "But he said nothing about the contents," Burroughs recalled with a pang.

By March 11 the Fords had returned. That morning before dawn the *Sialia* hoisted anchor and steamed out of Havana harbor. Burroughs went out on deck in the half light to watch the city fade away.

"Ten days of my life passed here," he thought, "and its longest and most important chapter closed."

As the *Sialia* slipped past the Morro fortress at the mouth of the harbor, the ship began to roll in the ocean swell. Before they reached Key West, everyone on board was seasick. Burroughs and the Fords had retreated to their cabins, coming on deck only, as Burroughs put it, "to pay tribute to Old Neptune."

On the way home Ford took the *Sialia* up the western coast of Florida so he and Burroughs could visit Fort Myers. They anchored off the mouth of the Caloosahatchee and took a power boat upriver. Burroughs found the speed—nearly twenty miles an hour—"exhilarating." It was like riding in a fast car on a smooth road. Edison was not at his winter house, but Ford and Burroughs went ashore and walked into town.

The next evening they sailed on to Tampa, where the *Sialia* ran aground in a thick fog. Newspapers were warning of an impending railway strike, so Burroughs decided to leave for home immediately. He went ashore by launch and made his way to the train station. Three days later he was back home at West Park. "Very sad, but very glad to be in a haven of rest once more."

Once he had settled back in the house he had shared with Ursula, his regret focused on the way he had abandoned his wife a month earlier. "I knew it was our last good bye," he said. "It was weak of me to go—but it would have killed me to stay."

A few weeks after his return from Cuba, Burroughs took his Ford car out for a drive to Port Ewen, New York, with his friend Clara Barrus, a fifty-three-year-old psychiatrist and writer who had become both secretary and biographer for the naturalist. On the drive home Burroughs encouraged Barrus to take the wheel. It was only her second time driving. Burroughs was impressed by how well she controlled the car and let his own attention flag. As they crossed a bridge near home, Barrus lost control and ran the car onto a roadside embank-

ment. The Ford rolled over, trapping Burroughs underneath and pin-
ning Barrus's legs. Burroughs heard a loud crack as the car went
over—the sound of his arm breaking. Barrus began to shout, and
her calls eventually caught the attention of some passing workmen,
who were able to right the car and free the two passengers. Barrus
was scraped but not severely injured. Burroughs's arm, though, was
badly hurt, and his ribs were bruised. He tried to ride out the injury
by putting the arm in a sling, but when he finally went to the hospital
in Newburgh a few days later to have it x-rayed, he learned that the
neck of the humerus was broken. It would be months before he could
use his arm normally again.

Although his injuries kept Burroughs close to home, Edison was
already plotting to lure him back into the wilderness. Back in January the inventor had begun planning for a camping trip in Florida
that winter. He was expecting Ford, Burroughs, and Luther Burbank
to join him in Fort Myers, and on January 15 he wrote to Firestone to
suggest that he and Harvey join the camping party, too. Earlier that
day, he told Firestone, he had arranged for his entire camping outfit,
along with four new tents, to be shipped to Florida. The only thing
missing was the cast of characters.

Firestone, though, was not enthusiastic about what came to mind
when he imagined camping in the semitropical south. "I must confess
that as much as I enjoy a camping trip with you," came the reply from
Lemon City, "I am too much of a coward to live in a camp in Florida.
Snakes and all kinds of insects just give me a fit, and I know how
much you dislike a coward or a timid fellow and I would not impose
upon you on a camping trip in Florida." Firestone said he was expecting to see Ford in Florida, and he proposed visiting Edison at his
house rather than in camp.

There the matter rested until world events reordered the pattern
of all their lives.

Just over two months later, on April 2, Woodrow Wilson went before Congress and asked for a declaration of war against Germany. The following day, which was clear and cool at Riverby, found Burroughs celebrating his eightieth birthday. News of the president's declaration lifted the old man on a great swell of emotion—"my best gift today." He believed that Wilson's courage in entering the still unpopular war would "play a great part in the future political history of mankind."

Before the week was out, newspapers were reporting that the imminent war was all but won, thanks to a one-man submarine that Edison had designed in a secret laboratory and that Ford would fabricate at a rate of a thousand a day. The truth behind the hyperbole was that Edison had redoubled his efforts on behalf of the navy department—and Ford, in a dramatic shift from the pacifist stance he had taken earlier, now made it known that he was prepared to commit his vast industrial resources to the war effort. Once the possibility of avoiding war evaporated, Ford, a practical man at his core, had no trouble shifting gears. If he could not prevent war, he would use all his resources to make it as short as possible.

Since signing on to head Josephus Daniels's Naval Consulting Board, Edison had directed nearly all his attention to combating the submarine threat. He first tackled the problem using a device called an induction balance, with which he was familiar from his investigations into electricity and magnetism. Essentially an arrangement of two coils, one of which had a rapidly interrupted current passed through it, the induction balance worked as a kind of metal detector. Any conductive material, such as a steel submarine, that entered the electromagnetic field set up by the pair of coils would alter the flow of current between them and could thus be detected.

The basic principle behind the machine had been known for decades. In July 1881, days after the shooting of then-president James

A. Garfield, telephone pioneer Alexander Graham Bell, expanding on a suggestion put forward by mathematician Simon Newcomb, had built an induction balance device for the purpose of locating the bullet that remained lodged in the president's abdomen. Bell connected a telephone amplification system to the apparatus in such a way that a tone was produced when a metallic object was detected. Although Bell's induction balance failed to determine the location of the bullet that had wounded Garfield—the president was to die of his wound some months later—Bell went on to improve his system, and by the time the world war began, induction balance devices were being put to practical use. As early as 1915 the French army was using the devices to clear shell fragments and unexploded munitions from battlefields so that land could be put back into agricultural production as quickly as possible.

All through the spring Edison labored single-mindedly to apply induction balance technology to the task of submarine detection. In theory the system should have worked perfectly. A submarine was after all a massive body of metal moving through an aqueous medium that presented few obstacles to detection. Nevertheless, Edison's experiments again and again failed to produce positive results.

Although he was ultimately compelled to set aside his hopes for the induction apparatus, Edison remained undeterred. If he could not use electricity to detect submarines, he reasoned, he could nevertheless improve on established methods of coastal surveillance. In the wake of the war declaration he turned his attention to an elaborate plan for a system of manned submersible buoys that would maintain a round-the-clock lookout network stretching from Nova Scotia to southern Florida.

The basic pattern for the buoys came from the floating markers employed by the Lighthouse Board to alert oceangoing vessels to hazards along the coast—essentially enclosed metal rafts some eleven feet in diameter that were anchored in such a way as to bob with the ocean swell rather than roll as a ship would. According to the Light-house Board, these buoys were all but indestructible. Edison's innovation was to make them both submersible and capable of sustaining a crew of three men, who would be supplied with all the equipment necessary—including a sound detection device and radio equipment—for both surveillance and communication with the shore.

"The buoy," as Edison described it, "contains tables for the wireless apparatus, and electrical parts of the sound detecting apparatus. It also contains bunks for the men, four weeks' supply of food and water, and cooking apparatus. It is lighted by storage battery." At most times the buoy would ride at the surface. But when an enemy vessel was sighted, or to evade the worst kinds of weather, it could submerge to a depth of a hundred feet. Edison proposed to use a two-horsepower compressor to pressurize enough air to sustain the crew during submersions and to eject ballast water when it was time to resurface.

In Edison's mind the buoy would not just be effective; it would be a comfortable base of operations for the men stationed there. While on the surface the crew would enjoy fresh air and a more stable platform than a ship could offer. The buoy's technological methods of detection would also give the crew an unprecedented margin of safety. "While watching in the daytime, the detector will warn of the presence of top ships or submarines before they can be seen. If in danger of being run down by a top ship or being shot at by submarine, they can submerge out of danger." At night the detector would offer protection against ships, friendly or hostile, that happened to be running without lights.

As Edison saw it, these buoys could be assembled quickly and cheaply, with no additional burden being put on the system of naval shipyards. The average boiler shop, he maintained, could do the work, and he estimated the cost would be well under ten thousand dollars each. Working in conjunction with a small fleet of destroyers, which could respond to the sightings reported by the buoys, as well as a modest network of supply vessels, the buoy system, Edison believed, offered real hope of shielding the East Coast against the submarine menace.

While most of the experiments Edison conducted for the navy were original in nature, he was also quick to adapt existing technology where he saw a way to improve it. In May, when he learned that Germany had begun extracting nitrogen from ammonia for use in explosives, he recalled experiments he had conducted nearly twenty years earlier in which ammonia had been produced as a by-product. He quickly rebuilt the apparatus he had used in the earlier experiment and was soon producing substantial quantities of cheap ammonia from little more than air and iron.

July found Edison roving the waterfront in New York in the company of representatives of the Cunard Steamship Company, investigating steamships with an eye toward making them less vulnerable to submarines. With the aid of a draftsman he came up with a system of camouflage that broke the silhouette a ship presented against the horizon. He also recommended removing masts and other superstructures that, with the passing of the age of sail, were now used primarily for supporting communication equipment. Edison devised a replacement system that employed small pipes and guy wires that could be quickly erected to transmit wireless messages, then just as quickly disassembled. He reasoned that merchant ships only became targets when they were detected by lookouts aboard the German submarines. If they were harder to detect, they would be harder to sink.

However, the ship itself was the least of the problems when it came to concealing a vessel. Smoke from the coal that powered a steamship's engines broadcast a dark plume visible some twenty miles away, making the ship vulnerable to a submarine anywhere within a 40-mile radius. The use of cleaner-burning anthracite rather than bituminous coal, he suggested, would greatly reduce the visible evidence of a vessel's passage. It would also allow a reduction in the height of smoke-stacks. Taken together, these measures would significantly diminish the area from which a ship could be spotted, a reduction, according to Edison's calculations, from 1,600 square miles to 144.

The Cunard company was much quicker to accept Edison's suggestions than the navy had proven to be. Before the month was out, they had begun to camouflage some of their cargo vessels in the manner Edison recommended. One of these, Edison later learned, operated for a year unmolested by submarines. Only when it was forced into a convoy with other, uncamouflaged vessels was the ship detected and sunk.

Edison believed that similar measures would help to protect American warships and make them more effective against enemy submarines. On August 16, William Saunders, the engineer who served as acting chairman of the Consulting Board, met with Secretary Daniels to explain Edison's plan. Daniels, quick to see the sense of the scheme, immediately relayed it to President Wilson. But Wilson was of an entirely different mindset. As he saw matters, the United States, when forced to enter the war, must take the lead in offensive measures against the submarine threat. Expending a great deal of effort and money merely to conceal ships would, he feared, make the United States appear weak, whereas similar expenditures on offensive technology might achieve the same goal while putting up a bolder front. On August 20, Daniels tried again, this time taking Edison along with him to meet with Wilson. Edison led the president through his arguments about anthracite coal and the shortening of smoke-stacks and then went on to detail schemes that were more to Wilson's liking: a plan for detecting submarines that Edison believed would make them vulnerable to attack and an aggressive turning method for protecting ships from torpedoes.

Edison also had some more overtly offensive schemes up his sleeve. He had come up with a plan for mining the German-held harbor of Zeebrugge, outside Bruges. Edison envisioned approaching the harbor on a moonless night and releasing a small fleet of unmanned, flat-bottomed boats powered by electric motors and guided by a gyrostatic rudder system. The boats, some fifteen feet long and four feet wide, would have a rounded deck that would give them a silhouette of only six inches above the waterline, making them all but invisible on a dark night. As Edison described it, the boats would be outfitted with mines linked to a triggering system that would detonate the explosives when they reached the harbor's breakwater.

(As it happened, the British Royal Navy conducted its own unorthodox raid against German forces at Zeebrugge the following spring. On April 23, 1918, British warships entered the neck of the harbor under cover of a smokescreen and destroyed three of their own derelict vessels, scuttling them in a position intended to block traffic into and out of the port. At the same time, a British submarine rammed the causeway linking German fortifications at the mouth of the harbor to the mainland. Although the raid did briefly disable the port, it came at a high cost to the British, who suffered more than five hundred casualties. Edison's plan might well have been more effective.)

On October 16 Edison again met with Daniels and showed him a detailed chart he had made that tracked seven months' worth of submarine attacks overlain with shipping routes. In Edison's view established patterns of shipping were making hunting easy for German submarines. Simple changes in routes, along with the camouflage strategies he had developed, could be as effective as actually destroying submarines. Daniels was impressed. "Edison full of subject & working hard," he noted in his diary. By October 29 Edison had expanded his chart with still more incidents and had created a plan for routing shipping that he felt certain would significantly reduce losses. The navy was, however, slow to respond to Edison's urgent suggestions.

When he met with Daniels next on November 21, his frustration at the situation was turning to anger. Over the course of a long conversation Edison made it clear that many of the naval officers with whom he was compelled to work seemed intent on sticking with the status quo rather than moving to implement his plans. It was clear to him that hundreds of ships and thousands of lives could be saved through the simple expedient of sailing into and out of the danger zones he had identified only under the cover of darkness. Of all the ships sunk in the incidents he had studied, only 7 percent had been attacked at night. Since it appeared to him that the U.S. Navy had no interest in acting on this information, Edison was now drafting a version of his report to send to representatives of the British Navy.

While the two men talked, they were briefly interrupted by a veteran officer—a man who had served in the Confederate Navy—who, on learning the nature of their meeting, expressed his regret that the Confederates had invented the submarine. The remark did little to lighten the mood. Daniels later recorded in his diary that Edison had been uncharacteristically "severe."

Altogether Edison proposed dozens of ideas to improve and in some cases revolutionize the wartime operation of the U.S. Navy. His innovations included a method for making navigation lights visible only within a convoy and not to submarines lying alongside, an underwater searchlight, a system of nets to protect vessels from torpedoes, one scheme for the detection of enemy periscopes and another for smudging them with oil to render them useless, an improved plan for evasive maneuvers at sea, a design for water-penetrating projectiles, decoys designed to resemble steamships, and a high-speed signal light operated by a telegraph key. He contributed several ideas toward the improvement of U.S. submarines, including a stabilizer system that allowed a submarine to remain in a stationary position and a detector that would alert sailors to the presence of hydrogen gas in the shipboard atmosphere. (Hydrogen was produced by the batteries that powered submarines and had caused a number of casualties in U.S. submarine operations.) Edison also devised a gas mask that would protect lookouts on surface ships from the hazardous gases that billowed from a ship's smokestack without impeding their vision. This he went so far as to test himself, "wearing it in a closed room filled with burning sulphur vapors." He "experienced no inconvenience whatever."

As Secretary Daniels was the first to admit, Edison had put together an impressive body of work in a remarkably short period. But the navy, even now that the United States had entered the war, was slow to change.

Unlike the hidebound commanders of the U.S. Navy, Ford quickly stepped into his new role with respect to the war, throwing himself wholeheartedly into the effort to defeat Germany. At Edison's suggestion representatives of the Wilson administration had approached the automaker to solicit his advice on methods for easing the shipping shortage caused by the successful German submarine strategy. Transportation of commodities had been disrupted all across the country, and the problem had been deepening since early February, when Germany had resumed the policy of unrestricted submarine warfare that had been suspended under U.S. pressure following the sinking of the *Lusitania*.

Shipping by sea was an obvious casualty of the U-boats—as the newspapers, drawing on the German name *Unterseeboot*, had now begun calling the German submarines—but shipping by rail had suffered to a nearly equal extent. Railcars were being held up at the ports, sidetracked with full cargoes that had nowhere to go when the ships they were destined for failed to appear. Grain was piling up in Chicago, while the East Coast was beginning to experience shortages of both wheat and more perishable produce. The president of the Chicago Board of Trade issued a statement warning of "riot and anarchy" if the rail slowdown was not rectified soon. Food prices had begun to rise all over the country. Meanwhile, an investigation by the

New York County district attorney found that farmers on Long Island and upstate were holding back produce in anticipation of still higher prices. It was clear that something had to be done to get ships, and with them the railcars, moving again. Wilson believed that the methods of mass production Ford had developed in his automobile plant could be applied to the shipping problem.

On November 7 Ford formally agreed to serve on the U.S. Shipping Board. By that time, however, the submarine war was rising to a new level of intensity. Two days after Ford joined the board, the *New York Times* carried the news that the American freighter *Rochester* had been torpedoed and sunk off the coast of Ireland. Four men were dead and fourteen were missing. The *Rochester* had been one of the first American steamships, along with the *Orleans*, to slip successfully through the German blockade in February, when unrestricted submarine warfare had resumed. But now it seemed that the U-boat net was tightening. The *Orleans* had been sunk in October. With the loss of the *Rochester* it was becoming clear that a new strategy was necessary if American ships were to continue to cross the Atlantic.

The same day the news of the *Rochester* disaster broke, Secretary Daniels issued a statement saying that the navy was giving up the search for the crew of the *Alcedo*, an American patrol boat that had been torpedoed earlier in the week. "It is believed that most of the missing men were killed by the explosion of the torpedo," Daniels had been forced to concede. The *Alcedo* was the first American warship to be sunk since the outbreak of the war, and in that sense its loss held a symbolic importance. But Daniels knew there was a more practical lesson to be learned as well. A converted yacht, the *Alcedo* was typical of the vessels pressed into service to patrol the coast. Daniels saw that the navy needed a smaller and swifter class of warship to supplement the destroyers that had up until then provided the fleet's primary defense against submarines.

Plans for such a vessel were already in development, and now Daniels asked Ford to weigh in on the design with an eye toward making the boats as quick to manufacture as possible. Ford mulled over the hull pattern and quickly recommended that it be modified to allow for the use of flat hull panels "so as to take full advantage of mass production methods." He had another suggestion, too. The plans called for power to be provided by a reciprocating steam engine. Ford recommended switching to a steam turbine, which would have a higher power-to-weight ratio.

As the plans evolved, the boats grew in size and complexity. The final design called for a vessel just over two hundred feet in length, with a beam of thirty-three feet at its widest point and a draft of eight feet—shallow enough, it was hoped, to let enemy torpedoes pass underneath. It was expected that the 2,500-horsepower turbine engines—Ford got his way on that score—would drive the ship to a speed of eighteen knots. Armament included a battery of fifty-caliber guns. It would also carry the latest radio gear, as well as an underwater listening device Edison had designed. The navy—in response to an editorial that ran in the *Washington Post* in December declaring that "the crying need of this hour is for an eagle that will scour the seas and pounce upon every submarine that dares to leave German or Belgian shores"—dubbed the new class of ship "Eagle Boats."


All through that summer, as Ford and Edison helped the nation tool up for the coming conflict, the prospect of getting away, however briefly, from the responsibilities they had taken on assumed a new significance for the two men, and camping was often on their minds. On June 12, Burroughs had written a letter to Edison in which he reported that his broken arm was finally mending and he had begun to make use of it again. But while his body was bouncing back from the crash, his mind was still stuck in what he called "this dripping, almost sunless spring" that had followed in the wake of his wife's death. The war loomed large in his thoughts as well: "I am impatient that with all our wit and ingenuity we can not yet find anything to get the better of those damnable U-boats."

When the inventor wrote back a few days later, it was evident that his mind was occupied with the same problem. "For sometime past, I have been giving all of my time to Government experiments, and it looks as though this work will continue for quite a little while," Edison confided. "We all share your feelings of impatience at the delay in getting the better of the damnable U-boats," his letter went on to say, "but let me assure you that the solution of the problem is as difficult a task as any one need wish for." Edison expressed his delight in learning that his friend's arm was on the mend, but he quickly turned the news of Burroughs's recovery to his own ends. "Evidently you still continue to grow younger," he added, "so I shall look forward to some more camping out trips with you."

Early in July, Ford telephoned Firestone and asked how plans were shaping up for an August trip. He, Ford said, would be game to go. Firestone told him that he had not heard from Edison about any further plans, and he knew that the inventor had been working around the clock on his experiments for the Naval Consulting Board.

A few days later Firestone wrote Edison to tell him of Ford's interest and to ask if Edison might be able to free himself up for a trip in August. He was quick to say he knew how busy Edison had been. "I was in Pittsburgh yesterday and picked up a Pittsburgh paper in which there were headlines stating that Pittsburgh was going to win the war by manufacturing your invention to eliminate submarines from the sea." He imagined, he said, that with the responsibility for winning the war sitting squarely on his shoulders, Edison might well be unable to get away for a camping trip.

Edison's reply brought two pieces of disappointing news. He was indeed too busy to leave his work in August, and the Pittsburgh story was, as he put it, "a fake."

   The following week Firestone and Ford met for dinner in Detroit, where the topic of camping again came up. Ford, Firestone gathered, was "very anxious to get out in the woods." He suggested that Firestone write to Edison again to ask if he would be willing to loan the others his camping gear for the last week in August. He and Ford would take care of the rest of the arrangements themselves, Firestone told Edison when he wrote a few days later. "I would not be surprised," Firestone added, "if Mr. Ford has an idea in the back of his head that if he gets everything ready and into the woods he can get you to jump in the car and join him for few days, at least, without anyone knowing it." Edison's reply suggested that his resistance was indeed breaking down. If Firestone got things arranged with Ford, the inventor might be able to join them for ten days at the end of August.

*Thomas Edison conducts smoke-screen experiments aboard a navy vessel on Long Island Sound, August 26, 1917.*

Wheels were soon set in motion, and on August 17, Edison received a telegram from Firestone saying that Ford was on his way to New York in the company of his secretary, who would consult with Fred Ott on the camping details. Ford, he said, wished to start on August 25. But Edison's reply brought the planning to an abrupt stop. "At last minute I find it impossible to go as Government has called on me for work I cannot possibly evade." But he did have one last proposal. He suggested the others locate a yacht and join him off Long Island, where he would be conducting antisubmarine experiments aboard a navy submarine chaser. "There is good fishing," Edison wrote, "& you will see lots of interesting things."

But the momentum had been lost. No trip would materialize that year.

A month after Edison sent his last letter, John Burroughs drove into the village of Roxbury from Woodchuck Lodge. On the return trip he realized that the outing in the car had soured his mood. "I often wish I had never seen a Ford car, or any other," he wrote in his journal that afternoon. "All such things create wants which we never knew before."

⌖

# 8

# A GREAT SLICE OF
# OUR GEOGRAPHY

At his farm near West Park, John Burroughs spent the early days of the new year of 1918 listening to the reverberations of the Hudson River as the stream iced over in the tightening grip of an especially cold winter.

"When the river first freezes over, it is more noisy," Burroughs noted in his journal. "Any change of temperature causes the ice to let off musical volleys. It is a whooping and a shouting, like boys coming out of school." As the ice thickened, however, the river's music grew more subtle. "Vague as a dream, everywhere, but nowhere, chords of sound floating on the air. To locate them would be like trying to locate the rainbow."

Burroughs was himself in good health. The arm he had injured when his Model T overturned the previous autumn was now nearly healed. His weight had rebounded—to 132 pounds—and he was feeling strong enough to spend his afternoons doing chores on the farm after writing through the mornings. "More easily tired than one year ago," he conceded, "but my interest in the War, in Nature, in books, as keen as ever."

Early in February, hoping to escape the cold weather, Burroughs traveled with Clara Barrus to Tryon, North Carolina, a picturesque small town situated at the edge of the craggy escarpment where the Blue Ridge Mountains descended toward the piedmont region of South Carolina. The town was famous for its temperate climate, and its mixed hardwood and pine forests were a haven for a variety of birds. Burroughs, however, was disappointed by what he found when he arrived. He identified the songs of the pine warbler and the cardinal, and he heard the drumming of woodpeckers. But his verdict on the Carolina forest was disparaging—"very little wildlife."

"I can see nothing beautiful in the Southern landscape," he wrote in his journal at the beginning of March, nearly a month after he had arrived in Tryon, "the everlasting blood-red soil, and the dark pine woods, the disheveled fields, the houses upon legs ready to run away, the mud-bespattered horses and vehicles and pedestrians, the absence of grass . . . all offend my eye."

Henry Ford had sent out a car and driver from his dealership in nearby Charlotte for his friend's use, but Burroughs showed little interest in automobile outings, and he extended even less courtesy to the driver. The aging naturalist was feeling out of place in the unfamiliar landscape, and he found himself thinking more and more about the death of his wife, which had occurred exactly a year earlier. The only thing that lifted his mood was the sound of military training underway on the firing ranges used by soldiers from Camp Wadsworth. "All day we hear the boom of the guns 5 miles away on the artillery range, where our boys from Spartanburg are learning the art of war," he remarked at the beginning of March. About everything else he grumbled.

Twelve days later, however, as he and Barrus were preparing to leave Tryon for home, his tune changed and he felt a "pang" at the departure. "Such a clean and salubrious land, with its breath of pine and its soil of granite—an ideal climate," he now felt. Now that he was turning toward home, the southern atmosphere that had first irritated him took on magical qualities. "A truly antiseptic air—I think. No mildew, no dampness. Our butter would not get old or strong or deteriorate at all on the open shelves in the kitchen. Meat kept a long time, though the mercury was at times above 80. I gained steadily in strength and spirits."

Barrus, who had put up with her friend's complaints throughout their stay in Tryon, was accustomed to this kind of retrospective change of heart. For Burroughs, she concluded, "Memory's geese are always swans." The past was always greener.

As it happened, Burroughs's change of heart about the southern mountains proved fortunate: the camping trip that did not come together in 1917 was soon on the horizon again. Edison was eager to give Ford a sampling of the camaraderie and rural pleasures he had cultivated with Burroughs and Firestone in 1916. At the end of July the inventor directed his secretary, William Meadowcroft, to write a letter to the U.S. Geological Survey office in Washington, requesting maps of the Blue Ridge and Smoky Mountain ranges of the southern Appalachians that sprawled across East Tennessee, North Carolina, and Southwest Virginia. "Mr. Edison expects to make a trip through the above region," Meadowcroft's letter explained.

Always on the lookout for the remotest camping grounds, Edison was itching to confront the steep terrain and notoriously bad roads of the southern mountains. Ford, meanwhile, normally reluctant to leave the work that absorbed him at his auto plant, had uncharacteristically gotten himself involved in a campaign for a Michigan Senate seat—an arena for which he was both empirically and temperamentally unprepared—and he was as eager as Edison for a respite. The others would soon fall in line.

Edison pored over the Geological Survey maps and got hold of a copy of the *Automobile Blue Book* covering West Virginia, Virginia, Tennessee, and North Carolina. By the end of July plans were coming together for a trip through the rugged southern mountains. On the last day of the month Edison's laboratory assistant Fred Ott wrote to Firestone, who was to supply a heavy truck for carrying camping equipment, recommending that the vehicle be outfitted with side curtains to safeguard the cargo from the weather and a cage of wire netting to keep everything in place, and that a second, smaller truck carry the suitcases, cooking utensils, and food.

When Ott's letter reached Firestone, it found the tire maker unsettled by automotive concerns of an entirely different sort. A day earlier Idabelle and Harvey Jr. had been involved in a terrifying accident. The two had been riding in a car driven by a chauffeur on Cleveland Road near Silver Lake, a few miles outside Akron, when another auto backed out into the roadway. Mrs. Firestone's driver had been forced to swerve to avoid the other car, but in doing so he had approached too close to an embankment, which gave way. The Firestone's car rolled over, ending up on its top. Miraculously, neither Harvey nor the driver was injured, but Idabelle suffered bruising and nervous shock severe enough to warrant an ambulance. By August 3, however, she was doing well enough for Firestone to commit to joining Edison and the others on the camping trip.

The same day, Edison drew up a list of automotive supplies he had not yet secured, including tires and tubes for the various vehicles, and had his secretary wire Burroughs the proposed date of departure. By August 9 it had been decided that the naturalist and his friend Robert DeLoach would rendezvous with Edison in West Orange, and the three would travel from there to Pittsburgh to meet Ford and Firestone, who would be coming from the Midwest.

Edison had hoped the party would be one stronger. Earlier in the summer he had invited Josephus Daniels to join the expedition, and for a while it looked as if he might be game. It was not until August 5, when a telegram arrived from Daniels, that Edison had his answer. With the American war effort now in full force, the secretary would not be able to tear himself from his work in Washington long enough to make the trip south. "It distresses me that it is impossible for me to give myself the pleasure," Daniels said. "Nothing ever appealed to me quite so much."

Though Daniels was out, Burroughs and DeLoach were definitely in. On Thursday, August 15, they caught the afternoon boat from Albany bound for New York. By 8:00 that evening, they had reached West Orange.

Traveling with driver Ivar Simpson in the inventor's dependable Simplex, Edison, Burroughs, and DeLoach left New Jersey early the next day. With Fred Ott following along in a baggage car, they motored southwest toward Philadelphia to the newly commissioned Lincoln Highway, a privately organized patchwork of existing roads and new construction that stretched across the country from coast to coast—or from Times Square to the Golden Gate, as the highway's promoters liked to put it. Billed as "America's Main Street," it was the first long-distance roadway of its kind.

But at times it did not strike Burroughs as much of a road. Despite the "furious speeds" it made possible, often upwards of twenty-five miles an hour, the highway was riddled with rough patches where "the car fairly kicked up its heels." Again and again the naturalist found himself bucked from his seat. As he pulled himself back into place each time, he grumbled about the luck of his more "cushiony and adjustable" companions, who always managed to remain upright.

Although a good deal of the Lincoln Highway east of the Mississippi was at least crudely paved with macadam or brick, long stretches were still gravel or, worse yet, packed dirt that was rutted and rough when dry and quickly turned to mud in the rain. At odd intervals, however, the Simplex skimmed onto silk-smooth strips of concrete roadway that the highway's promoters called "seedling miles." These upgraded stretches began unexpectedly in the middle of nowhere, ran on for a mile or so, and abruptly stopped, leaving the route to continue over unimproved road. The idea, according to the official Lincoln Highway guidebook, was to give drivers "an opportunity to note the striking difference" between a concrete road and "the mud in which it begins and ends." The promoters hoped that raising motorists' expectations in this way would help to raise funds for resurfacing the entire length of the highway. All Burroughs knew was that the Simplex certainly hummed along over the concrete. This, he felt, was motoring—no cushioning required.

Edison planned to cover just over 220 miles the first day, which would allow the party to spend the night in Gettysburg, Pennsylvania, where his second son, William, was training with the U.S. Army Tank Corps. A week earlier Mina Edison had paid a visit to Camp Colt, where William was stationed, and Edison was eager to do the same.

This was not William's first time in uniform. Now thirty-eight, he had enlisted in an army engineer regiment during the Spanish-American War, when he was just nineteen. Returning to the army now to fight in Europe, he had turned down an officer's commission in order to serve in the newly formed mechanized battalion.

Edison, despite a fair amount of grumbling on the part of his eldest passenger, managed to hold the party to his rigorous itinerary. Beyond Philadelphia the route took them through Bryn Mawr to Paoli—where, during the Revolutionary War, the British had wiped out a division of the Continental Army—and on through Downingtown and Coatsville to Lancaster. From here they continued west, shelling out a ninety-three-cent toll to travel along the macadam-surfaced Lancaster Pike to York. By evening the Simplex was rolling into Gettysburg. Edison pointed the party right onto York Street toward Center Square, where they checked into the Hotel Gettysburg.

Not long after 6:00 on Saturday morning, Edison was back on the streets, strolling around the square and taking stock of the produce market that had unfolded along the sidewalks in the predawn hours. It had been a good year for tomatoes in south-central Pennsylvania, he discovered. Residents of the town clustered around the famous inventor, many of them eager to thank him for the work he was doing for the Naval Consulting Board.

"Mr. Edison, I want the privilege of shaking your hand," called out one woman in the crowd. "I think you are the most wonderful man in America." Edison waved off the compliment as he clasped the woman's hand.

Around 7:00 Burroughs, dressed in a plain gray suit and a cloth hat, appeared at the hotel door and joined Edison out front. Once the naturalist had conducted his own tour of the produce market, he and Edison along with DeLoach made the short trip out to Camp Colt, southwest of town, where William, now Sergeant-Major Edison, was among the soldiers learning mechanized warfare at the army's only tank school—under the command of a young Captain Dwight Eisenhower.

What they found when they arrived was a rough-and-ready facility sprawled across the same muddy fields where, fifty-five years earlier, forces commanded by General George Pickett had mounted their ill-fated assault on Union positions along the adjacent ridge. A collection of makeshift buildings and barracks now clustered on either side of a rail line, and the area was buzzing with activity. So great an influx of men had arrived over the summer that many were now housed in horse stables, the horses themselves having been superseded by the new motorized armored vehicles that had come to be called tanks.

The tanks at Camp Colt were small, French-built vehicles propelled by steel tracks driven by a rear-mounted engine. A cannon protruded from a rotating turret mounted in the center of the vehicle.

Beneath this was the cramped crew compartment—a hot, noisy, and dangerous place to learn the art of war, as Sergeant-Major Edison could attest.

Edison the inventor took a great interest in the camp and its activities.

Leaving Gettysburg that afternoon, the travelers followed the Lincoln Highway westward through Seven Stars and McKnightstown, over well-maintained macadam roads as far as Chambersburg.

Where the highway mounted the Allegheny range, between Chambersburg and Bedford, Pennsylvania, the macadam surface ran out, and road grades quickly pitched skyward. The state highway department had provided concrete watering troughs from which motorists could fill their automobile radiators before attempting the climbs, and Burroughs was amused to see men standing beside their cars "at the foot of those long, winding ascents, nursing and encouraging them," as they might once have tended their horses, "preparing them for the heavy task before them." Burroughs appreciated the effortless way the more powerful Simplex floated up those same hills. It felt to him like "easy victory."

Much of the traffic Edison and his companions saw along the highway was headed in the other direction. The Simplex swept past several convoys of military vehicles heavily laden with men and equipment, great khaki caravans all trundling eastward, bound, as Burroughs and Edison knew, for the shipping ports of the East Coast and from there to Europe to join the war the United States had entered the previous spring. In these "silent, grim processions" Burroughs imagined he could see the "doom" of Germany's Kaiser Wilhelm "written large."

The long, slow-moving caravans of trucks radiated a mute, mechanical invincibility. Watching them crawl along, Burroughs imagined the vast resources of the United States converging on a German foe that had been unable, or unwilling, to perceive the material strength of the nation its aggression had now roused to anger. He could picture countless roads around the country along which similar caravans made their slow way toward battle.

By that afternoon, after two days and four hundred miles on the road, the Simplex was motoring through the outskirts of Pittsburgh. The day was sunny and breezy, but as the city grew nearer, a stifling atmosphere seemed to close in on the open-topped car. Burroughs felt "fairly suffocated" by what he soon realized were fumes pumped into the air by Pittsburgh's many mills and factories. "It might as well be the devil's laboratory," he told himself. As the party drove deeper into the brimstone landscape of the industrial city, he found himself imagining a cleaner future "when the oil and coal are all gone" and Americans might turn instead to what he thought of as "white coal" and "smokeless oil"—the wind and the sun—for their fuel.

Henry Ford left Detroit for Cleveland on Friday night, August 16. The next morning Firestone met him in Cleveland, and the two drove eighty-five miles southeast to Firestone's family farm, just outside the town of Columbiana, Ohio.

Once Ford had settled in, he and Firestone walked with Firestone's young sons Leonard and Raymond and two of their friends to a nearby stream, where Ford gave the youngsters a lesson in dam building. The two Firestone boys enlisted their father to provide brute labor. Firestone took off his jacket and, with his tie flapping in the gentle breeze, began heaving rocks into place. It wasn't long before they had constructed a makeshift barrier of stone and mud, and they stood for a while watching the water rise in the reservoir behind their dam.

To Ford's eye a flowing stream always looked like energy waiting to be tapped. On his own estate back in Dearborn he was still drawing the bulk of the energy for the house and farm from hydroelectric power. Even looking at a small stream like this one, he always seemed to be calculating its utility and scheming the best way to harness it. Here he had enthusiastic laborers to help him put the water to work.

Later that afternoon they took to the fields to try out a Fordson tractor that Ford had given his friend. Once they had plowed a small plot of land, Ford, true to character, took some time to tinker with the machine. Each of the boys hopped aboard the tractor for a turn at pretend plowing. Before evening Firestone saddled up horses for his older son Russell, Ford, and himself, and the three went for a ride, with Raymond and Leonard tagging along on their ponies.

Firestone had a dinner party planned for that evening. More than three hundred of his employees—foremen and superintendents from his factory—came out to the farm for a celebration every summer and would soon converge for this year's sumptuous feast. Since Ford was on hand, Firestone pronounced him guest of honor.

That afternoon dozens of members of the Ladies Aid Society of Columbiana arrived at the farm to help with the party, their starched white dresses bright in the afternoon sun. Idabelle Firestone rallied the women into a horseshoe rank on the grassy lawn next to the house, where, with American flag bunting flapping from the eaves of the porch behind them, they posed for a photograph with Firestone's famous visitor. Ford and Firestone sat cross-legged on the grass in front. Firestone's dog, a collie with shaggy hair and a white face, nosed its way into the shot.

As the guests began to arrive, the farm echoed with convivial voices, while the ladies of the Aid Society scurried about, laying supper dishes on long tables. Soon the party was in full swing. When Firestone rose to introduce Ford as the guest of honor, he was answered with shouts and applause. By the time the evening was over, Ford had been well fed and endlessly toasted, and Firestone's employees went home brimming with stories about the luminary with whom they could now say they had dined. It was a far cry from the campfire suppers Ford and Firestone would enjoy in the coming days.

The next morning at 10:00, the two men, traveling with Harvey in his Packard, left for Pittsburgh along the direct road that ran through Salem and Canton.

Once Edison got his bearings in Pittsburgh, his party motored along Penn Avenue as far as Tenth Street, where they stopped at the Fort Pitt Hotel and checked in for the night. The Fort Pitt was famous for its "Norse Room," a gothic salon with vaulted ceilings and chandeliers in the form of Viking ships. The tiles lining its walls formed an expansive panorama of images drawn from Longfellow's poem "The Skeleton in Armor," in which a long-dead Norseman recounts the adventures of the life he left behind. But the travelers from West Orange, weary from their own adventures, found themselves more interested in a meal and bed than in Longfellow.

After dinner that evening Edison selected a large cigar and made his way out to the lobby, where he found DeLoach listening to the hotel orchestra. Edison took a seat beside him and drifted into his own thoughts, quietly chomping away at his cigar, unbothered by the music. When a local reporter approached the two men, the trend of Edison's meditations quickly emerged. He had been thinking about the labor shortage he had heard manufacturers in Pittsburgh were suffering. Before the interviewer had spoken more than a few words, the inventor turned the tables on the man and began quizzing him about the labor crisis. To Edison's mind the solution to the problem was obvious.

"We have about 300 women working in our plant and are running a school to train others," he explained. "We find they can run a lathe and do almost every kind of work that men can do." He felt certain that the same tactic would work in Pittsburgh. "The places will be filled by the women and the work will go on."

Once he had said his piece about labor, Edison, less interested in the reporter's questions than in his own train of thought, fell back into his usual reticence. But when he was asked about the war, he grew more animated. While he refused to discuss his own work with the Naval Consulting Board, he was voluble on the subject of the American soldier, whose military value he put at twice that of the average German.

"The German is no good," Edison declared. "He is a soulless brute." German training turned the soldier into an "automaton," incapable of making decisions in the heat of battle. "The American is not that way," he said. "Shoot his leader and he leads himself." Edison attributed this self-reliance to the diversity built into American culture—"that melting pot they say America is." He likewise attributed his own success to the combination of elements in his own ancestry. "The mixture of various races is good," he concluded.

When the reporter wondered whether Edison's friend Henry Ford had experienced a change of heart about the war, the inventor let out a chuckle. He squinted for a moment at the ash of his cigar and then told the man, "Henry is going after peace in a different way now."

By this time Burroughs had already retired for the evening, but the reporter, when he had run out of questions for Edison, tracked the old naturalist to his room and found him in his slippers, reading and recovering from the nearly four-hundred-mile journey from New Jersey.

Asked about literature, Burroughs had little to say beyond granting that there was some good poetry being written. His own reading had lately been focused on the war. The topic consumed him. "I feel it very much," he said. Even the vacation he was embarking on failed to turn his attention away from the news. "I really don't know where we are going," Burroughs admitted. "It is a pleasure trip. But I do not want to get out of reach of newspapers. I want to see them every day so that I can keep in touch with the situation."

It was clear he was feeling his age and suffering some regret about signing on for another automobile excursion. With the journey just getting underway, he was already feeling the effect of days spent on the road. "It has been a hard trip for me."

On Sunday morning around 8:30, the chairman of the United States Shipping Board, Edward Hurley, arrived from Washington to join Edison's group. A broad-faced, barrel-chested man with dark hair clipped close on the sides and a thin mouth drawn straight across his face, Hurley was a native of Ireland. He had immigrated to the United States and set up shop in Illinois, where he founded a company to sell a new type of pneumatic drill he had developed himself. More recently he had expanded into other areas, forming a second company to sell the world's first fully self-contained washing machines. As head of the Shipping Board, he was charged with keeping the nation's vital maritime transport system operating in the face of submarine warfare, which, in the first three months after the German declaration of total war on the high seas, in February 1917, had cost the Allies nearly five hundred ships.

When Edison wrote to Hurley earlier in the month to invite him to join the camping party for a few days, the inventor had just learned that Secretary Daniels felt too pressured by war work to make the trip, so he went out of his way to convince Hurley that the excursion need not interfere with his own duties.

"You can get back by railroad in 8 hours," Edison assured him. Hurley could have his secretary forward his mail each morning and respond at the closest telegraph office to anything urgent that might arise. The vacation would offer a welcome respite, while allowing Hurley to continue his work. "Ford is getting a little nervous from the strain," Edison had added. "I am a little weary & I presume you are also." Hurley had telegraphed back the same afternoon to say he would make every effort to join the "distinguished group." Now he had made good on his promise.

At the hotel Hurley found the lobby and hallways all but empty. When he asked where to find Mr. Edison, the staff seemed hardly aware that such a guest might be registered there. Finally, Hurley discovered Edison and Burroughs in an empty dining room, where, they told him, they had been ensconced since 6:00, catching up on the latest war news. Burroughs told Hurley he made a habit of waking up "when the sun begins to shine." After arranging to meet them later, Hurley left to attend to shipping business elsewhere in the city. Pittsburgh had come to play a crucial role in the manufacture of ships for the war effort. From raw steel to electrical parts, local factories were busy producing the materials that made Hurley's merchant fleet run. "We are leaning heavily upon Pittsburgh," Hurley had told reporters earlier that morning. "There is not a city in the United States that is taking such an active part in this war as Pittsburgh."

Just as Hurley left the hotel, Edison's brother-in-law, Halbert Hitchcock, found his way to the dining room and joined the inventor and Burroughs. An affable fifty-three-year-old man with glasses and a fringe of hair around a balding pate, Hal Hitchcock was married to Mina Edison's sister, Grace. He headed a Pittsburgh company that manufactured plate glass, and he had lately been working with Edison to develop an improved process for electroplating glass. They also shared an interest in the electrical pioneer Werner von Siemens, who in the 1840s had created a graphical alternative to the sound-based Morse code telegraph system. Hitchcock slipped easily into his brother-in-law's conversation with Burroughs. The three sat chatting until almost 11:00, at which point they decided to take a leisurely drive to Hitchcock's house at 5710 Bartlett Street, where they planned to have lunch. Leaving Edison's friend Charles Hanford at the hotel to wait for the rest of the party, they set out immediately, taking a meandering path through Pittsburgh in order to see the landmarks of the city.

After enjoying a lunch with Hitchcock and his wife, Edison and Burroughs both settled in for a nap to pass the time while they waited for their friends to arrive from Detroit and Akron.

When Ford and Firestone reached Pittsburgh that afternoon, they stopped for lunch at the newly opened William Penn Hotel on Mellon Square, a few blocks south of Fort Pitt. From there Firestone telephoned his branch office and learned that Edison and Burroughs would meet him and Ford at the Firestone shop at 5932 Baum Avenue.

Ford and Firestone set out to meet their friends; not far behind them came Russell Kline, driving a Ford truck groaning under the weight of the supplies it carried. By the time Edison and Burroughs arrived, the camping gear and food stores were being transferred to a heavier and more powerful White truck, and the group was assembling for photographs and talking to reporters.

The crew this year included one veteran of the 1916 trip, Fred Ott. There were also several new faces among the men clustered around the vehicles. Russell V. Kline, Firestone's twenty-nine-year-old advertising manager, was a snappy dresser who sported a bow tie and goggles on the road; he would drive the heavy truck and serve as official photographer for the expedition. Twenty-six-year-old Harry Linden, who was making the trip as a driver and general crew member, would trade off stints behind the wheel with Kline. Linden was suited up for the journey in coveralls.

Near the kitchen van stood Thomas Sato, a handsome thirty-six-year-old Japanese immigrant, with upswept black hair. In 1915 Clara Ford had hired Sato through the Japanese Reliable Employment Agency to serve as a butler at the Ford house in Dearborn. Soon he was also cooking meals and overseeing the household laundry. Now Ford depended on him for everything. In his three years with Ford, Sato had garnered a reputation as both an excellent chef and a smooth operator among the hired girls at Ford's estate. Another driver, a man by the name of Willmott, would assist Sato with the kitchen van.

There was also a celebrity in the group. Edison's friend Charles Hanford was a widely acclaimed stage actor, best known for his performances in productions of Shakespeare plays, in particular as Mark Antony in *Julius Caesar*. He was also something of a polymath. Hanford had studied law before turning to acting and had then worked for the U.S. Geological Survey. He was now collaborating with Edison to develop camouflage for American shipping and army operations, helping the inventor by applying tricks of stagecraft to the task.

When the photos had been taken and the newsmen had been assuaged, the members of the party climbed into their vehicles, and the caravan pulled out onto Baum Avenue. With Hal Hitchcock leading the way, they motored through the city streets, headed southeast. On the outskirts of town the party bade farewell to the Hitchcocks, and, with Edison's Simplex in the lead—the inventor in the front passenger seat surrounded by his maps and guidebooks—they pushed out onto the state road. Their trip had begun in earnest.

By 6:00 the camping party had become separated from the supply truck, which was having a difficult time maintaining speed on the steep-graded roads east of Pittsburgh. When Edison spotted a wooded area just outside the town of Greensburg, he thought it best to call a stop for the day. The lead cars pulled into the yard of the next farmhouse they came to. As the Simplex rolled to a stop, Hurley leaped out and went in search of the owner. When he found the man, an elderly farmer named Miller, Hurley explained that he and his friends would like to camp on his property.

"Why certainly," Mr. Miller said, "I will be glad to let you camp here." As he and Hurley stood in the farmyard talking about the farm and how the crops were faring, the other vehicles began to arrive. The farmer directed the party toward a clearing in the woods, half a mile from the house. It was a beautiful spot. Burroughs, in particular, liked the lay of the land. "The camp was in an ideal place," he felt, "a large open oak grove on a gentle eminence well carpeted with grass." All agreed that it was a good location. In honor of the man who had secured permission to stay there, they dubbed the place Camp Hurley.

While the crew began setting up tents—a kitchen tent and one for dining, as well as the individual sleeping tents—Ford, Edison, Burroughs, and Firestone went about gathering dry branches for a campfire. Soon Sato announced that supper was ready. By then the evening had turned cool, and the campers gathered around the fire to enjoy the meal, which Firestone pronounced "delicious."

That evening Hurley was the center of attention: everyone wanted to learn from him what the Shipping Board was planning to do about

*Thomas Edison taking notes at Camp Hurley, outside Greensburg, Pennsylvania.*

the menace of German submarines. "How," as Burroughs put it, "could we help freeing our minds about the Huns"?

Hurley had been a busy man since becoming chairman of the Shipping Board the previous July. A week after assuming office he had issued an order commandeering the nation's shipyards, giving the Shipping Board control over their operation and ensuring that materials and manpower were directed toward the war effort. Over four hundred hulls then under construction were immediately earmarked for war use. Hurley had next commandeered German vessels that were interned in American ports and then many that had been detained abroad. Some of these went to the navy, but most remained under Hurley's control for employment in shipping that was deemed vital to American security. By the fall he was forced to press all active oceangoing American cargo vessels over 2,500 tons into service.

Although these measures had helped to avert a more serious crisis, they were not enough to solve the problem of wartime shipping. "Building new ships from the keel up necessarily became our chief concern," Hurley recalled. Even with all U.S. shipyards under his control, Hurley quickly saw that the demand for ships could not be met by conventional means. "The Germans were sinking vessels so fast that it became apparent we must adopt extraordinary methods." Working with naval architects, Hurley developed a plan to construct ships of prefabricated parts. "For generations it had been the practice to build ships, from the keel up, in the yard," he explained. "Every piece of wood or steel that went into the construction was shaped in the yard, and the shapes are extraordinarily complex."

Hurley instead wanted to manufacture ships the way Henry Ford produced automobiles. Parts could be fabricated in mills and shops all around the country before being shipped to the yards for assembly. Soon Hurley had a program underway to construct ships—out of steel, wood, and even concrete—to uniform plans out of standard parts. Hurley and his board had briefly consulted with Ford himself on this innovative plan—but events had taken the automaker into a different aspect of the maritime war effort when Josephus Daniels recruited him to help design the navy's new antisubmarine patrol boat.

As it turned out, Ford had become more deeply involved with the navy than he had anticipated. Once the plans for the Eagle boat were finalized and models were being tested, it had seemed that Ford's participation in the project was over, but Josephus Daniels hoped for more from the automaker than just his expertise. He wanted the Ford Motor Company to manufacture the new boats in the plant they then had under construction along the River Rouge in Dearborn. The idea was that the rough-finished boats would sail up the Rouge, navigate through the Great Lakes and Erie Canal to the Hudson River, and make their way to a navy yard in New Jersey to be outfitted for sea duty. Ford was hesitant to accept the idea. But by January 1918 he was ready to sign on, and on January 14 the navy placed its first order, for a hundred boats.

As was usual for him, Ford went into the project with a full head of steam—perhaps with even more enthusiasm than usual, because in this instance the U.S. government was footing the bill. He had the River Rouge dredged to create a deeper navigable channel and began construction on a massive steel-framed building in which to manufacture the boats. Designed by architect Albert Kahn, this facility, which Ford would call Building B, was, when it was completed that May, 1,700 feet in length and some 350 feet wide. The roof of the open-plan, glass-walled structure hung 100 feet above the floor. It was equipped with a rail system designed to move boats along through the various manufacturing areas, much as Model T cars were moved through the Ford plant in Highland Park. There were three production lines in the plant, each capable of working on up to seven boats at a time. Ford had banners hung along the walls that proclaimed, "An Eagle a Day Keeps the Kaiser Away."

The keel for the first of the new boats was laid on May 7. An unimag-

inably quick sixty-four days later Eagle boat number one splashed
into the Rouge and began its voyage to the East Coast. A lengthy article in the *New York Times* called Ford's achievement "extraordinary"
and marveled that he had managed to turn out warships "as if they
were just so many 'Flivvers.'"

This was what Edison had been alluding to when he told a reporter
in Pittsburgh that Ford was now working for peace in a different way.
"No man wanted to do his bit during the war more than Ford did,"
Hurley believed.

Ford was not, of course, alone in doing his bit for the war. The
furious pace of Edison's work for the navy had made the year that
had intervened since the last camping trip a trial for him as well.
It was not that the inventor resented the work itself, but he was not
accustomed to bucking the resistance to change that characterized
a staid institution like the U.S. military. Hurley, like Daniels, had
worked to encourage the navy to adopt Edison's ideas but to little
avail. While a few of Edison's proposals had been tested, months after
he had first pressed the issue, there was as yet little movement to put
them into use.

The inventor's frustration was evident to all those around the
campfire that evening, but he was not one to let setbacks sour his
mood. Despite the focus on the war, the talk that first evening often
took a humorous turn.

"Hurley, why did that farmer hesitate so long to allow us to go into
his woods?" Edison asked when there was a lull in the conversation.

"Why, he had some difficulty with campers a short time ago," Hurley answered. "Some of his cattle were killed and he naturally hesi-
tated to allow more campers in."

"Well, didn't you tell him who we are?" Edison wondered.

"Yes, that's the strange part of it," Hurley went on, working to conceal a smile as he did so. He said he had told the farmer that Thomas
Edison, the inventor, was in the party, but the man had never heard

of him. So he tried Henry Ford, the automobile manufacturer, but the fellow had never heard of him either. Same with Firestone, the tire maker, and Hurley himself, who was often in the news in his role as chairman of the Shipping Board. He had never heard of any of them.

"Have you ever heard of John Burroughs, the naturalist?" he asked at last. At this, Hurley said, he saw the man's eyes gleam.

"Is John Burroughs in your party? Well, you go right ahead! I have just finished reading his latest book!"

Chortles erupted all around the campfire. Hurley had, in fact, made up the scene to amuse Burroughs and the others, and the jape had the desired effect. Burroughs was soon shaking with laughter.

"Huh," the old naturalist exclaimed, "never heard of Edison, never heard of Ford! They have to have me with them to get them into the woods!"

Hurley's story was the hit of the evening, and it would turn out to give the party a chuckle on more than one occasion. Within a few days newspapers would be reporting this anecdote as fact.

At one point in the evening the talk around the campfire turned to presidential administrations. The campers discussed Wilson, with whom several of them were personally acquainted, and compared his character and his handling of the presidency to models set by Taft and Burroughs's old friend Roosevelt.

Burroughs told the others about a birding trip he had recently made with Roosevelt. They had traveled through Virginia for a few weeks and in all that time had come across only two birds that the former president could not identify. Impressed as he was by Roosevelt's knowledge of birdlife, though, Burroughs had been left cold by his friend's behavior after the trip. It seemed that Roosevelt, every time he had met Burroughs since then, had hounded him to write a book about their excursion. Burroughs had come to feel that Roosevelt was more interested in the book, and perhaps the publicity it might have brought to his recent attempt to reclaim the White House, than he was in Burroughs himself. "Just because he was insistent, I am not going to write the book," Burroughs told his fellow campers.

Although the trip was just getting started, the campers could not resist talking that evening about where they would go next year. They also floated ideas for improving their equipment to make subsequent excursions even more enjoyable.

Later on, when the campfire had burned itself low, Ford still had energy to expend. He popped out of his chair and declared that he could leap over the flames, which he then did. "He was as nimble and lively as a boy of eighteen," Hurley thought. "All of his cares had been left behind. He was with his 'Buddies,' Firestone, Edison and Burroughs and he was having a mighty good time." It was midnight before the talk dwindled and the first of the campers wandered off to their tents.

By the time Burroughs finally found his way to bed, the night had turned unseasonably cold. The naturalist who had spent so many nights outdoors sleeping on the ground could not make himself comfortable. "Folding cots are very poor conservers of one's bodily warmth," he discovered, "and until you get the hang of them and equip yourself with plenty of blankets, sleep enters your tent very reluctantly." Burroughs shivered and tossed until 4:00 in the morning, when he finally gave up trying to sleep and left his tent to sit by the fire. Once he had stoked up a good blaze, he could at least think the "long thoughts" that were troubling him in some degree of warmth. His friends, all considerably younger, seemed to be having no problems. "Youth was soundly and audibly sleeping in the tents with no thoughts at all," he noted.

From his camp chair by the fire, Burroughs watched the sun rise and listened as the dawn chorus of birdsong gradually filled the oak grove. Around 8:00 the others began tumbling out of their tents in search of breakfast. When they had finished eating, one of the men set up targets, and the campers spent the morning shooting at them with small-bore rifles. Burroughs managed to score a bull's-eye without rising from his camp chair. The others assumed various marksman-like poses as they took turns firing. Anyone watching could tell they were enjoying the opportunity to display their prowess in front of a fashionable young woman who had come out from Greensburg that morning with Firestone's son Harvey to see the camp that had begun to be talked about in town. She wore a dark woolen dress with brass buttons up the sleeves, its military look set off by a large, lacy white collar. A cloth cap was pulled down over her short, curly brown hair. A thin, mop-haired man named McClintock, the manager of the Pittsburgh Firestone dealership, had come to pay a visit as well, and stood smoking a cigarette as he watched the contest. The local newspaper had also sent out a reporter to have a look around. Word was that the mayor was on his way, too. By 11:00 the party's gear was loaded onto the trucks, and they received the mayor's ceremonial send-off as they motored out of camp.

Burroughs and his friends drove the two miles back into Greensburg in search of gas and oil for the vehicles. After the chilly night he had passed by the campfire, Burroughs spent some time looking around town until he found what struck him as the perfect remedy for the cool mountain air: a long linen duster, which he happily pulled on over the lighter jacket he already wore.

That afternoon, as the caravan rolled toward the town of Connellsville, twenty-odd miles to the south, the Packard car in which Hurley rode with Ford and Firestone rattled to a halt. The cooling fan, they discovered when they raised the hood, had torn itself apart and pierced the radiator. With no assistance in sight, Ford, using just the supplies they had with them in the car, patched the radiator and got the party moving again. Firestone marveled at his friend's "mechanical genius."

When the party reached town, they found their way to the Connellsville Garage on Apple Street, where they hoped to have a mechanic make a proper repair. As soon as word of their arrival got out, a crowd began to form around the famous visitors. But warm as the welcome was, there was little help to be found either among the bystanders or in the garage. The mechanics on duty surveyed the damage and, as Burroughs observed, simply "shook their heads." With all the blades of the fan broken away from the hub, they saw no way to make a repair. The only solution was to have a replacement part sent from a supplier in Pittsburgh. For Ford this was an intolerable idea, less because of the delay than for the lack of mechanical imagination the prospect entailed.

"Give me a chance," he said at last. Ford again pulled off his coat and took matters into his own hands. Using tools and material he found in the garage, he removed the fan iron and began drilling connection points for a system of wire lacing that allowed him to weave the mangled fan back into shape. Over the next few hours he repaired the broken part, soldered in a patch to seal the punctured radiator, and then reassembled the engine, giving the crowd of observers a look at the mechanical aptitude that had impressed Firestone earlier. It was a close-up show that recalled the day at the Panama–Pacific Exposition when Ford had rolled up his sleeves and assembled Model Ts as gifts for the group of naval officers whose hospitality he had enjoyed on his visit to the fleet. This time Ford had not just repaired the automobile; he had taken what might have been a dispiriting misadventure and turned it into one of the highlights of the trip.

That afternoon, as Hurley left his traveling companions to continue on their journey, he found that he had come away with a new sense of Ford and Edison, as well as their friends. "I can understand why they enjoy each other's society at any time, but particularly on these trips," he later remarked. "They were so carefree they enjoyed everything— the country, the farm, the people and especially the food. Every meal was a picnic." They even managed to enjoy the breakdowns. Hurley hoped he would be able to rejoin the camping party in a few days, but that would depend on the state of things in Washington.

With the Packard now in running order once again, Ford and the others were eager to press on. Although the White truck had not caught up during the lull while Ford made his repairs, the remainder of the party set out in a caravan made up of Edison's Simplex, the newly repaired Packard, and the two Model Ts. The route followed Crawford Avenue over an iron bridge spanning the Youghiogheny River and passed over a railway line that paralleled the far bank. Beyond the bridge they turned right onto a steeply graded road toward West Leisenring.

As the caravan motored along, Ford spotted a disabled Model T by the side of the road and called for a stop. He got out of the Packard and spoke to the driver, who told him that the machine had "bucked" so badly he had been forced to stop. Ford took a look at the drive mechanism and then explained to the driver that a part had broken. The automaker removed the damaged component and took it to a nearby blacksmith shop, where he oversaw the necessary repairs.

When the campers reached Uniontown, thirteen miles southwest of Connellsville, they stopped at the Firestone dealership, where they learned that Linden and Kline, in the White truck, had broken a drive shaft and were held up some distance back. They had phoned the agency to say that repairs were underway and they hoped to catch up in an hour or so.

Ford and Firestone managed to convince Edison that under the circumstances—the camping gear was all loaded onto the disabled

White truck—it made sense to find a hotel for the night. Although he had vowed not to spend any time indoors on this trip, Edison eventually agreed to a night of soft living. Firestone had learned of a seasonal hotel nearby, so he telephoned to reserve rooms. Since the lead party had been ahead of the supply truck all day, they had not eaten lunch. Firestone, feeling the effects of hours on the road without food, asked if dinner might be served early.

The Summit Inn, situated about seven miles southeast of Uniontown, was perched atop Summit Mountain, at the westernmost end of the Allegheny range. The relatively new Mission-style building—it had been built just eleven years earlier—looked incongruous in the mountain setting, its stucco architecture in contrast to the rough-hewn style cultivated by other mountain resorts in the East. But the staff gave the campers a warm welcome and served them an excellent dinner soon after they arrived.

After dinner, Ford suggested that the party venture out for a walk. Burroughs and Edison had already settled themselves in the lobby, but Firestone was willing. "Certainly," he told Ford, "I will join you in anything."

The two friends walked up the slope of Summit Mountain. When they reached the top, they could see Uniontown in the distance. Firestone thought it was a beautiful view, a cascade of shaggy green undulations tumbling down to a broad plain that then ran flat as the inn's billiard table to the western horizon. It was worth the demanding walk to the summit. Ford, though, needed more. After taking in the view, he led Firestone down the other side of the mountain.

By the time they returned to the hotel, having climbed the mountain twice, Firestone was ready to drop. He went straight to bed, but Ford went looking for Burroughs and Edison. He found them in the lobby, surrounded by locals. Word of the famous visitors had already gotten out.

After listening to the talk for a while, Ford, who was still full of vim after his evening stroll in the mountains, proposed an athletic contest. He took the cigar Edison was enjoying and placed it on the mantel over the inn's massive stone fireplace. Then he "dared" anyone present to kick it off. Turning to Edison, he made the challenge personal.

"You can't kick that."

Edison took a look at the smoldering cigar, some six feet above the floor. The inventor positioned himself in front of the fireplace and hiked up his trousers. Then, with no apparent exertion, he launched a high kick and, as one onlooker described it, "calmly landed his shoe squarely and fairly on the fiery nose of the burning weed." As if to rub in his victory, he then did it twice more. Not to be outdone at his own game, Ford put the cigar back on the mantel and took a turn himself. But the trip across Summit Mountain had left the usually limber automaker less flexible than he anticipated. It took him several attempts to make contact. He did eventually manage to knock it down but with none of Edison's aplomb. When the cigar finally hit the floor, it was a "battered and frazzled stump."

Burroughs, who had been watching the contest, was now invited to take a turn. But he said the exertion of watching his friends in action had satisfied his athletic needs for the evening.

Ford was just getting warmed up. Even as he congratulated Edison, his eyes darted around the inn in search of another challenge. When he noticed the stairway leading up to the second floor, he challenged his friends to a race up to their rooms. In no time he and Edison were bounding up the stairway at top speed. This time Ford redeemed himself, reaching the second floor a step ahead of Edison, who took three bounds to Ford's quick two. Soon Burroughs was drawn into the fray despite himself. The naturalist took a run at the stairs and leaped. But he landed badly and nearly tumbled back down before Ford and Edison caught him.

It was now nearly midnight. Once Burroughs regained his foot-

ing, the three athletes made their way, a little more carefully, to
their rooms.

Edison was up with the sun the next morning and out and about by
6:30. The others were not far behind him, and the party gathered to
enjoy an early breakfast. Sometime in the night the White truck had
arrived in Uniontown, along with Sato and Fred Ott in their Ford
truck. With the caravan reunited, the campers were soon off, retracing their path down Summit Mountain to rejoin the road toward Keyser's Ridge, thirty-two miles to the southeast.

After following a long downgrade into Chalkhill, they reached the
grave of General Edward Braddock, who was killed in a skirmish
along the Monongahela River at the height of the French and Indian
War. Shot through the chest and dying, the general had transferred
his command to a young volunteer officer named George Washington. Here, on a low, grassy knoll set against a backdrop of maples
and elms, the campers paused long enough to read the bronze tablets
affixed to the tall stone monument, which had been erected not quite
five years earlier. Thirteen miles farther along, they crossed a bridge
over the Youghiogheny River and passed through Somerfield, where
there was a bronze marker commemorating Washington's crossing of
the same river on his way to attack the French at Fort LaBoeuf in
1753. Beyond the bridge the road grade again climbed steeply upward
as far as Addison, then descended into Strawn, just beyond the
Maryland line. Here another monument, the Washington-Braddock
boulder, paid tribute to Braddock's ill-fated expedition against the
French. The morning drive, covering as it had some thirty hilly miles
from Uniontown, had taken the campers on a march through colo-
nial history.

In Braddock's day this journey through steeply undulating, forested terrain would have taken a day or more. Although the land-

scape itself remained largely unchanged from that time, the campers, traveling by automobile—even over winding roads in less than ideal conditions—had covered the same ground before lunch.

Just past Strawn tree cover along the roadway grew sparser as the cars climbed toward a high plateau ringed by taller mountains in the distance. Frost heaves gave evidence of the harsh winters that struck the region. Complaining about the state of the roadway here made less sense than marveling at the fact that it was passable at all. Two-and-a-half miles on, the lead cars came to a fork in the road. There was a store on the left and on the right a sign pointing the way to Oakland, the next town on their route. Firestone drew the others' attention to the sign; it seemed to him they ought to take that road. But Burroughs's friend DeLoach had arranged to have mail delivered to Keyser's Ridge, which Harvey also wanted to visit. They both voted for driving on into the town. While the others were busy weighing their options, Edison announced that he would like to have something to drink. Harvey went into the store to get the inventor a bottle of pop, and when he came out again, he announced that this—the store and the sign—*was* Keyser's Ridge.

When DeLoach had retrieved his mail and everyone had piled back into the cars, they took the right-hand fork toward Oakland. The road followed a downgrade before leveling off five miles farther along, where it crossed a concrete bridge. Two miles beyond that the lead cars drove into the ominously named Accident, Maryland. Edison's guidebook offered some clues to the origin of the town's name. One story held that George Washington, as a young man, was surveying the ridge on which Accident now sat when he accidentally knocked over his surveyor's transit and damaged the device. Another version said that two surveying teams had once crossed paths here by accident.

That afternoon the lead party stopped for lunch at an attractive spot where a grove of shade trees grew close to a spring-fed stream. A split-rail fence ran down the hillside, and beyond this a pasture rolled away into the distance. As the campers ate their meal, they noticed a young girl on the road above them carrying a pail of apples, which she wished to sell. When they called to her and asked her to join them, she came shyly into the camp. Ford said he would like to buy the pail of apples, and he handed the girl a dollar.

Burroughs noticed the girl's "shining eyes as she crumpled the new one-dollar bill" in her small hand, while the men introduced themselves. When the campers asked her where she lived, she explained that her family's farm was on the hill above the grove. Burroughs, listening to her answer, thought her "a very firm, level-headed little maid." After she returned to her house, the campers noticed an older man in the field above. He walked to the gate and gazed down at the party, as if to see whether the girl's story was true. A few minutes later he walked into the camp carrying a pail of cider for these unlikely visitors.

After lunch the caravan covered the few remaining miles to Oakland, a settlement of about two thousand, that was the hub of the road system in the region. From here roads fed out in all directions. The town itself was largely supported by the many lumber mills in the area, but it also had a certain renown as a health resort.

The lead cars stopped at a garage to take on gasoline and oil. While the drivers were seeing to the vehicles, Harvey went into a candy shop he had noticed nearby to pick up a treat for Burroughs, who was known to have a particular taste for caramels. When Harvey returned with the sweets, Ford caught wind of what was happening.

"This displeased Mr. Ford," Firestone noticed, "and he snatched the box of candy and threw it up the street." The locals who had gathered around the cars gasped at this display. Burroughs himself may have been shocked for a moment but not surprised. Ford held strong, some would say extreme, views on diet and health, many of which he shared with the naturalist: after all, the two had taken a similar interest in the pronouncements made by Dr. Kellogg when the famous physician had visited Edison's estate in Florida. To Ford's mind a sugary treat was the last thing his friend needed when he was already suffering digestive difficulties, as Burroughs had made clear he was.

Whatever tension Ford's outburst had created was soon soothed by a piece of good luck. The route from Oakland to Elkins, West Virginia, would take the campers over the 3,334-foot summit of Backbone Mountain. Yet while Edison's guidebook painted an ominous picture of the travel that lay ahead—"very winding and hilly roads, with some narrow, precipitous places," it warned; "should only be taken in dry weather"—the road out of town, at least, turned out to be one of the best they had encountered in days. Because the state was responsible for maintaining the roadway in front of the courthouse, which happened to be the road the travelers were taking, they were able to set out that afternoon over a superbly smooth concrete surface.

This stretch took them almost six-and-a-half miles, through Gortner, Maryland, before it ended, and they turned left onto a macadam road that, true to the guidebook, began to twist and turn as it climbed nearly a thousand feet toward the summit of the mountain. Around 5:00 they reached a broad, clear creek, which they were told was Horseshoe Run. A narrow lane ran alongside the stream.

It was growing late enough to begin searching for a campsite, so Firestone and Edison decided to take a look upstream. They drove along the creek half a mile until they spotted a well-maintained field on the far side of the road from the creek. This looked to Burroughs like just the place, but the smooth field was too soft a spot for Edison—"the rough, grassy margin of the creek suited him better, and its proximity to the murmuring, eddying, rocky current appealed to us all."

Edison's view won the day. The campers pitched their tents near the creek, where the limited space required a close placement, and more neighborliness, than usual. The only spot left for the kitchen tent was a slender stretch of ground bisected by a gully. Though the field would have offered greater convenience, "wild Nature, when you can manage her, is what the camper-out wants," Burroughs concluded.

To Ford's ear, however, the murmuring of the stream was not quite sufficient: he wished there were more of a fall to the water. When the automaker mentioned this to his companions, Harvey, as eager to please Ford as his younger brothers had been on the farm back in Columbiana, waded into the stream to build a dam, over which the water could tumble.

Firestone watched as his son set rocks into place to create the waterfall, but he was as unprepared as Harvey for what came next. When he had enough rocks in place to cause the water to begin backing up behind the makeshift dam, Harvey reached out to adjust one of the stones and lost his footing. Suddenly, he fell headlong into the water. "Thereafter," Firestone quipped, "the fall was complete."

As dusk came on that evening, first a few and then more locals began to wander into camp to see who these outsiders bivouacked by the run might be. Some had come from the nearby lumber camps; others were mountain people who scratched a living from the land on small farms thereabouts. They were unlike the onlookers who had gathered in towns the caravan had passed through. Firestone judged them "a very rough looking crowd." Eyeing the mob gathering at the fringes of the firelight, Kline proposed to stay awake and guard the camp. As he described the plan, the pugnacious driver pulled back his jacket to reveal the Smith and Wesson pistol he wore in a holster.

But Ford, the man whose Peace Ship had so famously failed to bring an end to the war in Europe, had not lost his aversion to conflict. He managed to convince the others that a warm welcome would do more to keep the party safe than Kline's pistol could.

"Thereupon," Firestone recalled, "we went out and made peace with the enemy, offering them cigars." And they found that Ford was right. The rough crowd was not merely harmless but quite amiable.

"They proved to be the most congenial and hospitable people we had met." In fact, gathered around the campfire with cigars and the food left over from supper, the campers and their visitors hit it off so well that by the end of the evening the lumbermen had pledged to come back in the morning.

True to their word, the men turned up again after breakfast. This time they had driven the logging engine—used to transport cut timber—to a stretch of track close to the camp so that Ford and the others could see it, and Ford, Firestone, and Edison were soon climbing all over the locomotive. Before long Ford was in the cab with the engineer, ready to give it a test drive. Firestone grabbed a shovel and prepared to add coal to the fire, while Edison, his hands in his pockets, stood nonchalantly on the steel-framed cowcatcher bumper mounted on the nose of the engine. Ford gave the whistle a pull, and a burst of steam shot a resounding hoot through the forest. The campers, grown men the night before, now looked more like boys set free with the world's largest train set.

By the time the campers finally tore themselves away, the crew had broken camp and loaded the gear onto the trucks. After bidding the lumbermen farewell, Ford and the others trundled back into their workaday internal combustion vehicles and left their boyhoods behind, driving on toward Parsons, West Virginia.

The road they followed descended into a hollow before turning right along a ravine and beginning to climb again. As the caravan made its way along a shallow mountain stream rippling over a bed of sandstone scree, tinged in places with a ruddy hue—it was known locally, they would learn, as Lead Mine Run—they caught a glimpse of a dilapidated grist mill. Ford, characteristically, called for a stop. The entire party clambered out of the cars to investigate the wide overshot waterwheel that had once powered the mill. As they looked around, Ford had an opportunity to calculate the horsepower the stream might have provided when, in his opinion, it was put to proper use.

Ford's interest in waterpower was almost obsessive. Whenever the campers passed a stream or river, he lost himself in assessing its potential and talked of his plans for a network of small water-powered factories. His fascination with this topic was contagious, and the others appeared happy to have a look at any mill they came across. But they also had hobbyhorses of their own. Burroughs seemed to be on a constant vigil against the neglect of land and looked at every fallow field and pasture the party drove past with the same eye toward utility. "If it was mine," he liked to say, "I'd plough the daylights out of it." For Firestone, the consummate salesman, it was the people they met who should be cultivated. Edison's eye was always alert to novel plants and minerals. Yet, though he was interested in everything he saw, he was becoming more and more focused on discovering a native replacement for the latex rubber that manufacturers like Firestone and Ford were forced to buy from overseas sources. Whatever their unique obsessions, they all cheerfully joined Ford as he poked around the waterwheel.

This mill, which had once been owned and operated by a family named Evans, would in its heyday have ground five or six thousand bushels of grain a year, turning the wheat and corn grown on the hillside farms of Tucker County into food for the hardworking mountaineers who populated the region. It had now fallen into disrepair, its siding broken away in spots, stones falling from its foundation walls, and its wheel long stilled. But to Ford it had the same air of elegant utility that had excited him about the logging engine that morning. He stretched his long arms up and pulled himself onto the wheel, paused, and then took a seat, arms on his knees, and looked around at what was left of the place. Soon the others joined him. Though no spring chicken, Burroughs followed Ford to the top of the wheel and perched beside him. It was an obvious occasion for a photograph, and the others clustered around. Edison clambered onto the wheel's hub and stood with his hand resting on the worn timber of its outer rim,

*Edison, Burroughs, Ford, and Firestone explore the Evans mill near Lead Mine, West Virginia.*

while Firestone balanced himself on the axle between the wheel and the mill, next to Ford. The photograph would become the most iconic image of their trip.

Not long after they left the Evans mill, the passengers in the lead cars got their first glimpse of the Cheat River. For the next few miles there were breathtaking views of the river cutting through its valley. Burroughs was struck by this "large, clear mountain trout-brook." But the views came at a cost. The road skirted a high ledge, where there was no guardrail, and sharp curves appeared without warning. About eight miles from Lead Mine, the road turned right over a timber bridge, and the party got a close-up view of the Cheat. It would not be their last.

"Every mountain we crossed showed us Cheat River on the other side of it," Burroughs remarked. "It was flowing by a very devious course northwest toward Ohio." Three miles beyond the timber bridge, the road descended a steep grade along a ledge and then crossed the stream again over an iron bridge. As the caravan worked its way toward the southeast, it would cross and recross the same river all day.

With no road signs to guide them, the campers found that the dirt roads were difficult to distinguish from each other, and they once wound up driving five miles down one mountain track before realizing they had made a wrong turn. After retracing their path they finally rolled into Parsons.

Twenty-five years earlier Parsons had been at the center of a "war" that pitted its residents against those of the nearby town of Saint George in a dispute that went back to the formation of Tucker County, of which both towns were part. When the county was incorporated in the 1850s, Saint George had been designated as the county seat, but after a fire destroyed much of the town thirty years later, it became something of a backwater. By the late 1880s residents of the new town of Parsons, which had sprung up along the railway line linking Pittsburgh to Elkins, petitioned to become the new county seat. After failing three times, the measure was passed in the election of 1892. But before steps could be taken to begin the move, the citizens of Saint George filed an appeal. The residents of Parsons, determined not to have what they saw as a fair vote overturned, banded together and, in a mob that may have been as large as a thousand men, marched into Saint George to collect the county court records and other documents and carry them back to Parsons. When Saint George residents turned out to stop them, their sheriff sent them home, hoping to prevent a violent confrontation. This left the Parsons contingent free to ransack the courthouse. After camping that evening outside of town, they returned to Parsons the next day and established a makeshift courthouse that served as the county seat until a permanent structure was built several years later.

Now, however, Parsons appeared to be a peaceful town; its residents showed the campers none of the aggression they had once launched against their neighbors. While the crew topped off the autos with gasoline and oil, Ford and Edison drifted into the drugstore. Edison bought milk and chocolate. Ford, perhaps recalling the shocked faces of the crowd that had watched his outburst over Burroughs's caramels, let the sweet purchase slide and turned his attention to the locals who had come in to shake his hand. He then wandered back outside and helped the crew repair a leak in the cooling-water jacket on the White truck.

That afternoon the campers made their way toward Elkins, first climbing a long ascent that leveled out along a ledge overlooking Shavers Fork, which flowed into the Black Fork at Parsons to form the Cheat. Even as they left the Cheat watershed behind, they were getting a last look at the river's childhood. When the road turned downward again, the cars rattled over a rough and rutted surface cut by drainage runs that had gouged deep, diagonal gullies across their path.

Along the way they stopped to pick up a young girl, "twelve or thirteen years old," Burroughs guessed, who was walking along the road. They gave her a lift of a few miles and learned a little about her as they drove along. "She had been on a train five times," Burroughs heard her say, "and had once been forty miles from home. Her mother was dead and her father lived in Pennsylvania, and she was living with her grandfather." When they asked her how much farther it was to Elkins, she gave them a bleak answer. "Ever and ever so many miles."

When the party reached Elkins, their cars were quickly surrounded by townspeople who had caught wind of their arrival. While Firestone and Ford scrambled into the telegraph office, Burroughs and Edison found themselves engulfed by locals holding up cameras or thrusting pens and paper into their hands for autographs. Edison took the crush of admirers with his usual nonchalance, and Burroughs quietly enjoyed it. Writing to a friend two days later, the naturalist said of the crowds that "Ford is our greatest drawing card," but sometimes "I had more worshippers than Edison or Ford."

Among the onlookers was the mayor, who extended an invitation on behalf of a group of local businessmen for the campers to put up for the night at their fishing lodge on Cheat Mountain. The place was some thirty miles away, the mayor explained, but it was along the route they had been traveling. It would make for a warm and comfortable night. This, of course, was antithetical to Edison's principles of camping. So Firestone and Ford dodged the invitation and, after taking on gasoline, the party drove on, planning to find a campsite in the mountains beyond town.

As the caravan was pulling out of Elkins, though, Edison's Simplex, which had been remarkably dependable thus far, suddenly sheared off the U-shaped bolt that held the car's long elliptical leaf springs to the frame. Burroughs's comments about the shaking-up he received in the car notwithstanding, the Simplex was known for its smooth ride due to the innovative spring system it used: a shackle bolt designed specifically for this model would be hard to come by this deep into the mountains. The car might be disabled for some time.

Firestone talked Edison into leaving the vehicle and driving on with Burroughs and Harvey to scout out a campsite, while he and Ford dealt with the Simplex. As the caravan rolled away, Ford took off his coat, slipped underneath the car, and began tinkering with its suspension. When he had a sense of the sort of fastener he needed, he crawled out and took a look around. Spotting a threshing machine at work in a field not quite a mile away, he led Firestone out through the grain and introduced himself to the men who were threshing the field. After looking around the machine he found a loose bolt he could

use to make the repair. Not two hours after the Simplex had rattled
to a stop, he had the car on the road again.

Ford and Firestone set off, but night was falling, and as they tried
to find their way over Cheat Mountain, they lost the light. Just as
they started to lose hope of finding the campsite, the road descended
toward a stream crossing. When the headlights of the Simplex swept
across the bridge, Ford and Firestone spotted a Packard on the far
side. It was Harvey.

"While we were happy to see him," Firestone recalled, "we were
very anxious to locate the dining tent." He and Ford had had nothing
to eat, and they were famished. Harvey had good news for them. The
crew had pitched camp at a beautiful spot along the Shavers Fork
River, barely a mile up the road. Harvey wheeled the Packard around
and led the Simplex to the spot. When they turned off the road, Firestone saw that they were entering the grounds of the same Cheat
Mountain Club that the Elkins mayor had invited them to visit. Firestone had trouble believing what was happening, "as Mr. Edison had
absolutely refused to go to any Club."

But Firestone and Ford were not themselves opposed to the idea
of a warm night and a good dinner. When they reached the Cheat
clubhouse, they saw a two-story timber lodge with a wide, roofed
porch. There were six symmetrically placed windows on each level. A
blocky, hip-roofed turret rose from the middle of the second story, and
a large chimney on the left side of the structure promised a warm fire
inside. As they entered the building, they came into a large, rustic
room with a massive fireplace at one end. The broad timber beams
that supported the ceiling were illuminated by the firelight. It looked
like the perfect haven after a day on the road, but the travelers' hopes
were soon deflated when they learned that they would have to wait
at least an hour for supper. There were, however, attractions to enjoy
while they waited. Upstairs there was a bathroom with hot and cold
running water. As the party looked around the clubhouse, Firestone

glanced into the bedrooms on the second floor. The crew had already pitched tents by the river, but Firestone felt himself yielding to the temptation of a proper bed.

Dinner was finally served around 9:30 that evening. When the talk began to flag later that night and the campers started to make their way to bed, Burroughs and DeLoach made up their minds to spend the night in one of those cozy rooms in the lodge. Members of the crew, who had never signed on to Edison's camping philosophy, did the same. Firestone, who had been drawn to the rooms himself, chose to avoid the taunts of "dude" and "tenderfoot" that Edison would certainly rain down on him if he slept indoors. He threw in his lot with "the old-time campers" who "stuck to their tents."

Some of the travelers slept in the next morning, but Ford and Firestone were up early enough to walk around the grounds. They found a stone basin fed by a spring, and Ford sampled the cool mountain water. It was going on 10:00 by the time the crew had stowed the tents and the caravan began to make its way back along Shavers Fork to Cheat Bridge, beyond which they rejoined the road headed southeast toward the town of Warm Springs.

Through much of the morning they followed winding roads that were sometimes dirt, sometimes shale. This was coal country, and here and there they could see signs of mining operations. Coming around one bend, Firestone spotted an odd-looking structure by the roadside—an arch-roofed shack with a gaping hole in the middle. Ford recognized this as a mine-shaft ventilator, and they stopped to take a look before continuing on their way.

For miles the landscape followed the same undulating pattern. When the road descended from one summit, it would quickly begin climbing toward another. Burroughs was awed by the mountains they were now traveling through.

"They were not rubbed down and scooped out by the great ice-sheet that played such a part in shaping our northern landscapes," he remarked. In the Catskills, the action of glaciers had smoothed off the edges, turning the V of a river valley into a softened U. Here in southern Appalachia, in contrast, the landscape was rugged and sharp. Many of the valleys they passed through were hemmed in by walls so steep they could not be cultivated. The few houses that were scattered about clung to the hillsides, leaving barely enough land for the road to pass through. When the road eventually spilled out into a broader valley, however, Burroughs could see how rich the soil was. "Everywhere," he observed of one valley, "were large fields of buckwheat, white with bloom." In another he saw "miles upon miles of beautiful farms in which hay and oats were still being harvested."

At one particularly verdant farm along the road outside the village of Bartow, some ten miles into the day's travel, the party stopped to watch farmhands harvesting ripe oats with cradle scythes. Ford and the others had not stood watching the work long before talk turned to their own experiences on the business end of a scythe on the farms where they had each grown up. Ford, as usual, managed to turn the occasion into a contest. Before long he had a scythe in his hand, his gangly arms swinging the blade vigorously and leaving a broad swath of felled grain in his wake. Firestone soon peeled off his jacket and took a turn himself. Burroughs, the only one of the three who had tried to scrape a living from a farm as an adult, was not far behind. Everyone enjoyed the contest. The farmer for his part took off his hat and scratched his head as he watched a couple of millionaires doing his morning work.

After lunch the travelers consulted a map and decided they could make Warm Springs by evening and camp there. With that goal in mind the caravan set off toward the south, tracing a scraggly line across Edison's map: his guidebook was of little use, given how far off the beaten path they were now. Sometime in the afternoon they took a wrong turn and crossed a bridge they should have bypassed. Just when they expected to descend into Warm Springs, the road began to climb again. Before anyone could figure out what had gone wrong, they drove into a shaded mountain hamlet called Bolar Springs, which sat on a ridge high above the road they had intended to follow.

By this point it was too late to retrace their steps and find their way back to the Warm Springs road. They decided instead to ask for help in finding a campsite nearby. A local man guided them to a spot a half mile from town, where they set up their tents on a stretch of level ground in a shaded grove that Firestone deemed "a splendid place." Just beyond the treeline a natural spring fed into a concrete pool. The water was warm and clean. The campers were more than willing to pay the fifteen cents they were charged for a bath.

The spring fed the bath with "Calcic-Magnesic Bicarbonated Alkaline Water," according to an analysis of the water carried out earlier that month by the Richmond testing laboratory of the Froehling and Robertson engineering firm. If you believed the testimonials amassed by the owners of the baths, the water would cure anything that ailed you. A visitor from Marlinton, West Virginia, had been cured of blood poisoning. One septuagenarian had used the water to treat a kidney malady that had him so weak he walked with two canes, and after six months of drinking the water, he threw away both. A man from Trimble, Virginia, had been afflicted so badly with poison ivy around his mouth and throat that he could not eat, but the Bolar Spring water had cured him in five days. Another visitor had a similar experience with poison oak. Even the testing laboratory that examined the water went on to indicate that it was "applicable to a wide range of diseases especially gouty and rheumatic troubles as well as diseases of the digestive organs."

But while the campers had the best bathing fifteen cents could buy (or $1.50, if you preferred to pay for your bathing by the week), they were running alarmingly low on supplies. The general store in town had no bread, but a tip from the proprietor led the party to a hotel located on a hill above the store.

"We went up to the hotel and inquired of the lady who came to the door if we could buy some bread," Firestone recalled. "She said no; that she did not have any to spare." Firestone put on his salesman's charm and chatted with the woman about the party of campers. He was not above dropping the names Henry Ford and Thomas Edison, and he joked about how the great inventor had a tremendous appetite for apple pie. Once he had struck up a rapport with the woman, Firestone made her a proposition. Since there was still some flour among the supplies on the kitchen truck, Firestone asked if the woman might be willing to bake bread for them, so they could have some for breakfast. After some hemming and hawing, she agreed, and later that evening Harvey and Kline ferried a bag of flour up to the hotel.

That afternoon a late edition of a Philadelphia newspaper issued a lighthearted admonition to the famous campers. "Before you do anything these days you should be sure to think whether it could possibly give aid and comfort to the enemy," the piece warned. And this advice was doubly vital for notables like those in Ford's party. Their current escapades were sure to be used to German advantage in Berlin, where newspapers might even now be reporting that "American magnates, terrified at German victories, take to the woods in panic. Food shortage in America compels them to forage for fish, locusts and wild honey."

Later in the evening as the campers were finishing their bread-less dinner, the woman from the hotel appeared at the camp. It turned out that she had enough flour to bake an apple pie, and she had brought one down for Edison. Everyone was eager to dig into the fresh-baked dessert—everyone, that is, except for Edison, who had already finished his dinner and had no room left for pie. He wanted to have his slice saved for breakfast, "so we took great care in doing this," Firestone noted, "but during the night the dogs got into our commissary truck and ate Mr. Edison's apple pie."

The campers rose early the next morning, eager to breakfast on fresh bread. While they waited for their baker to arrive, Ford stood chatting with a local who had dropped in to see the camp. Firestone hovered near the fire, warming himself after a chilly night. Edison came tumbling out of his tent after the others were up, "holding his hand in front of his face," Burroughs noticed, "in mock repentance for being up so late." By 8:30 the inventor had ensconced himself in a chair near the fire with a copy of William Ellery Channing's biography of Thoreau. Burroughs was busy writing a letter to his friend Clara Barrus.

"What scenery we have beheld!" he wrote. "Wonderful every day— grander Catskills—about the same climate, the same flora and fauna. Farmers are yet haying, the oats are in the shock, the buckwheat in bloom, the corn in the ear." He described the mountains they had traversed thus far, a few over six thousand feet, many others more than half that tall. "For 200 miles the roadsides have been lined with purple eupatorium, iron-weed, and, once, a great mass of monarda." On that occasion, after spotting the flowers, Edison had bounded from the car and returned with a handful for Burroughs to inspect; that was how the inventor learned the name monarda, or bee balm, as it was sometimes called.

"The woods are of sugar maple, yellow birch, beech, spruce and hemlock," Burroughs went on to say. While these forests indeed reminded him of the Catskills, there were some notable absences. The naturalist had not spotted a single woodchuck or chipmunk. He had, however, added a new bird to his list—the painted bunting. A striking bird of the cardinal family, the male had a blue head and red underbelly, with green and yellow markings on the wings and back, while the female's plumage was green and gray with yellow mottling. The bunting's call reminded Burroughs of the songster his neighbors in the Catskills referred to as the yellow-bird.

It was not much later that the woman from the hotel returned with loaves she had baked from the flour Harvey and Kline had delivered to her. But the campers were disappointed to see that the bread had not risen; the loaves were dense little bricks, less than two inches thick. The woman seemed to think that the flour had somehow been soaked in gasoline—not an improbable notion, given the bouncing around the goods stored in the truck had received on the mountain roads. This made for a less than satisfying loaf, but if the gasoline kept the bread from baking properly, it did act as an effective preservative.

It was not the best baking they had eaten. But, Firestone remem-

*The camping party is ferried across the Jackson River in Virginia on August 23, 1918.*

bered, "we had this bread for the next two or three days; we did not seem to find a town in which we could purchase the 'staff of life.'"

After a meager breakfast the crew started breaking camp, and by 9:30 they had dismantled the tents and loaded the equipment onto the trucks. The party was soon back on the road, heading southwest toward Warm Springs. For much of the morning the road followed the Jackson River, then the caravan turned more steeply south on a road that meandered through forested land to Warm Springs. From here it was six miles, and one twenty-five-cent toll, to Hot Springs. Around 11:15 they reached the day's first destination.

Situated in a mountain valley almost 2,200 feet above sea level, Hot Springs, Virginia, was a town of a thousand year-round residents, but its population was often inflated by the influx of tourists who came for the baths. Here, Edison's guidebook pronounced, "are several springs whose waters are considered efficacious in the treatment of dyspepsia, scrofula, and disorders of the stomach and liver."

On the way into town the caravan passed the train station and a drugstore before stopping at the Homestead Hotel, where they rested and waited for word from Hurley, who had tentatively planned to rejoin the party there. When a message arrived saying he regretted that he could not come, the travelers decided to drive on toward White Sulphur Springs.

Two miles out of town they paid a fifteen-cent toll, then drove through Healing Springs and followed a winding road through a valley. When they came to a bend where a pleasing stream skirted the road, they stopped for lunch.

While the crew prepared the meal, Ford and Burroughs and the others explored the countryside. A sizable concrete basin near the stream caught their eye. It looked to Ford like some sort of water-power system. Ford and Firestone crawled out onto a log positioned across the mouth of the pool to get a better look at the setup. Ford

*Henry Ford and Harvey Firestone investigate a water-power system in the*
*mountains above the O. C. Barber phosphate plant near Healing Springs,*
*Virginia.*

took off his socks and shoes and dangled his feet in the water as he
pondered the arrangement. As the campers inspected the odd structure and tried to understand how it worked, they managed to close a
sluice gate. Then they were called to lunch.

While they were eating, an angry-looking man appeared—"a gentleman," as Firestone saw him, "in a very bad frame of mind"—and
informed them that they had shut off the flow to the power plant he
operated, some two miles downstream. When they had made their
apologies and the man had restored the flow of water, Ford asked him
how the power plant worked and what it powered. It turned out the
facility Ford and his friends had deprived of power was a phosphate
plant owned by the "Match King," O. C. Barber.

Ohio Columbus Barber was the head of the Diamond Match
Company, the largest manufacturer of matches in the country. He

had also founded the Diamond Rubber Company, which, like the Firestone company, manufactured vehicle tires in Akron. Barber's most significant contribution to the rubber industry was an innovative method for recycling used rubber, which allowed him to prosper in declining markets and reduced his dependence on foreign suppliers of latex. On the strength of this innovation he had built a thriving company, which he sold to B.F. Goodrich in 1912. The mark of Barber's success was easy to see around Akron. His French Renaissance–style mansion, in nearby Barberton, a town he had created outside the city limits, was spoken of as the finest house between New York and Chicago. The fifty-two-room mansion had been built on three hundred acres in 1905 at a cost of six million dollars. All the marble used in its construction was imported from Siena. Its grand ballroom had a floor made entirely of teak. The estate even had its own rail connection. What interested Firestone and Ford, however, was that Barber, like them the son of a farming family—his family's grain company had evolved into Quaker Oats—shared their interest in improving the efficiency of agriculture. A three-thousand-acre experimental farm was attached to his estate, and Barber's many greenhouses enclosed some dozens of acres of land. Over a hundred Belgian thoroughbred horses were housed in one of his massive barns, of which there were several, one of them three stories high. His experimental poultry operation handled more than fifty thousand free-range hens.

As soon as they heard about Barber's phosphate plant, Ford and Firestone made up their minds to get a look at the operation. They drove down the mountain and spent a portion of the morning touring the plant and chatting with Barber himself, who happened to be there. What they found at the facility impressed them both. It was not just well designed and efficiently operated; it was, as Firestone, put it, "the most modern plant in the south." If he and Ford had not accidentally shut down the water supply, they might never have found it.

After the visit to the plant, the party drove on through a little town called Callaghan toward White Sulphur Springs. They crossed a small wooden bridge and then forded Big Ogley Creek, the first of several crossings they would make over the next fifteen miles.

When they reached White Sulphur Springs, Ford and DeLoach stopped in town with Firestone, while Edison and Burroughs drove on ahead with Harvey to scout out a campsite for the night. Firestone was determined, against Edison's inviolable camper's precept, to have a bath and a shave—but when he went to a hotel to ask for a room, he was turned away. The same thing happened at the next hotel. These two main hotels, the Greenbrier and the White, were both managed by the same concern that ran the Plaza Hotel in New York, and it seemed that Firestone, after many days on the road and in camp, did not appear to meet their standards.

Although White Sulphur Springs was a small town, home to barely a thousand residents, nestled two thousand feet up in the West Virginia mountains, it had a long history as an upscale resort. "It is the most popular resort of the Southern States," Edison's guidebook proclaimed, "and no holiday place is more famous by association with great names and high memories, or makes a more romantic appeal." Robert E. Lee had spent a handful of summers there, and Henry Clay's name could be seen in one of the hotel registers. The hoteliers in town liked to say that the summer temperatures approximated those in Nice and Madeira.

Firestone was eventually directed to a bathhouse, where he cleaned himself up enough for a visit to a barber. By the time he had made himself presentable enough for White Sulphur Springs, Harvey came roaring back into town in the Packard to take his father, along with Ford and DeLoach, to the spot along Tuckahoe Run creek where the tents had been pitched. It was already close to sundown by the time they arrived, so the campers settled in for a quiet night.

While White Sulphur Springs, like neighboring Bolar Springs, attracted visitors with the promise of restored health and vigor, the news Edison gleaned from the papers he picked up there pointed to a growing health threat that lay beyond the curative reach of a mineral bath. The day Burroughs and Edison left West Orange, the *New York Times* had run a story about a Norwegian steamer that arrived at the port of New York with nine cases of influenza among the passengers. The surgeon serving aboard the vessel was careful not to use the word "Spanish" in describing the illness.

Thousands of cases of what was being called Spanish influenza had already swept through Spain, Germany, France, and England since reporting on the illness first began to appear early in the year. Even in nearby Cuba influenza was spreading at an alarming rate. There had also been cases in the United States, and Americans were beginning to fear this virulent new illness.

When the sickest cases from the Norwegian vessel were transferred to a local hospital, it was determined that their symptoms were "probably brought on by Spanish influenza." Because there was as yet no specific quarantine policy regarding the illness, some sick passengers were allowed to continue their travel. When concern was raised about this, the city health commissioner Royal S. Copeland maintained that "the public has no reason for alarm." Thanks to what he called the "vigilance of the city's health authorities," he believed "all the protection that sanitary science can give is assured."

Now, with the campers a week into their trip, articles on the spread of the disease, which was reaching epidemic proportions in Europe, were turning up almost daily in the newspapers Edison tracked down in the towns they passed through. By and large, American reporters were still treating the outbreak as a foreign problem. An article in the *New York Tribune*, for instance, busied itself with the argument that the so-called Spanish influenza had actually broken out first in

Germany, "just like most of the other ills which have afflicted mankind since 1914." The local papers in Pennsylvania had echoed this
reporting, adding that Americans "will chalk up one more black mark
against the Hun to be settled along with other matters when the war
is over."

For now Americans maintained an ironic attitude toward news
about the flu. One small local paper commented on a dispatch that
carried a warning from the New York City department of health
advising citizens "not to kiss except through a handkerchief." The
author of the piece was left with a question. "That's alright, but how
about the handkerchief? One ought to carry a bottle of disinfectant to
sterilize the handkerchief."

Nevertheless, certain comforting myths about the flu's spread were
proving false. One of these held that only malnourished populations
fell victim to infection, a notion undercut when the disease began to
spread among the officers and sailors at an American naval base in
Ireland—"probably the best fed persons in Europe." Even so, papers
stressed the manageability of the illness. "The disease is not danger-
ous if taken in hand quickly enough and it has left no ill effects at the
destroyer base."

The influenza story was tailor-made to stir up speculation among
the campers, who themselves held some unorthodox views on health.
Edison, for one, assumed that his peculiar combination of long work
hours and skipped meals protected him from most ailments. He
believed that most people eat and sleep twice as much as they should.
"The person who sleeps eight or ten hours a night is never fully asleep
and never fully awake," the inventor argued. "He has only different
degrees of doze." Edison had gone so far as to comb through the files
of the *British Medical Journal* and claimed to have found no evidence
of a negative effect from lack of sleep. People who eat until they no longer feel hungry were overdoing it in a similar way, he thought. "Most
of their energies are taken up digesting what they eat."

Burroughs was of a similar mind. "Most of our physical ills drift in at the mouth," he maintained. He watched his own health the way a mechanic tends to a machine. He monitored his weight and kept close track of his digestion. Whenever he began to feel under the weather, he always assumed that an excess of food was at the root of the trouble. "Then I take in sail in eating." If that did not do the trick, he next turned to calomel to flush out the digestive system. "That sweeps the clouds right away." He avoided tobacco and alcohol as assiduously as Ford did, but he also shied away from fruit. Raw fruit, he thought, was the cause of a great deal of trouble. He was not sure eggs were good for you either.

The flu and other bugs did not worry the old naturalist as long as his digestion was running smoothly. Germs come and go all the time, he believed, but they needed an opportunity—"whether unsuitable food or overwork or worry"—in order to cause any difficulty. "If your system is in proper tone, tuberculosis could howl around you day and night and not effect a foothold."

Edison was beginning to think that the etiology of the Spanish flu could be fit into the broader idea he had been considering about the inception of life itself. For some time he had felt that the best explanation for the origin of life on Earth was colonization by drifting life-entities from more developed planets, which arrived here once the newly formed Earth had cooled sufficiently and then began to adapt to the environment as they found it. To his mind this idea better explained life on the planet than any of the beliefs that had arisen to fill in our lack of knowledge about how life began. "I think this theory will explain special abilities better than any other. It will rid the world of harmful superstitions such as those of spiritualism. It will bring order out of the chaos of much of that puzzlement which we endeavor to accept as reasoning with regard to the creation and genesis of man." It was beginning to strike him as possible that new elements in biological life, like the Spanish influenza, might be novel introductions reaching Earth in a similar way. As the year wore on, this idea would take firmer hold in his mind.

When the party broke camp at Tuckahoe Run, Edison and the others took advantage of the stream to wash up in the appropriate fashion, demonstrating their hardiness before Firestone, whose freshly clipped hair and clean-shaven face were to Edison's mind a mark of shame.

That morning the campers stopped at Sweet Springs, a nearly abandoned town sixteen miles south of White Sulphur Springs. Here a cluster of antebellum brick buildings caught their attention. When Firestone tracked someone down to ask about them, he learned that these gracious Federal-style structures were more than a hundred years old, some dating to the late eighteenth century, and the oldest were said to have been designed by Thomas Jefferson. Now, however, they were mostly unoccupied. The campers were shown a nearby spring and bathing pool. But the spring water did not taste good, they found, and the bathing pool, Firestone thought, "looked as if the frogs had been bathing more than the people and was very stagnant." The decline of these old summer resorts became a subject of fascination for Firestone, who kept his eye out for signs of their sad demise for the rest of the trip.

Ten miles farther along, at the town of Gap Mills, Ford caught sight of another water-driven mill. Burroughs, who would normally have been as interested in this as Ford, was feeling exhausted by the morning's slow travel over rough roads, muddy fords, and creaky wooden bridges. So Ford spent half an hour looking at the mill on his own, while the others waited in the cars, which were quickly surrounded by locals who recognized Edison. By the time Ford returned, one of the residents had disappeared into his house and run back with a gift for the inventor, a can of maple syrup to tempt his well-known sweet tooth.

They made camp that evening on Wolf Creek, outside the hard-scrabble railroad town of Narrows, Virginia, situated on a bend of the New River just over the state line from West Virginia. When the travelers stopped to inquire about a place to camp, no one recognized them, and they could find no place to buy groceries for the night. Although it was a relief to dispense with the clamorous receptions they had experienced elsewhere, here it looked as if they would find no help at all. Firestone was troubled by the handful of people they encountered, who looked to him "rough and uncivilized," just as the countryside they inhabited seemed to him "rough and wild." After looking about for a while, the party finally convinced one of the locals to guide them to a campsite, which they found upstream along the wide, flat creek that spilled into the river at the edge of town. Once they had set up camp, Harvey drove out with Kline—pistol-packing Kline, because Firestone had not forgotten the rough crowd he had

*Edison, Firestone, Burroughs, and Ford in camp along Wolf Creek, outside Narrows, Virginia.*

seen in Narrows—to ferret around the nearby farmsteads for provisions. They soon returned with milk, eggs, and chickens. That night no one visited the camp, and although the cold reception at Narrows had unsettled some in the party, they found that camping alongside Wolf Creek gave them one of the most peaceful nights they had experienced so far.

While the crew broke camp the next morning, Burroughs found himself a comfortable spot and took in the scenery. Ford came and sat nearby. He was working at a cedar log he had found: he wanted to have the members of the party inscribe their names, as a souvenir of their trip, and was carefully scraping at the bark to make the surface smooth and durable. While Burroughs watched his friend at work, he began to write a letter to Clara Ford.

"After a week of motoring in W. Va. filled with glorious experiences and now rather much discomfort over very bad roads, we are camping on the banks of this broad, lucid stream," he told her. "I see fish jumping, I hear the Carolina wren calling. I hear the cicada rasping." He went on to tell Clara about her husband, happily hunched over his whittling. "Mr. Ford looks as well as I ever saw him and is in excellent spirits—as usual."

Burroughs reported that the trip had gone well so far, though there had been some cold nights and the weather had now turned quite hot. For the most part the campers had enjoyed fine weather, and the scenery along the way had surprised even a jaded naturalist with its beauty and variety. Burroughs had seen nothing to compare with it on this side of the Rocky Mountains. For all the pleasures the excursion offered, however, he was himself suffering somewhat. His old complaint—indigestion—had nagged him for a few days. If he were able to eat and drink like the others—coffee to start the morning and big suppers to put them to sleep—he would no doubt feel better. He admitted that were the trip to wind down in a day or two, he would welcome the return to his careful routine at home. "But Mr. Edison cannot get enough of the rough and the wild," he wrote. "He and Mr. Ford need this sort of thing more than I do. My life is all vacation." He confided to Clara that he was considering taking a train home, but he did not elaborate. "I would write more," he said in closing, "but we are off."

Before the party left, Ford had Burroughs, Edison, Firestone, DeLoach, and Harvey sign the log he had been working on. Then he signed it himself and added an inscription that read, "Your best friend is the one who can bring out the best in you."

Despite the quiet night and a slow start to the morning, the group's senior member, Burroughs, was still in the grip of exhaustion and indigestion as the day's drive began. The unpaved roads did nothing to ease his discomfort as the party rattled north, following the New River. At Glen Lyn the route swung west toward Oakvale. The town of Glen Lyn was little more than a store built where the road forked, but it held an attraction that would have brought Ford to a stop had he been aware of it. It was the home of a man named Henry Reed, who was not only one of the best fiddlers in the region but also the composer of fiddle tunes that were shaping the style of music played throughout southern Appalachia. Ford had bought his first fiddle when he was a young man, twenty or thirty years earlier, and had taught himself to play a few tunes. He never managed to become the fiddler he wanted to be, but he never lost his love for the instrument or for the tradition of dance music it had inspired. Ford still clung to that first instrument, and as he got older, he was growing more and more nostalgic for the dance music he had listened to in his youth. But he missed the opportunity to hear that music in Glen Lyn as the party pushed on to the west.

By the time they reached Oakvale, Burroughs had had enough of bouncing over bad roads. He and DeLoach decided to catch a train to Bluefield, where they would rejoin the party at the end of the day. The train would cover the twenty miles smoothly and effortlessly, giving the old naturalist some rest while the cars spent the remainder of the day fighting their way through the mountainous terrain. With Burroughs and DeLoach settled, the rest of the group drove on toward Bluefield. Around 1:00 they took a break for lunch, over Edison's gentle protests; he always wanted to cover more ground.

The tires on the heavy White truck had been taking a beating from the rough roads for a few days, and no spare inner tubes in the right size remained among the stock Firestone had laid in. It seemed likely the truck would suffer at least one blowout over the course of the morning, which would require patching the tire, a slower process than changing the tube. As a precaution, before they set out that morning, they had moved lunch supplies to the Ford car driven by Sato and Willmott. That way, they thought, their lunch would never lag too far behind. But now they waited for the Ford by the side of the road only to see the White truck come through first. The Ford had suffered a puncture, and it was some time before Sato and Willmott caught up with the others.

"Sato was not in a good humor when he arrived," Firestone noted. As a result, lunch was pushed back still later, while the irritated chef collected himself. After lunch Ford flagged down a farmer and learned that gasoline could be found in the town of Princeton, just a few miles ahead. After they left Princeton, following the trolley tracks out of town and turning onto the Bluefield Road, they finally found their way onto a paved surface again, the first macadam road they had encountered since before Warm Springs. From there it was a smooth eleven-mile ride into Bluefield.

Compared to the towns they had visited over the last few days, Bluefield, West Virginia, a city of nineteen thousand that served as a coal distribution center for the vast Pocahontas Coalfield, was a bustling metropolis. When they arrived, Ford, Edison, and Firestone found Burroughs and DeLoach resting at a hotel where they had already eaten lunch after reaching town by train that afternoon.

While the camping party cooled their heels in the lobby, Firestone had the manager of the hotel telephone the post office, where he was expecting to receive a spare tube for the White truck. Although the post office had closed for the day—it was Sunday—someone picked up the phone, and Firestone was able to make arrangements to retrieve the tube.

With the day wearing on, Edison and Burroughs began to worry that night would catch the party still on the road. Having checked the map, they decided to push on quickly toward Tazewell, twenty-three miles to the southwest, over the Virginia state line. Here the roads followed the line of least resistance, skirting just west of the more rugged terrain of the Appalachian chain. The vehicles were able to make good time, but more open countryside also meant more roads branching from their intended route. The caravan became separated along the way, and when the car carrying Firestone, Burroughs, and Edison reached Tazewell, the others were nowhere to be seen. When they failed to show after a reasonable wait, it was clear they had become lost.

Firestone, knowing that his companions were eager to make camp, volunteered to wait for the stragglers and direct them onto the route Edison had in mind. He climbed out of the car and made his way to the hotel on the town's main street, from where he could comfortably keep an eye on the roadway. As each car or truck arrived, Firestone gave them instructions and sent them on their way. To pass the time he chatted with the staff and patrons at the hotel and made the acquaintance of a visiting circuit judge. More than two hours passed before the last car, the Ford driven by Sato and Willmott, rattled into town.

When Firestone had joined them, the three men then drove on to the southwest, following the directions Edison had given Firestone, but as the miles wore on, they saw no sign of the camp or of their companions. Finally, they came across a group of young travelers making their way to Bluefield, who said they had passed the camping party earlier in the afternoon. The young people shared their food with

Firestone and the others and took a great interest in Sato, who, with his Japanese features, struck them as exotic. Soon the three pushed on, and before long they ran into Ford and Harvey, who had become concerned about them and turned back to look for the lagging car. It was just after nightfall by the time they reached the camp, which had been pitched at the western end of a small, enclosed valley.

That evening, after the party had eaten supper, again delayed by Sato's late arrival in camp, Firestone took his son out for a walk through the countryside. As they wandered along, the father and son began to hear strains of mountain music drifting from one of the nearby farmsteads. Listening to the distant melodies, Firestone grew nostalgic for the country life he had known as a boy on the farm in Columbiana. It was a life young Harvey had never really known. His father could not help turning the moment into a tutorial on rustic contentment.

"I gave Harvey a lesson," Firestone recalled later, "telling him what

*Morning in camp on the Witt farm near Tazewell, Virginia.*

great pleasure and satisfaction there was in living a simple country life, and the enjoyment these people got out of life in general." Back at camp Ford, Edison, Burroughs, and the others were settling in for a quiet Sunday night. The coming week was to be an important one in Ford's public life, but that fact had for the moment slipped his mind. More likely, he had pushed it from his thoughts.

With Ford now turning the capacity of his factory more and more toward the production of war materiél, President Wilson wished to thank him for his support for the administration's war effort while encouraging him to do more.

Wilson had called the automaker to a meeting at the White House, where he suggested that Ford should run for the Senate seat that would open up when Michigan senator William Alden Smith's term expired. Smith, a Republican who had held the seat since 1907 and had chaired the committee that investigated the sinking of the *Titanic*, had decided not to run for reelection, leaving both parties scrambling to line up candidates for what had once seemed a solidly held seat. Appealing personally to Ford, Wilson told him he was "the only man in Michigan who can be elected and help to bring about the peace you so much desire."

Ford may have been flattered, but he was not exactly pleased. He saw the invitation, however Wilson might try to sweeten it, as a civic obligation. He would do as the president asked, but he did not have to like it. "If the people of Michigan chose to elect me to that office I would accept it," he said privately, "but I will not lift a finger to bring it about."

As it turned out, Ford's participation was hardly required. By the following May a faction of the Republican party in Michigan had announced that Ford was their man. They published a statement proclaiming that the "presence of business men in the Senate of the

United States would be of great value to the nation in this time of emergency" and pledging "to use every legitimate means to secure the nomination and election of Henry Ford as Senator for the state of Michigan on the Republican ticket."

In June the Democrats, in a move that had no precedent in Michigan political history, endorsed Ford as their choice, too, pressing him "to become our party candidate, although he is not within our fold." Meanwhile, two former governors and a veteran of the Roosevelt cabinet, Truman Newberry, had all announced their own plans to seek the Republican nomination.

By the middle of July the press was reporting that Ford's friend Edison had thrown his own hat in the ring for a contested New Jersey Senate seat. New Jersey Democrats had been struggling to find a candidate who could hold onto the seat that had been vacated by the death of William Hughes in January. A popular public figure like Edison, so the thinking went, had a fair chance of uniting the party and going on to win the general election against strong Republican opposition.

Edison had no public affiliation with the Democratic party. In fact, he was seen as "Republican in his leanings," as one report put it. But he was "known to be a strong Woodrow Wilson man." It was easy to see the Ford candidacy reflected in the rumors that were emerging about Edison. "If Mr. Edison would become a candidate in New Jersey," announced a dispatch in the *Brooklyn Eagle*, "he would at once be looked upon as an administration candidate, and the New Jersey fight would become of nationwide interest."

Edison's "campaign" turned out to be short lived. When a reporter called at Edison's house in West Orange to confirm the story, he found the inventor away and pressed Edison's son Charles for a comment. The younger Edison dismissed the entire story as a "wild rumor." "My father is too busy to even contemplate such a thing," he said. Charles was quick to connect the rumor to Ford. "The report probably started because Henry Ford is running in Michigan and some one thought Mr. Edison, who is one of his close friends, might do likewise in New Jersey."

Unlike Edison's candidacy, Ford's had been real enough. But he seemed to have given it no more thought than Edison had given his fictional campaign. Ford had not given a speech, spent any money, or done any of the things candidates traditionally thought necessary to solicit the votes that would get them elected to office.

Whenever talk around the campfire had turned to Ford's entry into politics, Edison could not conceal his skepticism.

"What do you want to do that for?" he asked Ford. "You can't speak. You wouldn't say a damned word. You'd be mum."

Ford knew himself well enough not to argue the point. Instead he tried to interest Edison in the role the newspapers had already sketched out for him: he could join Ford in the Senate. But Edison would have none of that.

"I'm too deaf. I couldn't hear anything," he said.

"It isn't what you hear that makes you useful," Ford countered. "It's what you do or say—what you tell the people."

Although Edison mulled this over, he remained unconvinced.

"But if I did go," he eventually added, "I'd try to repeal all the patent laws. They've never done me any good or any other inventor."

Here, like two lawmakers reaching across the aisle, they found a point of agreement.

"That's so. The profits in inventions go to the manufacturers," Ford admitted.

Burroughs had little to say about Ford's political endeavors, but Ford could not fail to register his friends' lack of enthusiasm.

The campers were up and on the road again by 10:00 the following morning. On the way out of Tazewell they paid a visit to a farm before driving on to Lebanon, where they spent a few minutes taking on supplies. The roads were passable this far, but just beyond Lebanon, at Hansonville, the route turned southeast, climbing into the mountains toward Abingdon. The roadbed here all but disappeared. For more than six miles the caravan banged and rattled along a rutted track that inched its way through the rugged mountains.

Burroughs, with his bony, uncushioned frame, seemed to bear the brunt of the punishment. Complaining more vociferously than he had since the first leg of the trip, he insisted that "the Germans had built the road" as an act of sabotage and that these mountain roads were the "most damnable and despicable roads in the United States." The only pleasure the naturalist could take in the day's journey was the satisfaction of knowing that Edison, who had selected the route, was himself jouncing along the same poor excuse for a road.

When the party finally reached Abingdon, Virginia, they turned southwest onto a paved road that carried them, with considerably less complaining among the passengers, toward the Tennessee border. Around noon they arrived in Bristol, a bustling railroad town of sixteen thousand residents that was perched on the Tennessee–Virginia line. Along the main thoroughfare, State Street, you could step out of a car on one side and find yourself in one state, while your companions exiting on the opposite side were in the other. Unlike the one-horse towns they had passed through in the previous days, Bristol was just big enough to get lost in, and it took some searching to locate Harvey, who had driven ahead to scout out a spot for lunch. They eventually found him at the Hotel Bristol, conveniently located across the street from a back entrance to the Sheldon and Company garage.

No one in the hotel seemed to recognize the illustrious visitors as they ambled into the dining room. When Firestone got the attention of one of the apathetic waiters, he asked if there was a table large enough to allow the party to dine together, but the waiter replied that this would be impossible. They could find seats at the available tables or take their business elsewhere.

Disappointed, but too tired and hungry to put up a fight, they took their seats. Soon after they sat down, however, the man came bustling back out of the kitchen and began to rearrange the tables after all. Word of the celebrity visitors had finally caught up with the travelers themselves, and the waiter, now realizing that Edison, Ford, Firestone, and Burroughs were Edison, Ford, Firestone, and Burroughs, went out of his way to make up for the lukewarm welcome he had given them before. Once he had his guests seated, he disappeared into the kitchen again. "I think he cooked the meal himself or at least looked after it," mused Firestone, evidently pleased by this turn of events.

By now news of their arrival had spread around town, and locals began to wander into the hotel to get a look at them. When the party had finished lunch, Ford stood for a spell chatting with a group of residents, while Edison, as usual relying on his deafness to excuse himself from the conversation, read the day's newspapers, and Burroughs, exhausted from the morning's travel after a sleepless night, disappeared to snatch a nap in one of the hotel's empty rooms.

Before long Ford and the others had been joined by the mayor and the heads of the local Ford, Firestone, and Edison Phonograph dealerships. The talk in the dining room was of the war. When Ford was asked how long he thought the conflict would last, he said he did not know, but he guessed another year. His own factory, he pointed out, was churning out war supplies at a steady rate—"tanks, submarine chasers and Liberty motors"—all under the supervision of his son, Edsel. Ford had been criticized for keeping Edsel out of the fighting, and he was eager to call attention to what he saw as an important wartime job, implying that it was manufacturing might, managed by men like Edsel, that would turn the tide of the war. "I think it is safe to say that the Allies have retreated for the last time," Ford pronounced. "The retreating hereafter will be done by the Germans. We want peace on the right terms and we'll get it."

The locals also wanted to talk about Ford's Senate campaign, but he had little to say about that. He told the crowd he would not put up a fight for the office, and he had not spent a single penny campaigning.

Someone asked him what he thought about attacks launched against him in the press by George Harvey, a right-wing railroad magnate and newspaperman who was editor of the *War Weekly*, put out by the *North American Review*. Two weeks earlier he had published a diatribe against Wilson and Ford that called the automaker "disloyal."

"He is not helping to win the war for his country's sake, as a patriot," Harvey had complained of Ford. "He is participating 'to prevent future wars' as a pacifist." If Ford were to be elected to the Senate, he might well be expected to work to win the war and undertake the necessary reconstruction, "not in the interest of his native land," as Harvey put it, "but 'for humanity's sake,' as a man without a Country." Of the complaints that might legitimately have been lodged against Ford, this was perhaps the most convoluted in its logic: as a senator, Ford would win the war, but he would not have the right patriotic attitude about it.

Reminded of all this, Ford replied simply, "I do not know the gentleman." Ford was not just being coy: he had other things on his mind. The camping party's visits to waterwheels and grist mills and power plants all across the region had stayed with him, and what he wanted to talk about now more than anything was waterpower and how he would put it to use. With a captive audience, he began to explain his scheme to disperse the manufacturing process by setting up small "village" factories in farming districts. "I am buying up a number of small waterpower plants over the country with an idea of making separate parts in each plant." Local workers, including farmers in the off season, would provide labor and thereby help themselves through what were otherwise lean times.

The fact that Ford wished to spread what he saw as the benefits of his factories around the countryside came as no surprise to Burroughs. "Mr. Ford always thinks in terms of the greatest good to the greatest number," the naturalist believed. "He aims to place all his inventions within reach of the great mass of the people."

"One plant will turn out a certain valve," Ford continued, "another one kind of bolt and so on." The country around Bristol, with its rich farmland and network of rivers and streams, looked ideal for what he envisioned. "The country in this section is magnificent," Ford told the crowd. "I was really impressed with the mountain scenery through Southwest Virginia." And he was not alone in his assessment. "Mr. Edison," Ford added, "was favorably struck with this region from several standpoints." Edison, Ford knew, shared his interest in waterpower, but the inventor's deafness kept him from chiming in. "He seemed content," as one observer noted, "to let others do the talking and enjoy the effects." As Edison listened to Ford speaking, "his face was wreathed in smiles, hardly discernible behind the two-days' growth of beard."

After lunch Edison sat smoking a cigar on the piazza attached to the hotel, his newspapers stacked around him, while Ford went for a walk around the town. Firestone and Kline paid a visit to the local Firestone dealership on Cumberland Street, where they picked up a spare truck tire and talked shop for a while before posing for a photograph with the manager of the agency.

Ford met them at the shop, and they drove together to the telegraph office, where Firestone sent a telegram to the proprietor of the Grove Park Inn in Asheville, North Carolina, to make arrangements for their visit there. The plan, however, was not to stay at the hotel but to camp on the steep upper slopes of Sunset Mountain, which rose precipitously to the east of the inn.

When Firestone came out of the telegraph office, he and Ford returned to the hotel to find Burroughs revived by his nap, so the entire party decided to accept an invitation to inspect a farm on their way out of town. By 2:30 they were on the road.

The farm, Maplehurst, was owned by a man named Cox, who treated Ford and the others to fresh buttermilk and gave them a tour of his operation. Burroughs, Firestone, and Edison were all impressed by what they saw—both the natural beauty of the land and the efficient management of the farming. Ford called it "one of the best tracts of land" he had come across on the trip.

Cox, who had ridden from Bristol with Ford and Firestone, could not persuade his wife to come out and meet their famous visitors, so Firestone and Ford decided to look in on her themselves. They found the woman baking. She was startled to see the two strange men at her door, but Ford quickly put her at ease. Soon they were talking warmly, and Firestone suggested to their new friend that she come out to the car to meet Edison. When she said she would need a few minutes, Ford and Firestone returned to their car.

Five minutes later the woman appeared at the door, now dressed in what must have been her best dress. Firestone joked that she had looked better in her everyday clothes, and then the group assembled, with Edison, for a photograph with the now elegantly dressed woman and her husband. Soon the caravan was moving again.

That afternoon the campers crossed the south fork of the Holston River at Bluff City and drove as far as Elizabethton, twenty-three miles south of Bristol, before a rain shower halted their progress. They took refuge at a garage in town and waited there for the weather to clear. Ford and Edison passed the time talking with a handful of the town's leading citizens, including two colonels and a judge. When the rain slackened, they drove on, taking a right turn beyond the courthouse onto a long iron bridge. At the nearby hamlet of Milligan they picked up a winding macadam road that took them into Johnson City.

It turned out that a crowd of more than five hundred people had gathered at the center of town to watch for the arrival of the famous travelers, whose visit had been announced in a one-paragraph article in the previous day's newspaper. Burroughs, DeLoach, and Kline rolled into Johnson City first, in a car driven by Harvey. When Burroughs, wearing his linen duster, stepped out of the vehicle to stretch his legs in front of the Majestic Theatre on Main Street, two men on the street recognized him and brought over members of the Chamber of Commerce to be introduced.

Burroughs was surprised to have been recognized on his own in such an out-of-the-way place. He grew more animated than usual and chatted warmly with bystanders, recounting the ground he and his friends had covered in the trip so far. All he and the other campers asked, Burroughs announced, was "to pitch their tents by the side of a good spring and spend the night fairly rolling on mother earth."

When Ford and Edison arrived, a local man rushed to meet the car, where Edison sat in the front seat, and told the inventor he wanted "to shake hands with the greatest man in the world." Edison grinned and shook his head as he took the man's hand. Edison's reputation as a news hound had preceded him as well. No sooner had he freed himself from his first admirer than he was accosted by a boy offering to sell him the latest edition of the local paper. Firestone learned later that this had been the editor's son.

"His father," Firestone recalled, "had said to the boy he would give him a good whipping if he did not sell Thomas A. Edison a paper." Edison gave the boy a dime before grabbing a second paper, which he passed over his shoulder to Ford in the back seat. It was a lucrative transaction for the newspaper boy, who was later offered five dollars for the dime that had once belonged to Thomas A. Edison.

A reporter from the same paper buttonholed Ford to inquire about his Senate bid. "Mr. Ford," he asked, his inflection barely turning the provocation into a question, "you will have a little trouble in Michigan in the primary?" Without pausing for a moment's thought, Ford answered back, "I hope so." It seemed that the dubious reaction Ford had received from his friends Edison and Burroughs had further withered his interest in politics. Ford now turned the talk toward the war matériel his factories were churning out, as if acknowledging that he had more to offer the nation as a manufacturer than as a senator.

Solicitous as the crowd was, the press of admirers soon made the visitors uncomfortable, and they decided to drive on rather than wait for the always-lagging trucks to catch up. With Kline staying behind to direct the stragglers to camp, the others followed a trolley track to the edge of town. They took a road to the left under a railroad overpass and soon came to a group of dormitories clustered around a building fronted by a clock tower that was mirrored at the back of the structure by a looming smokestack. In front, a gazebo sat at the center of a circular drive. This was the Soldier's Home, a refuge for disabled veterans that would soon see the number of its residents growing as the fighting in Europe continued. Edison and the others had expected to find a suitable campsite nearby, but they found nothing that looked appropriate, so they drove on toward Jonesborough.

When the caravan stopped for a break that afternoon, they found that the only water available was drawn from a cistern. They missed the sweet spring water they had taken for granted earlier in the trip.


The party reached Jonesborough, the oldest town in Tennessee, late in the day. An inn built in 1797 still stood on the main street, which had itself once been a section of the Great Stage Road that linked Washington, D.C., to the frontier outpost at Nashville in the eighteenth century. But as far as Edison was concerned, the inn's rich history did nothing to justify a night in a hotel, and he was as determined as ever to spend the night outdoors. Though Jonesborough residents had heard that the famous travelers were headed their way and were scrambling to assemble the town band in order to sound a proper welcome, the visitors were not inclined to wait.

They drove on past the courthouse and clattered over railroad tracks that marked the edge of town. After about two miles they spotted a sloping pasture ringed by trees that looked like an ideal campsite: there was even a spring behind a nearby farmhouse. The owner of the place, a farmer named Will Lee, invited them to stay. Since it was growing late, they decided to pitch camp there for the night.

As they started to set up, however, the promise of the location began to fade. They had to drive through a barn in order to reach the pasture, and it turned out that the first truck through was too tall for the opening. Harry Linden, who was behind the wheel that afternoon, tried to coax the vehicle through but managed only to rip the top off of his truck and get himself stuck in the barn door. It was necessary to dig out underneath the wheels to lower the truck enough to free it.

As if that were not enough, the distance from the spring to the campsite seemed much greater when carrying water than it did viewed from the comfortable seat of an automobile. To make matters still worse, the campers were not, as they would learn later in the night, alone in the pasture.

When the truck hauling camping gear arrived, Burroughs began to rifle through the equipment and pulled out a set of tent stakes. He had decided to pitch his own tent some distance away from the others, at the top of the field near the treeline. He complained that Kline, Sato, and the other members of the crew went to bed too late and made too much noise for him to get any sleep, not that he expected to have a peaceful night in any case. He had noticed cattle grazing across the pasture, and he was sure they would do the work of keeping him awake even if the crew did not. Still, it was worth a try. He set to work pitching his tent before the ground became wet with dew.

*The Ford party encampment on the Lee farm outside Jonesborough, Tennessee, August 27, 1918.*

The evening meal that night was especially appetizing, or at least it seemed so after the long day on the road. After supper the party sat around a blazing campfire, for which, for once at least, they had not had to gather wood. After arriving late as they did, Edison had recruited some local boys to gather fuel, and he had paid them for the service. Now his wisdom in doing so was clear. But as the campers relaxed at their ease around the fire, they caught sight of lights playing along the road below. Soon these began to move up the slope of the pasture.

They turned out to be searchlights employed by a delegation of Jonesborough residents, led by the town's mayor. Having missed the opportunity to entertain the travelers in town, the party had ventured out into the countryside to track them down. What they found surprised them. Illuminated by the lighting system Edison had brought along on the trip, the camp looked like "a small city." Its illustrious residents were busy acting like ordinary folk. Ford was sawing wood, while Edison, a pair of reading glasses perched on the tip of his nose, sat by the fire combing through the Knoxville newspapers. Burroughs was carrying a bucket to draw water at the spring, but he let himself be distracted by a passing moth or butterfly and chased after the fluttering insect.

Ford was overheard chatting with a boy who lived on the farm.

"Sonny," he asked, "do you know you are sawing wood with Henry Ford?" The reply, when it came, sent the party into peals of laughter.

"And do you know you are sawing wood with Robert E. Lee?" the boy had shot back. The two took such pleasure in joshing each other that the boy presented Ford with a walking stick on which his historically resonant name was carved.

Another local boy, a nine-year-old named George Devault, approached Edison as if they were kindred spirits and told him he had been reading all about him.

"You have, and what was it you read?" Edison asked.

It seemed that the boy had come across a story about experiments Edison had conducted involving the incubation of eggs. The youngster's impression of the work was, however, somewhat vague.

"Why, I read about you settin' on those eggs to hatch them," he announced.

Edison gave a whoop of laughter that was echoed by the others nearby.

"Don't you ever try it son," he cautioned his new friend. "It won't work."

A sizable group gathered around the fire and regaled Ford and the others with stories about the town. The locals were proud of their town's antiquity, and they made a point of mentioning that it was the oldest settlement in the state, older in fact than Tennessee itself.

Jonesborough had been founded in 1779. Five years later it was named capital of the State of Franklin, a short-lived territory carved out of land west of the Appalachian chain that had previously been held by North Carolina. In the 1820s Jonesborough, by then a part of Tennessee, was home to an antislavery movement driven by a local newspaper, the *Emancipator*, believed to have been the first abolitionist organ in the country. By far the proudest claims of the locals, however, had to do with Andrew Jackson, who was said to have begun his law practice there in the county court in Jonesborough around 1788. Some could even point to the house where he had boarded, and a few recalled the widow who had owned the place.

There were darker stories too. It was said that on certain evenings, the ghost of Jackson could be seen making its way up Main Street toward the log building that had served as the courthouse. The other local hero was Daniel Boone, the frontiersman who had explored the western slopes of the Appalachians around the time of the Revolutionary War. Boone, one of the visitors told Ford and the others, had carved his name on a beech tree that still stood just outside Jonesborough. This struck Ford as particularly interesting, and he wanted to know just where the tree stood. Such talk continued around the campfire late into the evening.

When there was a lull in the storytelling, Edison took a few of the visitors on a tour of his camping setup. He was eager to show off the intricate lighting system he had designed for the expedition.

The ebullient colloquy stretched on until nearly midnight, far later than usual. The group from Jonesborough was left with the impression that "big folks are easy to get to."

After the Jonesborough group made their way back down the pasture slope and departed, the campers retired to their tents for the night. As it happened, though, they had not seen the last of the evening's visitors. In the middle of the night the cattle that Burroughs had worried might cause trouble began ambling into the campsite. And they were not alone: the farmer's hogs paid a visit as well. By the time the campers awoke the next morning, the kitchen tent had been ransacked. Kitchenware and supplies were left in complete disarray, and it was necessary to clean up before anyone could think about breakfast.

Burroughs had been wise to pitch his tent away from the others; he slept through the night unmolested. And despite the rampaging cattle and hogs, it had been a good night for the entire group. "Everyone was happy," Firestone concluded, "and this undoubtedly was our most enjoyable and interesting evening."

After breakfast the crew had begun to break camp when a half dozen or so men came tramping up the pasture. A remnant of the party that had visited in the night, they had come to show their new friends a photograph of the Daniel Boone tree they had described. It showed a crudely incised message that read "D. Boon CillED A. BAr on tree in the YEAR 1760." The group hoped to convince the camp-

*Crew members Harry Linden, R. V. Kline, and Thomas Sato take a break from changing a tire outside Jonesborough, Tennessee.*

ing party to return to Jonesborough to look at still more historical artifacts that were housed at the city hall, but Edison and the others had in mind that they might be able to make Asheville by lunchtime. The route, they thought, would take them some eighty miles over the mountains, so they had no time to spare. The visitors presented them with a huge watermelon and departed.

Ford, Burroughs, and DeLoach climbed into Harvey's Packard and left first, with Edison, Firestone, and Kline following in Edison's car. They stopped at a garage in Limestone to buy gasoline but were told there was none to be had; with the war on and operations in France putting a strain on resources, gasoline was in short supply. The government fuel administration had recently issued a statement asking citizens in states east of the Mississippi to comply with a voluntary "gasless Sunday" policy. Only tractors, freight haulers, emergency vehicles, and utility equipment were exempt. Even midweek, as the campers discovered, fuel was becoming difficult to find. Harvey eventually convinced the proprietor of the garage to sell them a few gallons to see them through to Greeneville, some ten miles farther along.

Just outside Tusculum they had to ford a small stream. These primitive bridgeless crossings were still a novelty to Burroughs, although they had crossed a good number of them already. The naturalist was amused each time he heard Edison call them "Irish bridges." Roadbuilders throughout the mountain south relied on fords because they were cheaper to construct than bridges, though they were likely to become impassable in heavy rains. Edison and his party were fortunate to have the weather on their side, and they forded the stream with ease.

By 11:00 the lead cars had reached Greeneville. Now perilously low on gasoline, the party made a stop at the first garage they could find. Here, too, fuel was in short supply, and the garage tank was down to

its last few gallons. While a crowd gathered around Edison's car to
gape at the famous inventor, Firestone slipped away and walked to
a nearby store, hoping to find a replacement for a pair of glasses he
had mislaid.

He found that the shop had the glasses he wanted, and, what was
more, they had a gasoline pump. Firestone made his way back to the
garage to tell his companions he had struck oil, but he found them
mobbed by locals who, like their neighbors in Jonesborough, wanted
to show the visitors the town's historical landmarks.

Like Jonesborough, Greeneville had for a time served as the capital of the State of Franklin, and the town had a similar abolitionist
story to tell. (The antislavery newspaper published there had been
called the *Genius of Universal Emancipation*.) What particularly distinguished Greeneville was that the town had been home to Andrew
Johnson, who had lived and worked there for several years. He had
even served as its mayor in the 1830s, just before taking up a post in
the Tennessee state legislature.

The townspeople were eager for Edison and his friends to see the
tailor shop where Johnson had practiced his trade, as well as the tomb
where the former president was laid to rest, on Monument Hill, just
south of town. With the crowd gathered tightly around the cars, there
was no way to move, and for a time it appeared that the day's progress
would grind to a halt. Firestone stepped in to talk with the mayor,
who headed the delegation, and "explained how greatly we regretted that we could not see all their points of interest." Firestone mar-
shaled the full force of his salesmanship to convince the locals that,
as much as they might wish to, their tight schedule would not allow
them to stay in Greeneville. At last the mayor relented and offered to
provide an escort to the city limits.

By the time the camping party reached Newport, just before noon,
the day had grown oppressively hot. Ford and Burroughs, riding in
the Packard with Harvey, arrived first and were met just outside of

town with a welcoming committee led by the mayor and the former governor, Ben Hooper, who escorted them to Mims Hotel, where they were to be given lunch. When Firestone arrived, the woman who ran the hotel was hovering near the table where Burroughs and Ford sat. She shooed the crowd away and made room for the newcomers, putting Edison and Firestone alongside their friends.

"She was more interested in Mr. Burroughs than in the rest of the celebrated gentlemen, and impressed Mr. Ford very favorably," Firestone noticed. Ford was more genuinely pleased to see others share his admiration of Burroughs than to be admired himself. By the time lunch was served, the automaker had promised to send their hostess a complete set of Burroughs's books.

After the meal a parade of schoolchildren filed into the hotel to meet Burroughs, many eager to know if the author of more than a few of their school texts was still writing books. The old naturalist assured them that he was hard at work and that he would have three new books coming out soon.

Meanwhile, Ford and Edison shook hands with a few of the hundred or so citizens who clustered around the hotel hoping to catch a glimpse of the famous visitors. As soon as he could, Edison found his way into a quiet room where he could sit and pore over the day's newspapers. Ford stayed behind to talk with some of the onlookers.

One of them had just returned from a trip to Michigan. He reminded Ford that it was primary election day and that back home voters were going to the polls; many of them, Democrats and Republicans alike, would be casting their votes for him.

Ford gave the man a puzzled look before answering. "Well," he said, "I had forgotten it was today but knew it was set for this year sometime."

When asked what he would do if he won nomination by both parties, Ford let loose a boyish laugh and answered without a thought. "Why, I will pitch a penny to settle it," he said. "I would give a million dollars to be out of the matter and I wouldn't have been in it except for the request of President Wilson."

By 1:00, Ford, Burroughs, and the others had separated themselves from the crowd and were climbing back aboard their vehicles. Just beyond the town line they joined the Dixie Highway, a route that, like the Lincoln Highway, had been pieced together from existing roads to give travelers an easy-to-follow overland route across long stretches of the country. The DH—as it was designated by roadside signs—was intended to connect the Midwest, starting from Chicago, to the southeast, ending at Miami.

From Newport the campers followed a section of the highway that climbed into the mountains toward Mars Hill, North Carolina, which lay nearly fifty arduous miles to the southeast. The grades were mostly moderate but very long, and the curves on the mountain switchbacks were sharp enough to test the nerve of the drivers—not to mention their passengers. For the first ten miles the road, which ran alongside the French Broad River, had a good macadam surface, but this gave way to gravel as the route corkscrewed through a series of blind curves near the North Carolina border. From here the road began a descent into a valley hemmed in by mountains on every side.

When the party reached Hot Springs, a town of 450 people situated on a bend of the French Broad, they were ready to stop. Although Edison was accustomed to spending the midday break relaxing on the front seat of his car, a newspaper folded across his face, on this occasion Firestone convinced the inventor to accompany him on a visit to the internment camp on the edge of town.

The camp had been set up a year earlier to house German internees, mostly merchant seamen whose vessels had been in American ports when war was declared. It occupied land that had once been a health resort, where the south's well-to-do enjoyed a spa-like environment and took in the fresh mountain air. There were similar, if less attractive, internment camps at Fort McPherson, outside Atlanta, and Fort Oglethorpe, also in Georgia, near the Chickamauga battlefield east of Lookout Mountain.

When Edison and Firestone reached the camp, they were met by an officer who took them on a tour of the facility. At its center was a majestic turreted building that had once been the Mountain Park Hotel and now housed some seven hundred German officers. The rest of the detainees—two thousand in total—lived in barracks they had constructed themselves.

Since the ships they worked on had to function like self-contained communities while at sea, the maritime crews were made up of all manner of skilled workers, including carpenters, plumbers, and electricians. The buildings were well made and looked comfortable.

Under the agreement signed at the Hague Conference, where Ford's peace delegation had hoped to stop the war, the prisoners were treated humanely, and if they were asked to work, they were paid a wage equivalent to what men of the same rank in the army would receive. A number of the prisoners worked in the kitchen, while others maintained the facilities. Some had taken up projects of their own. Near the river they had constructed what looked like a German or Swiss village "suggestive of Old Heidelberg, the crooked streets of Nurnberg, or some little village in the Black Mountains," as one visitor observed.

The small houses they had built were brightly painted and shingled with tin cans that had been flattened and nailed on in overlapping layers. They were warmed in winter by stoves constructed of river stone. The diminutive structures were not simply decorative. One was used as an art studio, while two others served as woodworking shops. There was also a miniature Gothic church, complete with pews for twenty worshippers.

Using lumber and building material donated by the YMCA, the

men had also constructed a large hall, nearly 200 feet long and 150 feet wide, where formal classes were taught by German volunteers. More than 400 prisoners were enrolled in courses that ranged from English, French, and Spanish to chemistry, geography, shorthand, navigation, and marine engineering.

Among the prisoners were several musicians who organized themselves into bands, including a German-style brass band and an orchestra. One visitor likened performances given by the orchestra to "those that one might hear from the Boston Symphony orchestra or other great orchestras of our cities."

The men also operated a canteen, a barber shop, a laundry, and a cobbler's shop. They had refurbished the spa facilities at the hotel, so they could now enjoy baths and hydrotherapy treatments. A seven-acre garden provided fresh produce, and there were many avid gardeners among the detainees. Some tended vegetables, some flower gardens, while others raised rabbits or kept pets.

Pleasant as their surroundings were, the fact remained that the men held there could not go home. The Hot Springs camp was not free of what some called "barbed-wire sickness." Few of the detainees tried to escape, but they did clamor for more to do—more classes, more recreation. Most of all they hoped for release.

Firestone, for his part, was impressed by the order and apparent humanity of the camp. A practical man, he did not concern himself with the privations of internment. "They all looked well-kept and well-fed and certainly were having a nice vacation," he remarked.


Edison and Firestone spent an hour exploring the camp, then made their way back to the town, where they found their friends ready to continue their journey. Leaving Hot Springs, they crossed a bridge over the French Broad and began winding up a long grade flanked by cliffs on one side and a precipitous drop on the other. The views were stunning, but neither the drivers nor the passengers had much leisure to enjoy them. As the cars snaked along the narrow switchbacks, the risk of plunging into the ravine below alternated with the danger of colliding with the rock wall of the mountain's upper slope. Firestone was particularly troubled by fear of a mishap. "I took no chances and I changed seats with my companion every time the side of the mountain changed," he recalled. "Mr. Edison said I always wanted an inside room, and part of the time I was riding on the running board because the drop was too far and the slope too steep to light comfortably in case of a fall."

Some twenty miles beyond Hot Springs the road nosed downward, and the caravan began a winding descent into a narrow valley. Where the grade finally leveled out, they passed through a town so closely flanked in by the mountains that there was barely room for a row of houses on either side of the road. By this time Edison was becoming agitated. It was nearly 5:00, and he felt it was time to begin looking for a campsite. But Ford and Burroughs, riding with Harvey and DeLoach, had outdistanced Edison's car on the precipitous descent. They were now somewhere ahead. When the inventor grumbled about this, Firestone revealed that the others were hoping to reach Asheville in order to spend the night at the Grove Park Inn. Edison was not pleased at the prospect of sleeping indoors, but he put up no fight. They drove on toward Mars Hill.

Burroughs and Ford had already arrived at this small college town, where all the residents seemed to be out on the streets waiting to meet them. A delegation of schoolchildren and young women from the college greeted the travelers with flowers. Some in the crowd displayed a service flag with 128 stars—one for each local boy serving in France. When Edison and Firestone arrived, the crowd called on the famous inventor to make a speech, the last thing Edison was ever inclined to do. Firestone stepped forward to calm the crowd, then persuaded Edison to stand up so everyone would have a chance to see him. Relieved that he would not have to speak, Edison rose and "in his gallant way," Firestone thought, "bowed to all sides of the automobile." With the crowd assuaged, they drove on.

But they had covered hardly ten miles when, just shy of Weaverville, they were met by another welcoming delegation. This group, which had driven out from Asheville, was headed by a man who identified himself as the secretary of that city's Board of Trade. He was proudly driving a Ford car and, with two companions, welcomed the travelers to Asheville, which he said "had been specially talcumed and perfumed for the occasion."

The party was still some ten miles from the city, and there were yet more delays to come. When they reached Weaverville, another throng of well-wishers flagged them to a stop and surrounded the automobiles, "probably the largest reception we had received," Firestone thought.

The local Red Cross had set up a booth, and the women who manned it asked Edison to come have tea. Again, the inventor was called on to speak, this time by the head of the local college. Edison, riding in the front seat as always and still holding a bouquet of flowers he had been given at Mars Hill, swiveled around to face Firestone and implored him to do something. "Firestone, you make a speech," he shouted, trying to make himself heard above the crowd.

The tire maker stood and did his best to give the crowd the show they wanted. At one point he called his friend Edison "the greatest man in the scientific world, the man who has done most for humanity." One onlooker observed that "Mr. Firestone said a good deal more about Mr. Edison than the 'wizard' would himself have said."

Edison, wearing his customary public smile, accepted another bouquet—asters—and the party continued on toward Asheville. By now young Harvey was growing impatient to reach their destination, and the lead Packard sped along at a fast clip. As the party neared the Beaverdam Creek north of town, the Ford car sent out by the

Board of Trade to escort the visitors into Asheville suddenly shut down and limped to the side of the road as Harvey zipped past. The owner of the car poured a pint of water into the radiator and tried to restart the engine but with no luck. By this time rain clouds were rolling in, so the man and his companions flagged down a passing car and hitched a ride into town, leaving the Model T abandoned by the side of the road. This was one story the locals would keep under wraps until Henry Ford was out of town.

When the lead cars finally reached the Grove Park Inn, it was nearly 8:30; negotiating mountain passes and thronging crowds over the last twenty-five miles had taken half the day. To Firestone it had seemed like a much longer trip, but Burroughs, despite the protracted journey, was in especially good spirits. He told a reporter that some of the roads were "pretty rough," but he left the man with the impression that it had been "a perfect day of travel through the mountains."

Asheville was familiar territory for most of the campers. Harvey had graduated from a nearby boarding school just two years earlier, and his father had been in town frequently to visit him when he was a student. Burroughs had passed this way on his visit to Tryon earlier in the year. Edison had made stops here as well. It may have been that sense of familiarity that led the campers to open up more to the press here than they had done so far.

When a reporter from a local newspaper asked Edison what he thought about the war, the inventor simply shook his head. "Man's foolishness," he said. "That's all you can make out of it. Man is a fool."

For his part, Ford was manifestly pleased to learn that American and French forces had made advances in the fighting in Europe, pushing German units back across the Hindenburg Line. The former pacifist seemed to have absorbed some of his friend Burroughs's zest for victory against Germany. One onlooker observed that Ford had "beached his ark of peace" and "rolled up his sleeves to make engines of war."

Ford was then asked what he thought of the criticism put forward the day before by Congressman William August Rodenberg, a Republican from Illinois, who challenged Ford's fitness for a Senate seat. Newspapers all over the country were repeating Rodenberg's allegations, by now familiar to Ford from other sources, that Ford had used his wealth and influence to gain a deferment from military service for Edsel. (As one newspaper jokester put it, "The only soldier Henry Ford ever got out of the trenches was his son Edsel.") Rodenberg also maintained that Ford had shown his unpatriotic colors months earlier when he said, "I don't believe in the flag; it is only something to rally around; when the war comes over these flags shall come down, never to go up again."

Ford said he had no public comment to make about these charges. But he let it be known, off the record, that he believed he "had made no such statement, but that he had never denied various untrue statements made about him."

The manager of the Grove Park Inn, Fred Seely, had selected a campsite for the party at Chunn's Cove, in the mountains east of the hotel. But as the evening wore on and the truck hauling the camping gear failed to appear—it would turn out that the driver had been delayed by torrential rains—everyone, even Edison, began to warm to the idea of putting up at the inn for the night.

For most of the trip the inventor had been content to knock about in disheveled clothing, a stubble beard on his face. But now that he had consented to a night indoors, he began to bemoan the fact that his suitcase and toiletries, which were stowed aboard the delayed truck, had not caught up with him. For once he wanted to get a clean shave and put on a starched collar before dinner. But even as he complained, Firestone noted, "he was most congenial."

Before dinner was served, the travelers, who had grown accus-

tomed to gathering around a campfire in the evening, instead con-
gregated in the inn's lounge, where Seely had set up a motion-picture
machine to entertain his guests. Edison, whose company had produced both the projection mechanism and the movies themselves,
took the keenest interest in this diversion. He wanted to watch every
reel. Firestone deemed the show "a high-class line of films."

After dinner Edison returned to the lounge, where he read until
midnight. Ford, if he was aware that results were beginning to trickle
in from the primary voting in Michigan, showed no interest.

The next morning, however, he kept to his room well beyond his
usual early hour, as if he did not want to face the news of a loss or,
perhaps worse, a win. Edison, after his late night in the lounge, was
also slow to rise. About 10:00 the party finally gathered for breakfast,
after which Ford walked out to the nearby golf course with Firestone.
The two then took a stroll up a mountain trail behind the inn.

Over the course of the morning the group, who had set out with
no ultimate destination in mind, decided that Grove Park made a
natural end point for their camping excursion. From here they would
part company with the trucks and camp gear and, unencumbered,
make their way north to Hagerstown, Maryland, where the routes to
the Midwest and Northeast divided. Burroughs and DeLoach would
catch a train home from Asheville. With the end of the trip now close
at hand, they packed a full itinerary of sightseeing into the rest of
the morning.

After touring the Grove Park grounds, the party made a foray to
Chunn's Cove, where they had been expected to camp before Edison
acquiesced to a night at the inn. Seely then took them to visit Over-
look Castle, a remarkable stone reproduction of a medieval stronghold,
complete with crenellated turrets and battlements. Seely had built it
as a private house on thirteen acres of forested land given to him by
his father-in-law, who had himself built the Grove Park Inn. The castle sat on a rounded peak, fringed by pines, and looked out over a vast

mountain panorama. Mount Pisgah was visible in the distance, and it was said that on a clear day, unlike the morning of their visit, you could see all the way into South Carolina, some forty miles distant. Elk and angora goats roamed the park that surrounded the castle. A casino and dance pavilion on the grounds had, until ten years earlier, attracted enthusiastic crowds to the site, which had been served by a light rail line. It was the kind of self-contained world Ford imagined when he dreamed of his water-powered factories.

By the time the travelers had returned to the hotel, eaten lunch, and packed their things, it was nearly 3:00 in the afternoon. A heavy rain was falling. The party posed for photographs with Seely in front of the inn. Then Ford and Firestone climbed into the back seat of the Packard, and Edison took his place in the passenger seat beside Harvey. Ivar Simpson and Willmott were to follow in Edison's Simplex, with Sato in the Ford. Burroughs and DeLoach were already bound for New York by train. The remainder of the crew would make their own way home with the supply trucks. There were still many miles to cover on the return journey, but the Grove Park Inn, the southernmost point on their itinerary, marked the end of the most memorable adventure the campers would ever share together.

Ford and the others drove that evening to Hickory, North Carolina, ninety-odd undulating mountain miles east of Asheville. Just outside Marion, where they stopped for supper, a spring broke on the Packard, and Ford was forced to make another roadside repair. When they reached Hickory, they put up at a hotel for the night. Evening newspapers were already beginning to report election results. Ford, as one headline put it, was "Both Victor and Vanquished." He had lost the Republican primary, in a landslide that went in favor of his opponent Truman Newberry. But he had won the Democratic primary.

Far from being galvanized by his nomination, Ford talked even less about politics in the coming days and instead fell back on his old interests. Passing though Winston-Salem the next day, Ford visited a trade school, where he talked about the Fordson tractors his factories were now building. Before he left, he offered to donate one to the school.

He and Edison then stopped by a warehouse where Camel cigarettes were manufactured from the fine tobacco grown in the region. Neither man had any personal interest in "the little white slaver," as Ford called the cigarette, but both were captivated by the processes that transformed natural materials into practical commodities. Ford, back in his element, examined the operation of the factory from stem to stern, inspecting the machinery and raw materials, even looking into the bookkeeping. When he and Edison drove away, they were hunched over a sample of loose Camel tobacco, which they were dividing up so each could take home a specimen. Edison's theories about the dangers of cigarettes—he blamed their harmful effects on acrolein, a chemical that arose from glycerine used in the manufacturing process—would now have new data to incorporate.

Leaving Winston-Salem the Packard became stuck in mud caused by the heavy rains that had swept through the region earlier in the week. Ford and Edison began trying to free the car by jacking the encumbered wheels clear. Firestone, meanwhile, walked to a nearby farm to get help. He returned with a mule team but no way to fasten it to the stuck car. When Ford borrowed a chain from a woman who lived in a nearby house, he became concerned by the fact that she had no teeth. Like the couple with the burned-out farm he had encountered while traveling with Burroughs in New England five years earlier, this woman stayed on his mind. He would later arrange for her to have a set of dentures made at his expense.

On the outskirts of Martinsville, ten miles beyond the Virginia state line, the group stopped to visit another factory, a fabric mill owned by Marshall Field and Company. It operated along the lines

Ford envisioned for the small, rural factories he hoped to build, using a local labor force that had previously been largely unemployed. "They were doing much good in bringing down the mountaineers and furnishing them with nice homes for the rental of a dollar a month per room," Firestone observed. The company had also built churches and schools and, according to the man Ford and the others talked to, was paying the workers a fair wage. If the man could be believed, the factory worked according to principles that would not have clashed with the ideas of compensation that Ford, under the tutelage of Burroughs, had drawn from Emerson.

That afternoon the party reached Roanoke, Virginia, where they paused for a rest before pushing on in the afternoon toward Lexington. Along the way they made a stop, around 5:00, to see the Natural Bridge arch in Rockbridge County. While Edison waited in the car with his maps and newspapers, Ford and Firestone hiked with Harvey along the trail that passed under the arch. Ford and Harvey then walked down into the canyon carved by the stream and crossed a low bridge made of wood planks. They stood for a while in the middle, surveying the scene. Looking at the walls of the arch and the stream flowing through, Ford naturally thought about how to harness the stream's power. The limestone arch over their heads, more than two hundred feet high, had been cut over time by a small stream flowing gently toward the James River. It was all the evidence Ford needed of the magnificent power of flowing water.

The following day, Ford spotted an abandoned grist mill just off the roadway, near Lexington. As usual he could not pass it by. He called for a stop, then he and Firestone climbed out to inspect the massive overshot waterwheel that had once powered the mill.

That same morning the party visited Washington and Lee University, where they were given a tour that took them through Robert E. Lee's office, preserved just as it had looked in his lifetime, as well as the tomb where the Confederate general was interred.

Taken together, the waterwheel and the glimpse at Lee's history put a cap on the camping trip. The waterwheel recalled the running obsession that Ford shared with Burroughs, Edison, and Firestone, each of whom for their own reasons appreciated the idea of clean, free power. For Burroughs the water-driven mill was a step back in time and a step closer to nature than the noisy steam or internal-combustion engines that polluted the modern environment. To Edison convenient power opened up a door to new experiments and new discoveries. Firestone liked the idea of reducing costs and increasing the efficiency of his manufacturing processes.

The expression on Ford's face as he gazed up at the tall arc of a disused waterwheel suggested that all of these ideas and more were running through his mind as he imagined the stream's flow being diverted across the wheel and it beginning once again to turn.

The tour through Robert E. Lee's office recalled the night outside Jonesborough when Ford had sawn wood with the Confederate general's younger namesake. That earlier evening on the Lee farm, which Firestone now regarded as their "most enjoyable and interesting," stood in memory as a kind of snapshot of the camaraderie and mutual interest and respect that the four friends shared.

In the afternoon the travelers drove through Staunton and stopped at a small town to have lunch at a hotel dining room. While they were eating, a man came in and invited them to come to a local fair that was underway. When he mentioned that a senator was scheduled to speak at 3:00, Ford had heard all he needed. He declined the invitation. He had no interest in listening to politicians.

By the time they reached Winchester, ninety-odd miles northeast of Staunton, it had begun to rain. They stopped at a garage to put the top up and then drove on toward Hagerstown, Maryland. On that leg of the trip, Firestone was careful to note, they paid nineteen tolls. Had they traveled a little later, he and Ford might have pocketed the $3.80 they spent. The toll gates were scheduled for closure the following day.

In Hagerstown they took rooms and ate dinner at the Hamilton Hotel. After dinner Ford and Firestone took a walk around town, while Edison napped. Firestone bought a pair of socks and was pleased with the bargain he got. When the two returned to the hotel, they went to Edison's room, where they sat talking with the inventor about the trip. Each of them expressed regret that they would soon part company.

After breakfast the next morning they drove to a private spot outside of town and said their goodbyes. Then Edison set out toward New Jersey, as Ford and Firestone turned west toward Pittsburgh. All were left with, as Firestone put it, "happy thoughts and pleasant memories." Traveling and camping with Burroughs, they had set their worldly affairs aside and "returned to nature and youth."

This "return" was more than simple nostalgia; it was a balancing of the industrial element in their lives with the pastoral and agrarian values that had always tugged against notions of progress in America's idea of itself. The history of the nation rested on this paradox: the building of cities and the flight from the city, advancement into the frontier and regret over the closing of the frontier. In their ordinary lives Ford and Edison had tipped the scale toward the factory and the laboratory. Their travels with Burroughs, who had himself rambled with the likes of Walt Whitman, John Muir, and Teddy Roosevelt, allowed them to uncover if only briefly their own deep, rural roots and reattach themselves to the nation's rooted, agrarian past. As Ford had carved on the log he found at the Wolf Creek camp, "Your best friend is the one who can bring out the best in you."

For the rest of their lives all four men would speak of this as the best trip they had ever taken. Soon after he reached home, Burroughs wrote to his friends about the experience. In a letter to Firestone he recalled the "beauties and wonders" they had seen—"what glory of

*Thomas Edison enjoys an afternoon nap as John Burroughs catches up on the war news.*

mountain tops and what summer ripeness and repose in the broad river valleys!" He thanked Firestone for his "serenity and good nature and spirit of helpfulness" and praised Harvey's character as well as his skill as a driver. ("He is a treasure—even with the cigarette habit. But this he will outgrow.")

Burroughs went on to express something that all the men seemed to feel, each in his own way. "How much more than a mere geographic division will West Virginia henceforth mean to all of us!" he wrote. "Yes, and the Great Smoky Mountains. Their smoke cannot blur the impressions they made." For men like Ford, Firestone, and Edison, whose success in the world had given them access to any *thing* they might want, these impressions had a value beyond calculation. Like Burroughs, they would carry forward a sharpened image of the nation they had helped to shape and an invigorated sense of the role they might play in its preservation.

Writing to Edison, Burroughs said that he hoped the inventor found himself "all the better for the thorough shaking up" the roads of the southern mountains had given them. "I am aware that I whimpered and grumbled a good deal on the trip," the naturalist admitted. But this, he said, was just the habitual groaning of an old man, and it did not reflect his deeper feelings. "I really had a wonderful time and got a large slice of our geography very vividly impressed upon my memory." Then, with a wink that could not be missed, even through the mail, he added, "to say nothing of the impression made upon some of my posterior muscles."

# Epilogue

In the coming years Ford, Firestone, and Edison would take several more vacations together, some in the company of Burroughs, others not. The scale of these excursions grew more monumental with each passing year. They involved larger crews, larger crowds, more cars, more equipment, more cameras, and more reporters. The campers began to bring their families along. On one occasion Firestone even transported a string of saddle horses to keep his companions entertained in their idle hours. Two presidents of the United States would take their places by the campfire—Warren G. Harding in 1921 and Calvin Coolidge in 1924.

For all the ballyhoo surrounding these later vacations, however, only the camping trip Ford, Edison, Firestone, and Burroughs took through the Green Mountains in 1919 would come close to recapturing the rustic magic of the Great Smoky Mountains adventure of 1918. Indeed, the notes Burroughs made in his travel journal in 1919 echo the themes and threads that had emerged in 1918. Both the shared interests and the points of friction among the campers came into bolder relief.

By the late summer of 1919, Henry Ford was emerging from months of rough weather. In the general election of 1918 he had lost his half-hearted Senate bid to Truman Newberry. The political establishment of both parties had been wary of Ford, who was taken to be both a free-trade capitalist and a pacifist. But the deeper complaint against him was that he simply had no preparation for the job. The kinder of the many assessments of Ford that appeared in newspapers around the time of the election put forward a view of him that his friends Burroughs and Edison shared. "Mr. Ford is a splendid man and a true patriot, and has been of inestimable service to the government in the construction of motors, sub-chasers and other things," one such article read, "but Mr. Ford is a mechanical genius, not a statesman."

In the wake of the election Ford had become embroiled in a libel trial that sprang from a series of articles published in the *Chicago Tribune* a few years earlier. On June 22, 1916, the newspaper had reported, falsely it turned out, that Ford's company would not hold jobs for employees called up by the National Guard. The following day an editorial under the headline "Ford Is an Anarchist" reiterated the charge, arguing that the policy showed that Ford did not believe in the basic functions of American government. "If Ford allows this rule of his shops to stand he will reveal himself not merely as an ignorant idealist, but as an anarchistic enemy of the nation which protects him and his wealth."

The automaker fired back with a libel lawsuit seeking one million dollars in damages. When the trial on the matter opened in May 1919, Ford quickly found himself the central exhibit in the *Tribune*'s defense effort. The newspaper's lawyers put the automaker on the stand and subjected him to questioning intended to show that the *Tribune*, in calling Ford an ignorant idealist and anarchist, had merely stated the facts.

While under oath Ford was quizzed on elementary points of American history and civics. The answers he gave revealed the paucity of his understanding of things outside his own field of expertise. Asked if he had heard of Benedict Arnold, Ford declared that he had: he believed that Arnold was a writer. He went on to pinpoint the American Revolution in 1812. He showed himself to be similarly ill-informed on other basic topics.

"Has Henry Ford ever heard of Christopher Columbus, of Jamestown, of Plymouth Rock, of Bunker Hill, of Yorktown, of the Declaration of Independence," one editorial wondered, echoing sentiments expressed in newspapers across the nation. In the press Ford was made a laughingstock. Yet throughout the questioning the automaker maintained his calm, folksy demeanor. "Henry Ford, sitting in court with crossed legs," one observer noted, "suggests the country store philosopher."

When the trial ended, the jury found that the *Tribune* had indeed committed libel, but Ford received only six cents in damages, a sum that seemed intended to underline the absurdity of the entire proceeding. It soon became clear, however, that the people of the United States had reached a different verdict. Hundreds of letters streamed into Ford's office from ordinary people who felt that his treatment at the hands of the *Tribune*'s lawyers was the real injustice in the case. These communications, which came from all parts of the country, all delivered a remarkably similar message: "You have done more good and accomplished more than any man living. Do not let them discourage you."

On August 4, as jurors sat listening to a Columbia University political science professor parsing the definition of the term "anarchist" and lawyers for both sides prepared their closing arguments, Henry Ford arrived in Albany, New York, having slipped away from Detroit on the overnight ferry to Buffalo, where Harvey picked him up. In Albany that afternoon Ford and the Firestones were reunited with

Burroughs and together they traveled to Green Island, eight miles to the north, off the west bank of the Hudson River, where they found camp already set up.

That evening Edison arrived from New Jersey, and the veteran campers gathered around the campfire once again. The mood was cheerful; Ford was understandably more eager to talk about his plans at Green Island than about the libel trial. Edison had introduced Ford to this stretch of the Hudson River, a spot where the inventor had long enjoyed fishing and that was close to his power plant in Syracuse. When the two waterpower enthusiasts realized that the dam constructed across a portion of the river at Green Island was not being used to generate power and that the great river's force was "being allowed to escape unharnessed," Ford had sprung into action. He quickly filed an application to construct a power plant at the dam site, one that would power a new Fordson tractor factory, and then arranged to purchase an adjacent tract of land. That was where he and his friends were now camped less than a year later.

The next morning the air was still and warm as the campers assembled near the dam that spanned the river from Green Island to Troy. In the grove of mixed pine and oak where their tents were pitched, an indigo bunting could be heard singing. With the mayors of Troy and Albany looking on, Ford had each of the campers chisel their initials—B E F F—into a fifty-pound chunk of sandstone that he intended to use as the cornerstone of the new water-powered factory. The inscribed stone gave a kind of solidity to the daydreams Ford and his friends had entertained through the many afternoons and mornings they had spent inspecting abandoned mills and waterwheels the previous summer.

Less than four years later the power plant and factory would be in operation. By the summer of 1923 the power facility was generating 8,000 horsepower, or nearly 6 megawatts of electricity, using four low-head turbines designed for the site by Allis-Chalmers. The adja-

*With the mayors of Troy and Albany in attendance, Ford, Edison, Burroughs, and Firestone chisel their initials into the cornerstone for Ford's Green Island hydroelectric plant.*

cent factory employed 625 workers in the manufacture of radiators and ring gears, and there were plans to bring on another 400. As Ford had envisioned, many of the employees were farmers who hired on in the winter months and worked their farms in the summer.

By 1925 Ford, expanding on his plan to give farmers work in the off-season, had built a total of nine water-powered plants in rural areas. The majority of these "village industries," as Ford called the plants, were built on the sites of abandoned mills and often incorporated the mill structure, or its architectural style, into the new facility. The buildings themselves were clean and well illuminated by natural light. As one industrial analyst remarked at the time,

"For beauty, safe and comfortable working conditions and convenience, these small plants are ideally designed." To highlight his belief in the efficiency of waterpower, Ford liked to showcase each plant's turbine generators, housing the machinery in glass-lined structures that left the turbines visible to passersby. When the manager of one of these plants, the Phoenix facility located on the River Rouge north of Detroit, had an internal combustion generator installed to supplement the hydroelectric power, Ford ordered the device removed.

"We built these plants to run on water power," he declared. "When I want any other kind of power in, I'll let you know how to do it!"

Available waterpower served as the basis of hiring at the plants as well. Initially, Ford employed one man—or woman, since the automaker favored women for work requiring precision—for every unit of horsepower produced by a given plant's generating turbines.

The manufacturing plant at Green Island eventually employed 1,500 workers in a town of some 3,000 residents. Although the factory was closed down in 1988, the hydroelectric facility continues to operate as a public utility. During refurbishment and expansion of the plant in the 2010s, provisions were added to allow fish to bypass the dam, and the generation capacity was increased to 48 megawatts.

After the cornerstone ceremony at Green Island, Ford, Burroughs, Edison, Firestone, and Harvey retraced part of the route of the 1916 trip through the northeastern highlands, first motoring through Saratoga Springs, where they had lunch with race driver Barney Oldfield. Over the course of three rainy days they camped near Long Lake, Lake Placid, and Plattsburgh. At Chazy Landing they again boarded the ferry to cross Lake Champlain, as they had in 1916. They camped near Stowe, Vermont, on a farm where they inspected the owner's sugaring operation, which once again reminded Burroughs of the favorite farm chore of his boyhood. After they crossed into New Hampshire they stopped near Meredith so Ford and Firestone could

get a look at a towel factory there before continuing on into Massachusetts to camp near the town of Hatfield. Heading farther south, they
passed through Springfield and Hartford before turning west toward
Waterbury, where Burroughs left for home. The following day the others were back in New York City.

Through all of this, the familiar pattern of camp life reemerged.
Burroughs observed the wildlife—bass and bullheads in Loon Lake,
a hermit thrush and red-eyed vireo near Long Lake—and speculated
about the geology of the region. He imagined that the origin of the
rocky landscape they had driven through the previous year now lay
all around them. "Not any drift boulders in Green and White Mountains," he explained, "because the old Ice-sheet plucked them from
these mountains and dropped them over the landscape of the south;

*Henry Ford and John Burroughs picking raspberries near Long Lake,
New York.*

here they lie like a herd of slumbering elephants with their calves, sleeping the sleep of geologic ages."

Ford remained as active as ever. Wherever the cars rolled to a stop, he was out, walking, chopping wood, even climbing trees. Spotting the carefree automaker scrambling up a tree in a beech grove one afternoon, Burroughs quipped, "If we could only tree all the multimillionaires!"

As usual, Edison read during breaks—he had the June issue of the *Atlantic Monthly* with him—and told stories around the campfire. He and Burroughs traded information about the plants and minerals they came across. Burroughs had a well-honed naturalist's sense of the outdoors, but Edison looked at the natural world through the eyes of an engineer and chemist. He showed Burroughs how the tiny hairs on an elm leaf are slanted toward the tip so as to sluice water off the leaf. And while Burroughs had once figured out a safe way to handle skunks ("clasp him firmly by his plumelike tail"), Edison knew, at a minute level, why such care was necessary. "He told us, among scores of other things," Burroughs recalled, "of the chemical compounds that give the odor to the secretion of the skunk," including mercaptan, which Burroughs recognized as a chemical cousin of the mustard gas that had been used to such devastating effect in the war that had by then mercifully ended.

Not all the campfire talk was as educational or as agreeable as Edison's disquisition on skunk chemistry. Burroughs had for years been troubled by Ford's inclination to rant about "capitalists" and "bankers," a category that over time had become increasingly indistinguishable from "Jews." By 1919 this inclination toward antisemitism had grown more virulent.

As the party clustered around the fire near Lake Placid one cool August evening, sheltering themselves against the occasional spray of wind-blown rain, Ford began to complain about the various ills perpetrated by Jewish interests. "Mr. Ford attributes all evil to the Jews or Jewish capitalists," Burroughs confided to his journal. "The Jews caused the War; the Jews caused the outbreak of thieving and robbery all over the country." The previous evening Edison had been grumbling about the navy's inability to implement the innovations he had tried to usher in during his tenure on the Naval Consulting Board. Now Ford blamed that on Jews as well. "He would probably attribute an eclipse to the Jews," Burroughs concluded.

But when Ford began running on about the "Shylock" Jay Gould, the nineteenth-century railroad baron, Burroughs finally felt obliged to intervene. Gould, Burroughs knew, was not Jewish but Presbyterian, and he always had been. It was the young Jay Gould, in fact, who had first told Burroughs about a mysterious figure called Santa Claus, since Burroughs's own family had observed the Christmas holiday as a strictly religious affair. "My folks didn't cultivate the Santa Claus myth," he recalled.

Gould had been a classmate when Burroughs was a boy, and the old naturalist still had fond memories of their schooldays in a small, red clapboard building perched on a hillside not far from a brook where the boys liked to swim and tickle for trout, reaching under the fish and trying to flip them onto the bank. Gould had sat behind Burroughs in class, and the two boys had quickly become friends, with Gould sometimes helping Burroughs when he struggled with writing assignments. When Gould eventually left school to make his way in the world, Burroughs had tried to help him along. He gave his friend eighty cents for a geology book and a book on German grammar. The naturalist liked to think he had given Jay Gould his financial start in the world.

Burroughs also recalled a time when a traveling phrenologist had turned up at the farm where he lived with his parents. The man had made a show of pawing and prodding the young Burroughs's head and finally pronounced, "This boy is going to be rich." "Well, if he'd gone up the road to the next house he'd have found Jay Gould," Burroughs added, "and if he'd said the same thing of him, he'd have been a pretty good prophet, wouldn't he?"

The way Burroughs saw it, the story of his boyhood friendship with Gould gave the lie to Ford's theory of racial types. Gould, by methods fair or foul, had built a financial empire because of who he was as an individual, not because of the religion he happened to have been born to. And as a Protestant he had closer ties to Henry Ford than to the stereotype of Shylock. A person's race or religion was no more a predictor of his character than the head-bumps by which the charlatan phrenologist had long ago professed to read Burroughs's own fortune.

Ford was not the first to imagine that Gould was Jewish. Henry Adams, writing about the gold panic set off by Gould's manipulations of the market in 1869, described him as "small and slight in person, dark, sallow, reticent, and stealthy, with a trace of Jewish origin." Nor was Ford alone in associating Jews with wider market conspiracies. But in the coming years he would give these antisemitic ideas a wide circulation. This was one area in which his camp friends had little influence on his thinking.

Earlier in 1919 Ford had taken over a struggling newspaper and begun publishing it under his own name as the *Dearborn Independent*. The format of the paper included a regular column titled "Mr. Ford's Own Page," which initially doled out the automaker's stock of "plain facts" and "helpful suggestions." When the first edition was printed in January, Ford had sent copies to each of his fellow campers. Each responded to Ford through his secretary.

Firestone, the most diplomatic of the bunch, wrote back to say that although he did not feel qualified to judge the paper on its journalistic merits, he had noticed that the type Ford had used was easily legible and the paper stock itself was light yet took the print well, giving evidence of Ford's "economy, service and practicability." He and Idabelle, he went on to relate, had particularly enjoyed Ford's own contribution, and each had read it twice.

It came as no surprise that Edison offered the bluntest criticism. "Take the paper as a whole," he wrote, "it is a dreary proposition for the man whom Ford wants to reach." The inventor pointed out that the design of the publication presented would-be readers with a wall of text that few would be willing to comb through. Even the illustrations were badly managed. Edison suggested that Ford read his way through a year's run of the *Literary Digest* and the *Geographical Magazine*, the two publications Edison thought most successful at presenting intelligent content in an engaging fashion.

As a writer himself, Burroughs no doubt felt particularly compelled to respond with encouragement. "It is surprisingly good," he said of the first issue. He then singled out the column that appeared under Ford's byline. "Mr. Ford's own page is alive to the last word," Burroughs wrote, before going on to give Ford an editorial nudge in the direction he thought the column would most fruitfully take. "This page gives him a pulpit from which he can weekly preach his gospel of work and opportunity to very large audiences." Burroughs concluded with a prediction that the newspaper would enjoy "a great future." Edison, somewhat more grudgingly, concurred. Both were wrong.

In the year following the 1919 camping trip, Ford began to pepper his newspaper with the antisemitic conspiracy theories that had galled Burroughs around the campfire. A front-page article published on May 22, 1920, launched a series of articles about the role of Jews in the modern economy, under the title "The International Jew: The World's Problem." When the articles were eventually published in book form, these ideas spread well beyond the circulation of the *Dearborn Independent*. During the Nuremberg trials a former leader of the Hitler Youth would point to the German translation of the book as "the decisive anti-Semitic book" that had inclined him and his comrades toward the ideas of National Socialism. This was not the bright future Burroughs or Edison had hoped for.

Ford's factories continued to employ a "significant number" of Jewish workers, and Ford counted Jews, including his neighbor Rabbi Leo Franklin, among his personal friends. "Ford's friends and associates, both Jew and gentile," a later historian would observe, "were at a loss to explain what had suddenly motivated the great industrialist to embark on the most profound hate campaign in the nation's history."

In other ways, however, the members of the camping party remained as favorably disposed to each other's ideas as ever. Even where particular views differed, their interests overlapped. They enjoyed discussing matters of health and diet, for instance, almost as much as they enjoyed ribbing each other about departures from the practices they espoused.

Edison, in particular, put forward health strictures that he was little bothered to follow himself. "He inveighs against cane sugar, and yet he puts two heaping teaspoonfuls in each cup of coffee," Burroughs noted, "and he takes three or four cups of coffee each day!" Nor was sugar the only vice the inventor disparaged even as he indulged in it. He encouraged Ford's demonization of smoking, while smoking several cigars a day. Publicly Edison espoused light eating and limited sleep, but Burroughs noticed that when the inventor tumbled out of his bed late for breakfast, he ate heartily—"fried eggs and a big piece of ham, with bread and a cup of coffee." Burroughs himself preferred "Minute Brew," a caffeine-free cereal coffee, and he ate lightly, capping off his breakfast with dry toast, half a peach, and a ripe tomato. "He eats more than I do, and yet he calls me a gourmand," Burroughs gibed. "He eats pie by the yard, if he can get it, and he bolts his food. Oh, Consistency, thy name is not Edison!"

Even as they chuckled at his foibles, however, all the campers admired the inventor. "He is a big-brained man, genial and good-natured," Burroughs felt. By lunchtime, the naturalist, having scoffed at his friend's inconsistency about sugar over breakfast, had come around to Edison's way of thinking. "I guess Edison is right about cane sugar; it is unwholesome," Burroughs concluded. "I have long known that ordinary sugar did not agree with me. I shall try maltose."

Health had become a more pressing issue in the twelve months since the 1918 trip ended. Just as that earlier outing came to a close, there had been an outbreak of influenza among naval officers and men at the port of Boston. More than two thousand men had become infected in a very short period, but most, although they suffered high fevers and reported feeling as if "they had been beaten all over with a club," had recovered. In the coming months, however, new cases began to appear in several eastern states. By the middle of September newspapers were reporting that at least one U.S. military health official believed that "German submarines have traversed the ocean loaded with Spanish influenza germs, which have been promptly released in this country." While experts spun such theories, the illness continued to spread.

Two weeks later the disease had swept across the nation, as far south as Louisiana and straight across the west to San Francisco. Bath, Maine, was soon under siege as well. At the same time, the nation was engaged in an effort to raise money for the war effort. Throughout the country officials allowed plans for Liberty Loan parades to go forward, although they knew these mass gatherings might speed transmission of the virus. When Chicago put on a huge parade that drew thousands in October, just as the death rate in the city reached its highest point since the outbreak began, the local board of health distributed instruction cards intended to help forestall transmission of the virus. "As soon as through marching," it read, "go home, remove all clothing and rub the body dry and put on warm clothing. . . . Take a laxative when you reach home and you will minimize your chances of catching the disease." Over the next four weeks some five thousand Chicagoans would die of the flu and related pneumonia. By the time Ford, Edison, Burroughs, and Firestone set out on their camping trip in August 1919, the Spanish influenza pandemic had killed nearly 675,000 Americans, many of them in the prime of life.

As the campers sat around an especially large campfire on the evening of August 12, 1919, it came out that Edison believed that the influenza was of "cosmic origin." As evidence he pointed to the sudden nature of its onset around the globe. This, Edison maintained, showed that "the earth passed through a zone of some form of Benzol vapor." Burroughs wondered whether germs were capable of surviving in space. But Edison, who still thought it likely that life itself had reached the earth from space, was confident that they could. He predicted that "there would be some recurrence of the distemper" in the coming autumn. "Edison's mind is a storehouse of facts and figures on nearly all subjects," Burroughs believed. The inventor had an encyclopedic memory for chemistry and mineralogy. Almost any subject that came up fell within the range of his intellect. On the topic of the influenza, though, Burroughs felt his friend had gone astray.

Although there was indeed some recurrence of influenza in the fall, as Edison had predicted, his postulation of a cosmic origin of the illness has yet to be borne out. (More than a hundred years later, however, experts still struggle to understand the origin and proliferation of pandemic disease. At the beginning of April 2020 the Ford Motor Company began manufacturing ventilators and other emergency medical equipment in an effort to stem loss of life in the largest outbreak of pandemic illness to strike the United States since 1918.)

One afternoon early in the 1919 trip, Burroughs was busy identifying a bough of striped maple for a friend of Ford's who had joined the group for part of the journey. The party had stopped for lunch at a fork in the road where starflower and heal-all carpeted the ground. While Burroughs relished the Latin names of these small woodland flowers, *Trientalis* and *Collinsonia*, Edison discovered another intriguing plant that exuded a milky fluid when he broke its stem.

The inventor thought it possible that this latex-like sap could be used to make rubber.

That evening Firestone, intrigued by the idea of a native rubber source, sought to draw Edison out on the topic. He found the conversation that followed was like opening an encyclopedia entry on the history and properties of rubber. "I was astounded at the knowledge of rubber he had at hand," Firestone later recalled. "I had been working with rubber for many years, but he told me more than I knew and more than I think our chemists knew."

Edison had tested the properties of many types of rubber and had developed a minute understanding of the chemistry that made the material so useful. He was determined to find domestic plants that would yield similar materials, thus freeing American manufacturers from reliance on foreign rubber sources. In his New Jersey greenhouse Edison had recently experimented with the cultivation of guayule, a desert shrub capable of producing large amounts of latex. Now he was becoming interested in milkweed, which, although not as productive as guayule, could be grown quickly in large amounts to meet the nation's rubber needs during a shortage. He had "no doubt" that rubber-yielding plants could be grown in the United States.

Their interest in the botanical world as an industrial resource had united Ford, Edison, and Firestone throughout their travels together, encouraged early on by the botanical wizard Luther Burbank on their visit to Santa Rosa in 1915 and then blossoming during their camping trips with Burroughs. Although Ford and Edison viewed the natural world with a modern eye toward the extraction of industrial resources, while Burroughs took an interest in botany in a more fundamental way, for its own sake, his influence on their thinking was profound. The old naturalist's readiness to identify any plants the party came across, and his familiarity with their habitats and properties, had served to fan his friends' enthusiasm. In the coming years Ford, Edison, and Firestone's growing obsession with these ideas would influence the work of all three.

Ford and Firestone soon launched their own rubber operations abroad. After exploring possibilities in the Philippines and Dutch East Indies, Firestone eventually settled on Liberia as the location for his company's rubber plantation. The West African nation had a suitable climate, with daytime temperatures in the eighties and nineties tempered by cool nights, and it received the necessary rainfall. Along the coast it was not unusual to see 150 inches of rain a year. Like Brazil, where the most productive rubber tree, *Hevea brasiliensis*, grew wild, Liberia also experienced a dry season, which had the beneficial effect of killing off diseases and pests that threatened trees grown in Asia.

There was the added attraction, as Firestone saw it, of Liberia having "sprung from our own country," when it was established as a settlement colony for freed slaves and free-born Americans of African descent in the decades leading up to the Civil War. Liberia was also close to the United States, or at least relatively close compared to the established rubber-growing regions of South Asia and Indonesia. This "unique little republic," as Harvey termed it, had a familiar feeling and was "about the size of the State of Ohio."

In 1926 Firestone leased a million acres of land in Liberia and launched the Firestone Natural Rubber Company. The company began clearing land and planting what is now the largest rubber plantation in the world, sprawling across some two hundred square miles.

Two years later Ford followed Firestone's lead, securing a three-million-acre tract of land along the Tapajós River, a tributary of the Amazon, in Brazil. After constructing a town on the site—which came to be called Fordlandia—Ford began planting rubber trees in vast groves. Analysts at the time predicted that if even half of the territory Ford had acquired were put into production, it would yield some 375,000 tons of rubber—more than had been used in the United

States in the previous year. Unlike Firestone's operation, however, Ford's never took off. Although it was thought that the productive *Hevea brasiliensis* trees were immune to pests in their local environment, the species did not thrive when closely planted. Ford also faced difficulties with labor, in large part because he tried to impose middle-American values on the local culture. In less than ten years he had abandoned the original site and established a new operation farther south, where conditions were thought to be more favorable. But the results there were little better than at Fordlandia. By 1945 the Ford Company had abandoned both sites.

While Ford and Firestone were busy making plans to supply their manufacturing operations with rubber by growing rubber trees abroad, Edison took a renegade approach and threw himself into the project of extracting rubber from plants that were native to North America or could be grown there. He scoured the pages of a 1921 study, *The Rubber Content of North American Plants*, underlining key passages, highlighting some of them as many as six times. Two years later, in concert with Ford, he had focused his attention on *Asclepias syriaca*, the common milkweed. When Ford's researchers had grown the plant in the company's Dearborn greenhouses, they found that extraction from milkweed yielded just over 4 percent rubber. Soon Edison was attempting to grow both milkweed and guayule, while also experimenting with harvested specimens of both in his laboratory. In the summer of 1923 he wrote to Firestone to say he was "having good luck" with both plants. Around the same time, he told Ford that his experiments suggested it would be possible to harvest as much as 680 pounds of rubber from an acre planted with guayule. The following spring found Edison planting the Madagascar rubber vine, *Cryptostegia madagascariensis*, in his Fort Myers gardens. Meanwhile, Firestone arranged for the inventor to consult with rubber experts from Liberia on the cultivation of traditional Hevea rubber plants there in South Florida.

By the summer of 1928 Edison, now over eighty years old, had set up a new laboratory in Fort Myers that was specifically devoted to his burgeoning rubber research. In this low-slung sunlit building, constructed next to a banyan rubber tree that Firestone had planted three years earlier, Edison became increasingly single-minded in his search for new sources of the material.

"With his accustomed thoroughness, he is ransacking the world for every bit of information he can obtain in regard to rubber and its cultivation and manufacture," his secretary William Meadowcroft observed at the time. "The books he has so far read would fill two five-foot bookshelves, to say nothing of domestic and foreign magazines and periodicals devoted to the subject. Mr. Edison has undertaken a stupendous task. However, he glories in it, and has attacked the problem with his old-time completeness, vigor and enthusiasm. I have never seen him *more* thoroughly wrapped up in and concentrated on any of his investigations."

Before his death in 1931, Edison, working in cooperation with botanists from the New York Botanical Garden and Rutgers University, would investigate the rubber potential of more than ten thousand plants, testing their properties and noting characteristics with the same determination he had brought to the search for an effective lamp filament half a century earlier. One of the prolific inventor's final patents, granted at the end of 1929, described a process for "the extraction of rubber from small plants, such as herbs and shrubs, having but a small content of rubber."

The excursions that Burroughs, Ford, Edison, and Firestone undertook together also had the effect of making automobile travel easier for the masses.

At the end of August 1918, in the wake of the Great Smoky Mountains trip, Edison received a letter from the chairman of the American Automobile Association, which explained that one mission of his organization, which had been founded in 1902, was "to convince the

Federal Government that the time has come for a Federal road system." He hoped the inventor could help.

As it happened, Edison held firm opinions on the matter. His travels with Ford, Firestone, and Burroughs had shown him the state
of roads in rural areas of the United States, while his trips through
France had given him a point of comparison. He believed that the
federal government ought to have a hand in training engineers in
the sciences of road and bridge construction, as the French government did.

"It is my opinion that the Government, utilizing these engineers,
should build all the main arteries of wide and deep concrete and keep
them in repair, leaving the feeding roads to be built by the States," he
wrote. "All these roads should be built with an idea of possible military use, which, of course, would include the operation of very heavy
trucks." The French roads Edison had traveled—more than four
thousand miles of them—showed him the benefits travelers enjoyed
when the government became involved in the construction and maintenance of highways. "I note with pain and humiliation the mess that
is made by us in our road building," he concluded.

Several months later Firestone was given a similar opportunity
to weigh in on the subject of roads. On July 13, 1919, a young army
officer named Dwight Eisenhower stopped off at Firestone's farm in
Columbiana. Eisenhower was an appointed observer on a transcontinental convoy that had set out for San Francisco from Washington
with the mission of testing the utility of the existing road network for
military transport. Firestone treated the convoy's officers to a chicken
dinner and passed along what he had learned from his trip through
the Great Smoky Mountains the previous summer. With Eisenhower
he also discussed improvements in tire construction. Pneumatic tires
of the type Firestone manufactured had proven far more reliable on
the road than the solid tires with which some of the convoy's trucks
had been equipped.

At dinner that afternoon Harvey sat next to Eisenhower, and the two struck up a friendship. Decades later, when, as president, Eisenhower returned to the idea of a nationwide network of highways, he would turn to Harvey for advice.

Despite the many benefits that had derived from the group's friendship, however, Ford, in the wake of their epic excursion through the Great Smoky Mountains in 1918, seemed to experience a moment of regret at all he had done to tug Burroughs into the modern age. That December, as the fifth anniversary of his first contact with Burroughs approached—the introduction that had also launched the naturalist's friendship with Edison and Firestone—Ford, perhaps giving in to nostalgia, had arranged to have an unusual gift delivered to Burroughs at his Riverby farm.

Christmas Day along the Hudson that year was unseasonably mild, with sunshine breaking through the clouds off and on throughout the afternoon. Burroughs had traveled to his son Julian's house in Kingston for dinner. Although he enjoyed the company of his grandchildren, he could not rise above a current of melancholy that undercut the holiday. "Christmas is always a rather sad day for the old," he felt, "such a flood of memories does it bring!"

When he returned home that evening, he found Christmas cards and telegrams waiting for him. One of these announced that his friend Ford was sending him an unexpected present by express mail: a donkey. The telegram explained that the animal was saddle trained and would arrive with all the equipment Burroughs might need for riding. It was Ford's hope that the new mode of transportation would allow Burroughs to continue his sojourns into nature, even as his age began to slow him down.

"I trust I shall get much good out of him," Burroughs thought. "His four young legs ought to be much better than my two old ones."

Three days later, at noon on Saturday, the little beast arrived.

"Hope we shall get on well together," Burroughs wrote in his journal.

This was an odd echo of the first gift Ford had given Burroughs, more than five years earlier. At the beginning of 1913 Ford had sent the naturalist a Model T, hoping to convince the famous outdoorsman that the automobile, far from spoiling the experience of nature, would make more of the natural world accessible to more people. At the time, Burroughs had believed that wisdom was more likely to be found "riding on an ass" than in an automobile. Now it was as if the automaker wished to turn back the clock, nudging the naturalist he had once ushered into the twentieth century back to the nineteenth. The donkey, however, proved to be a less successful gift than the flivver.

"The little beast is very free with her heels," Burroughs wrote to a friend. "She kicked the hired man the other morning. I shall be on my guard when I ride her."

A few weeks later the naturalist, who had shown remarkable composure when the Model T had "kicked up her heels" while he was learning to drive, had exhausted his patience with the burro. "The donkey is no good for me," he told his friend. "I am going to have to give her away or shoot her." A local man eventually took the feisty donkey off Burroughs's hands, and the old naturalist went back to his now customary mode of travel: Ford's Model T.

Where Ford had once hoped to convince Burroughs that modern technology was compatible with his love of nature, the automaker had come, over the course of his travels with Burroughs, to admire the traditional mode of life that the naturalist represented to him. The failure of Ford's Christmas gift underlined the fact that Burroughs's era was passing. Even the naturalist himself, an old-school outdoorsman who had hiked with John Muir and sauntered over the countryside with Walt Whitman, had grown dependent on the technology that Ford and Edison had introduced. Yet while Ford's automobile made possible the brief escapes he and his friends enjoyed on their camping trips each summer, it had also helped to create the need to

escape. Before the advent of automobiles and the electric light, everyone by necessity had lived in closer harmony with the natural world
and its rhythms. The conveniences that Ford and Edison introduced
made life easier, but they also expanded the gulf between that life and
the natural environment. To experience nature now required a turning away from these conveniences.

As Ford grew older, his own mode of escape was increasingly a
flight into the past. This nostalgic retreat most often took the form of
preserving or reconstructing the material culture of earlier times. On
the fiftieth anniversary of Edison's light bulb—October 21, 1929—
Ford threw a party for his old friend in Dearborn. Guests included
Herbert Hoover and industrialists Charles M. Schwab and John D.
Rockefeller Jr., as well as such science luminaries as Albert Einstein
and Marie Curie, the latter of whom traveled from Paris to honor
Edison. The celebration was held at Greenfield Village, to which Ford
had relocated the original Menlo Park laboratory where Edison had
created his light bulb. Ford had also moved both the railway station
where the younger Edison had worked as a telegrapher and the Smith
Creek station of the Grand Trunk Railroad, where he had been, as
Ford put it, "dumped off the train with his first little laboratory" after
his experimenting started a fire. The assembly of buildings included
even the boardinghouse where Edison had eaten while working on his
early inventions. (Edison reportedly complained that the floor in the
reconstructed laboratory was too clean to be an accurate re-creation
of his old workplace.)

When it came to Burroughs, Ford's nostalgia took on an even more
personal and mournful quality. The two friends met for the last time
in the fall of 1920, at Riverby, as Burroughs was preparing for a trip
to California. Together they cooked Burroughs's signature "brigand
steak" over a campfire they built on a hillside overlooking the family
farm Ford had helped Burroughs buy.

"I had found an ax imbedded in the soil of the garden, an old ax,"

*In November 1920, four months before Burroughs's death, Henry Ford records his friendship with Burroughs and Edison on film.*

Ford recalled. "It had the name of 'Kelly' stamped on it. Mr. Burroughs was quite excited about it. 'Why, that's my grandfather's ax,' he said. 'Well,' said I, 'let's bury it here again, and then some day you and I will come here and dig it up again.'" It was characteristic of his relationship with Burroughs that Ford wanted not simply to revive the past with him but to rediscover it again and again. Burroughs, however, sensed that his own story from then on would be about endings rather than rediscovery.

"Maybe you will be here to dig it up," he told Ford, "but I won't."

As Burroughs was leaving Woodchuck Lodge to make the journey to California, something caused him to linger for a moment on the front porch. Taking a pencil from his pocket, he inscribed a brief, enigmatic message on the siding that lined the back wall of the porch: "October 26, 1920. Leave Today." These were the last words the old naturalist, a lifelong journal-keeper and author of some thirty books, would ever write at the homestead he loved so dearly.

Burroughs spent the winter in California, dividing his time between La Jolla and a cabin in Pasadena Glen. By February his health had taken a turn for the worse, and he was forced to undergo surgery to remove an abscess from his chest. As soon as he had recovered sufficiently to travel, he started for home by train in the company of his friend Clara Barrus. His condition declined as the train made its way across the continent, and he was still several hours away from home when, at 2:00 on the morning of March 29, he died, outside Kingston, Ohio.

According to his wishes, Burroughs was buried at Roxbury, "beside the rock on the hill above Woodchuck Lodge, which I have frequently spoken of as my 'Boyhood Rock.'" Ford, Edison, and Firestone were all present at the funeral, at which passages from Emerson and Whitman were read, along with an excerpt from Burroughs's last book, *Accepting the Universe.*

"There was no sadness in John Burroughs's death," Ford maintained. He had lived a life true to his values and had wrung from it every measure or worth, working up to the very end. "When the grain lies brown and ripe under the harvest sun, and the harvesters are busy binding it into sheaves, there is no sadness for the grain."

In his final journal entry, recorded on February 4, 1921, just weeks before his death, Burroughs noted that he had gone for a drive that day to visit the post office in Sierra Madre, California. As had often happened in the years since Ford sent him the Model T that had marked the beginning of their friendship, the naturalist found that he returned from the automobile outing with buoyed spirits. "Life seems worth living again," he wrote. "Now, at 7 pm, I hear the patter of rain."

As a memorial to his friend, Ford turned a section of his Fair Lane estate into a bird sanctuary, which he referred to from then on as Burroughs Nook.

Ford, Edison, and Firestone remained friends, traveling together on several further occasions, each encouraging the others in their work and, when necessary, offering gentle rebukes, as was the case in 1924 when there once again arose a movement to draft Ford into politics, this time to run as the Republican candidate for the presidency.

Ford's wife, Clara, felt this was a notion he had no business pursuing. She knew her husband had extraordinary abilities, but she also knew that "Henry was a man of sudden impulse; he resented advice, was intolerant of restraint, and fired anyone who opposed him." Ford was gifted in mechanical matters, but the libel trial in Chicago had shown that his education in other areas was woefully inadequate. As Edison had pointed out years earlier, he was also no orator.

At the Daughters of the American Revolution convention in Washington, D.C., in 1924, Clara was surprised to see "Ford for President" campaign buttons. Again and again, speakers rose to tout Ford's strength as a candidate. When a delegate to the convention gave a speech in which she alluded to Clara as the perfect model of a first lady, Clara had heard enough. "Mr. Ford has enough and more than enough to do to attend to his business in Detroit," she told the chair of the convention. "The day he runs for President of the United States, I will be on the next boat to England."

Edison, who had been dubious about Ford's quest for a Senate seat, offered even less encouragement when the presidency was in question. "Yes, he's a remarkable man in one sense, and in another he's not," Edison told a reporter. "I would not vote for him for President, but as a director of manufacturing or industrial enterprises, I'd vote for him—twice." Burroughs would certainly have sided with Edison.

"Ford missed the quartet in later years," the son of a close friend would later note. "He always spoke nostalgically of the camping days."

Always a man with more acquaintances than close friends, Ford experienced the dissolution of the foursome as a genuine loss.

Each member of the camping party had contributed to the group in his own manner. As unlikely as their friendship appeared, the men's particular interests—nature, science, industry—in fact overlapped in ways that were already coming to define the young twentieth century and indeed the era that would follow.

Burroughs, for one, could already sense the acceleration of daily life at the dawn of the automobile age, when further developments like the interstate highway system and air travel, not to mention computers, the internet, and mobile phones, as yet lay below the event horizon of a far distant future. It worried him that attention spans (though he would not have used that term) were growing shorter. He saw that the "dilatory and meandering" literature of the nineteenth century, on which he had once modeled his own writing, now tried the patience of modern readers.

"We want the story to move rapidly," as we ourselves were beginning to move in our Model Ts. The age demanded an electrical experience, more like Edison's motion pictures than an essay by Emerson: "We want currents and counter currents—movement and reality at all hazards."

In the years immediately preceding his friendship with Ford, Burroughs had thought deeply about the pressure science and industry were exerting on our experience of the natural realm that had always been the focus of his attention and his writing. "Why is it that the scientific explanation of the universe, and of the mind and body of man, seems to shut us in a narrower and lower world," he wondered, even as he relished the scientific facts of biology and geology—the kind of facts he would soon gleefully exchange with Edison.

The danger of the scientific worldview, Burroughs came to believe, was in the way it could transform the mystery of existence, which once filled us with "awe and reverence," into a series of puzzles to be solved, displacing imagination in favor of reason and analysis. The same could be said of the products of industry: "Machinery is a beautiful application of mechanical principles; it surprises and, in a way, pleases us, but it does not touch the imagination and the emotions."

The way forward was not the rejection of the automobile or the electric lamp but rather their incorporation into the imagination. The world of the future was one in which the inventor, the mechanic, and the artist would naturally rub shoulders. "Specialists in science, experts in industry . . . and realists in literature," Burroughs concluded, "seem to be in the line of the mental evolution of the race."

What Ford, Edison, Firestone, and Burroughs found in their travels together was a lighthearted premonition of that evolution. As they explored the still-wild parts of a nation on the verge of a new era, they found themselves captivated as much by the beauty of a grist mill as by the waterfall that drove it. They were by all accounts as happy climbing trees or cradling oats as exploring a manufacturing plant or clambering aboard a locomotive. They looked upon the farm track and the state motorway with equal anticipation of the adventure they might provide. And for all his grumbling about rough roads and late nights, it was the oldest member of the party, the venerable naturalist whose era was passing, who radiated the basic optimism that nurtured this new kind of receptiveness among his companions.

"My faith as a naturalist," Burroughs declared near the end of his life, "is like that of a man who takes out a life policy in an insurance company. He believes that the company is sound and will meet its obligations. So I believe that the universe is solvent, and can be trusted."

# Acknowledgments

I owe a great debt to John Glusman and Helen Thomaides, my editors at W. W. Norton, whose efforts improved this book in innumerable ways. Both were a pleasure to work with from start to finish. I would also like to thank Neil Olson, who helped shape the proposal and place the book with Norton. Wendy Levinson read the manuscript at a crucial juncture and offered advice and encouragement that propelled the project forward, and Pat Wieland helped to root out errors in the copy and notes.

My research was aided by a number of librarians and library support staff. In particular, I would like to thank Linda Skolarus and Jim Orr at The Henry Ford and Dean Rogers at the Archives and Special Collections Library of Vassar College. The Center for Research in the Humanities at the New York Public Library provided research support as well as work space. I am indebted to the directors of the library's Research Study program, Rebecca Federman and Melanie Locay, and to all my quietly typing colleagues in the Wertheim Study.

Thanks to my parents, to whom the book is dedicated, and to their 1968 Ford Galaxie, for providing my first glimpses of the mountain roads over which Henry Ford's party had traveled long before. The late Fred Crouse, traveler and troubadour, encouraged the project from its inception, as did Pat Willis, who was generous with his knowledge of Appalachian byways. Finally, I am grateful to Jessie, Willa, and Alice, who make all journeys worth taking.

# Notes

## 1. The Spark

1 **Babcock Electric ... on a single charge:** Curtis D. Anderson and Judy Anderson, *Electric and Hybrid Cars: A History*, 2d ed. (Jefferson, NC: McFarland, 2010), 33.

2 **"to make them all alike":** Peter Collier and David Horowitz, *The Fords: An American Epic* (New York: HarperCollins, 1988), 34.

2 **"Ford Car a Paradox":** *Salina Evening Journal* (Salina, KS), Jan. 5, 1912, 3.

3 **"one of the small-car sensations":** *Boston Globe*, Mar. 5, 1911, 61.

3 **"Until the advent of the motor car":** *Inter Ocean* (Chicago), Dec. 31, 1911, 22.

4 **"that automobiles are to be classed with":** "Lewis v. Amorous et al.," *Southeastern Reporter* (St. Paul, MN: West Pub. Co.), vol. 59 (1908), 340.

4 **"I don't claim that every man":** Simeon Ford, "On the Automobile," *Life,* Jan. 4, 1912, 82.

4 **a substantial library:** The invoice Ford received from Houghton Mifflin is held in Acc. 1, Fair Lane Papers, Box 34, Benson Ford Research Center, The Henry Ford, Dearborn, MI (hereafter THF).

5 **reading to him from Charles Dickens novels:** Louise B. Clancy and

Florence Davies, *The Believer: The Life Story of Mrs. Henry Ford* (New York: Coward McCann, 1960), 35.

5   **"When I visit Mrs. Ford"**: Clancy and Davies, *Believer*, 176.

6   **"I remember the nest"**: Quoted in Steven Watts, *The People's Tycoon: Henry Ford and the American Century* (New York: Vintage, 2006), 6. The note is held in "Loose Notes," Acc. 1, Box 14-2, THF.

7   **the Detroit *Free Press* ran an article**: "Sage of Slabsides," *Detroit Free Press*, Mar. 31, 1912, 3.

8   **"Mr. President . . . you must be mistaken"**: The sparrow story is recalled by Corinne Roosevelt Robinson, in "My Brother Theodore Roosevelt," *Scribners Magazine*, vol. 52, no. 1, July 1921, 89.

9   **"They started new currents in him"**: John Burroughs, with Clifton Johnson, *John Burroughs Talks* (Boston: Houghton Mifflin, 1922), 326.

9   **"that the automobile was going to kill"**: Henry Ford, with Samuel Crowther, *My Life and Work* (Garden City, NY: Doubleday, Page, 1923), 237.

9   **"habit of mind"**: This and subsequent quotations are from "In the Noon of Science," *Atlantic Monthly*, Sep. 1912, 323, 331.

10  **let his "emotions" carry him away**: Ford and Crowther, *My Life and Work*, 237.

10  **"I had a surprising letter"**: Clara Barrus, *The Life and Letters of John Burroughs*, vol. 2 (Boston: Houghton Mifflin, 1925), 185–86.

10  **"I didn't know what in the dickens"**: *John Burroughs Talks*, 325.

10  **"Some folks object"**: Quoted in "Sage of Slabsides," *Detroit Free Press*, Mar. 31, 1912, 3.

11  **"a happy combination"**: *Ford Times*, Mar. 1912, back cover. Buck later corrected himself, describing the wings as "sacred ibis wings." See Glen Buck, *Trademark Power: An Expedition into an Unprobed and Inviting Wilderness* (Chicago: Munroe & Southworth, 1916), 96.

11  **"The best piece of business literature"**: Glen Buck, *Quirks and Quadrates* (Chicago: Buck & Hammesfahr, 1919), 25.

11  **"big, artistic, prophetic"**: Elbert Hubbard, in *The Philistine*, vol. 38, no. 2, Jan. 1913, 57.

11  **"The man who today doesn't understand"**: Buck, *Quirks and Quadrates*, 46, 48, 56.

12  **"A spark may consume a city"**: Buck, *Quirks and Quadrates*, 16.

13  **strictly an open-air motorist**: Burroughs's neighbor Harriet B. Shatraw is quoted in *John Burroughs in Roxbury*, unpaginated (Roxbury, NY: Roxbury Burroughs Club, 196-?), New York Public Library.

13 **"It was a pathetic meeting"**: John Burroughs to Clara Barrus, hand-written note by Elizabeth Burroughs Kelley on back of typescript journal page, Jan. 1913, John Burroughs Papers, Series I. Writings: Journals and Notebooks, Archives and Special Collections, Vassar College Library, Poughkeepsie, NY (hereafter *Burroughs Journal*).

14 **"unexpectedly contented"**: Burroughs to Barrus, handwritten note by EBK, *Burroughs Journal*.

14 **"silent as a sphynx"**: *Burroughs Journal*, Jan. 14, 1913.

14 **a few days with him at his camp**: "Chronicle and Comment," *The Bookman: A Review of Books and Life*, vol. 34, no. 1, Sep. 1911, 12.

15 **"hauling stone, manure"**: *Burroughs Journal*, Jan. 15, 1913.

15 **"a fine ride"**: *Burroughs Journal*, Jan. 21, 1913.

15 **"Modern surgery"**: *Burroughs Journal*, Jan. 27, 1913.

16 **"The trouble with driving"**: Shatraw quoted in *John Burroughs in Roxbury*, n.p.

16 **"I looked back"**: *Burroughs Journal*, Apr. 8, 1913.

16 **"The blind, desperate thing"**: *Burroughs Journal*, May 8, 1913.

16 **"A run to Highland in the car"**: *Burroughs Journal*, May 8, 1913.

17 **"the degeneracy of"**: *Omaha Daily Bee*, Apr. 19, 1913, 10.

18 **"Clover blooming"**: *Burroughs Journal*, June 3, 1913.

18 **"Mr. Ford pleased with me"**: *Burroughs Journal*, June 5–8, 1913.

18 **"I was running it when the bobolinks"**: Ford and Crowther, *My Life and Work*, 21. Some automotive historians dispute Ford's memory of the date.

19 **"earnest, big-hearted man"**: *John Burroughs Talks*, 326.

19 **the setup astonished Burroughs**: *John Burroughs Talks*, 326.

19 **"a wilderness of men and machinery"**: *Burroughs Journal*, June 5–8, 1913.

20 **Ford was "astonished"**: Glen Buck, "The Factory Has a Distinguished Guest," *Ford Times*, July 1913, 399–400.

22 **"The Ford cars grow before your eyes"**: *Burroughs Journal*, June 5–8, 1913.

22 **"While we stood looking at the cars"**: *John Burroughs Talks*, 326–27.

22 **"The place is still home to me"**: *John Burroughs Talks*, 274.

23 **"When I'm up in the Catskills"**: *John Burroughs Talks*, 332.

23 **let himself get "rattled"**: *Burroughs Journal*, June 29, 1913.

23 **"I went into the barn"**: *John Burroughs Talks*, 332.

23 **"it burst through"**: *Burroughs Journal*, June 29, 1913.

23 **"Only for that I'd have been in eternity"**: *John Burroughs Talks*, 332.

23   **"I just got rattled"**: Quoted by Shatraw, in *John Burroughs in Roxbury*, n.p.

24   **"You mustn't go fast in ticklish places"**: *John Burroughs Talks*, 333.

## 2. Compensation

25   **he "is said to have more actual cash"**: *Wall Street Journal*, July 3, 1913, 7.

26   **"Lightness is what we are striving for"**: *Washington Times*, July 19, 1913, 11.

27   **"A fine rain"**: *Burroughs Journal*, Aug. 7, 1913.

28   **"I would enter the barn with fear"**: *John Burroughs Talks*, 9.

28   **"Money I get now"**: *John Burroughs Talks*, 35.

28   **"We pried it up"**: *John Burroughs Talks*, 48.

28   **cleared debris from Burroughs's spring**: Barrus, *Life and Letters*, vol. 2, 196.

29   **"They tried it and then scolded us"**: *John Burroughs Talks*, 329.

29   **"This is the first place where I ever studied"**: *John Burroughs Talks*, 350.

29   **"to see the world"**: *John Burroughs Talks*, 47, 48.

30   **"I started the horses"**: *John Burroughs Talks*, 48.

30   **"A fine drive"**: *Burroughs Journal*, Aug. 29, 1913.

30   **"fumbled in his pocket"; tears running down their faces**: *John Burroughs Talks*, 328, 327.

31   **"The moment you strike"**: Quotations are from *John Burroughs Talks*, 25.

31   **"a stream of motor cars all day"**: *Burroughs Journal*, Aug. 30, 1913.

32   **"the absence of a billiard room"**: *Boston Globe*, Sep. 8, 1897, 4.

32   **"most superb and complete hostelry"**: *Boston Globe*, Sep. 8, 1897, 4.

33   **"There was a little party of us"**: *John Burroughs Talks*, 336.

34   **"I was like Jonah in the whale's belly"**: *John Burroughs Talks*, 177.

34   **"I like Sanborn"**: John Burroughs to Walt Whitman, Aug. 10, 1877, "Life and Letters," Walt Whitman Archive, https://whitmanarchive.org /biography/correspondence/tei/loc.01128.html.

34   **Sleepy Hollow Cemetery**: See photo "Standing in front of the Walden cairn, photographer Glen Buck, Aug. 31, 1913," in John Burroughs Papers, Series IX: Photographs, Candids of Burroughs, 59.63, Archives and Special Collections, Vassar College Library, Poughkeepsie, NY.

34   **"I had walked up from Cambridge"**: All Sanborn quotations are from

Franklin Sanborn, *Personality of Emerson* (Boston: C. E. Goodspeed, 1903), 8, 9, 10.

36  **"All mean egotism vanishes":** Ralph Waldo Emerson, *Nature* (Boston: J. Munroe and Company, 1836), 13.

36  **"His dining-room, his study":** *Burroughs Journal*, Sep. 1, 1913.

36  **"With Emerson dead":** Barrus, *Life and Letters*, vol. 1, 235.

36  **"He was a mighty good talker":** *John Burroughs Talks*, 326.

37  **"He had so saturated himself":** Ford and Crowther, *My Life and Work*, 239.

37  **"With exercise of self trust":** This and the following Emerson quotation are from Robert Lacey's discussion of Emerson's influence on Ford in Lacey, *Ford: The Men and the Machine* (Boston: Little, Brown, 1986), 112–15, which also informs my depiction here of the interest Ford and Burroughs took in Emerson. Ford's attention to particular ideas in Emerson's work is indicated by the jacket of an Oxford edition of *Essays: First and Second Series* with page numbers noted by Ford, held in Acc. 1, Various Boxes, Fair Lane Papers, Box 14, Folder 14-3: HF—Notes—Vagabonds & Heroes, THF.

37  **"telegraph, loom, press, and locomotive":** Ralph Waldo Emerson and Lewis Mumford, *Essays and Journals: Selected, and with an Introd., by Lewis Mumford* (Garden City, NY: Doubleday, 1968), 399.

37  **might well view the Model T:** See Lacey, *Ford: The Men and the Machine*, 115.

37  **"To be great is to be misunderstood":** Ralph Waldo Emerson, "Self-Reliance," in *Essays* (Boston: Ticknor and Fields, 1865), 45.

38  **"class of men":** Emerson, "Character," in *Essays*, 375.

38  **"It is as easy for the strong man":** Emerson, "Self-Reliance," in *Essays*, 52.

38  **"the most beautiful cemetery":** *Burroughs Journal*, Sep. 1, 1913.

38  **"laugh a good deal":** *Boston Globe*, Aug. 24, 1913, 46; and *Burroughs Journal*, Sep. 2, 1913.

38  **"If you happen to touch":** *John Burroughs Talks*, 321.

38  **"the more practical man":** *John Burroughs Talks*, 328.

38  **"I can not afford to waste my time":** "Anecdote of Prof. Agassiz," *The R.I. Schoolmaster*, vol. 6, 1860, 109.

39  **"to live as Adam did":** "Naked He Plunges into Maine Woods to Live Alone Two Months," *Boston Post*, Aug. 10, 1913, 1.

39  **"I am not interested in money":** "The Nature Man," *New Yorker*, June 18, 1938, 21.

39   "The artist Knowles": Burroughs to William Sloane Kennedy, Sep. 28, 1913, quoted in Kennedy, *The Real John Burroughs* (New York: Funk & Wagnalls, 1924), 91.

39   **more than thirty thousand copies:** "Nature Man," 21.

40   "Mr. Ford is the man": Quoted in Kennedy, *Real John Burroughs*, 89–90.

40   "trying to bash each other's brains out": Lacey, *Ford: The Men and the Machine*, 116.

41   **Ford recalled Emerson saying:** In his biography of the automaker, *Ford: The Men and the Machine*, Robert Lacey provides a thorough discussion of Emerson's influence on Ford's thinking with respect to the five-dollar day. I have drawn on his work in the account I give here.

41   "In labor as in life": Emerson, "Compensation," in *Essays*, 89.

41   "Today he is just as he was": Gertrude Price, "Henry Ford Plans No More Dull Seasons in His Factories," *Day Book* (Chicago), Jan. 8, 1914, 26.

42   **more than thirty articles about Ford:** David E. Nye, *Henry Ford: Ignorant Idealist* (Port Washington, NY: Kennikat, 1979), 13.

42   "economic blunders, if not crimes": Quoted in Nye, *Henry Ford*, 13.

42   "It gives him the pick": *John Burroughs Talks*, 331.

42   "If the gatherer gathers too much": Ralph Waldo Emerson, *Essays: First and Second Series* (London: Humphrey Milford/Oxford University Press, 1936), 68–69. In later life Henry Ford owned and annotated a copy of this edition.

42   "I guess you and I are": Typewritten letter from Burroughs in Roxbury to Ford, dated Sep. 9, [1913], [Letters] Acc. 1, Fair Lane Papers, Box 111, 106-G-1, THF.

### 3. Trial Runs

45   **Edsel's fellow motorist:** The friend was Philip Worcester, who lived at 51 Rowena Street in Detroit. For details of the accident, see *Detroit Free Press*, Mar. 22, 1910, 7.

46   **graduated three years earlier:** Edsel Ford's biographer is unsure whether he graduated: "There are no records of Edsel graduating, nor is his photo in the school yearbook for 1912." Henry Dominguez, *Edsel: The Story of Henry Ford's Forgotten Son* (Warrendale, PA: SAE International/Society of Automotive Engineers, 2002).

47   **Bob Gray . . . rounded out the group:** The names of the young men were, in full, Thomas Cram Whitehead, Horace Caulkins Jr., Herbert Book, and Robert T. Gray Jr.

47  **"If a young man comes out of college":** Ralph Waldo Trine and Henry Ford, *Power That Wins* (Indianapolis: Bobbs-Merrill, 1929), 34–35.

47  **"to waste time at college":** Quoted in Dominguez, *Edsel,* 41.

48  **an adventure in itself:** For a published account of Edsel Ford's travels to the fair, see "Touring the Exposition," *Ford Times,* Oct. 1913, 117–24.

48  **a new Stutz touring car:** The vehicle was most probably a Stutz Bulldog.

49  **"If the place were to come into my possession":** Typewritten letter from Burroughs at Woodchuck Lodge, Roxbury, NY, to Ford, dated Sep. 18, 1913, marked received by Ford, Sep. 23, 1913, [Letters] Acc. 1, Fair Lane Papers, Box 111, 106-G-1, THF.

50  **either "dreamy" or "addled":** Neil Baldwin, *Edison: Inventing the Century* (New York: Hyperion, 1995), 24.

50  **"Broadway is as quiet to me":** Baldwin, *Edison,* 35.

51  **"Maybe he would have a bungalow here":** Typewritten letter from Burroughs at Woodchuck Lodge, Roxbury, NY, to Ford, dated Sep. 18, 1913, marked received by Ford, Sep. 23, 1913, [Letters] Acc. 1, Fair Lane Papers, Box 111 106-G-1, THF.

51  **"to go down to the Everglades":** *New York Times,* Feb. 12, 1914, 1.

52  **"an ideal vacation":** *New York Times,* Feb. 22, 1914, 1.

52  **just over three thousand:** Population data from *Florida Health Notes,* vol. 10, no. 1, Jan. 1915, 27.

53  **watched the rest of the parade:** *News-Press* (Fort Myers, FL), Feb. 23, 1914, 1.

53  **"At another place":** *Fort Myers Tropical News,* Apr. 25, 1928. Also quoted in Tom Smoot, *The Edisons of Fort Myers: Discoveries of the Heart* (Sarasota, FL: Pineapple, 2011), 7.

54  **"Up the Caloosahatchee":** *Fort Myers Press,* Oct. 17, 1885.

54  **"It was a small cattle village":** *News-Press* (Fort Myers, FL), Feb. 11, 1925, 1.

54  **referred to as his "playhouse":** *News-Press,* Feb. 24, 1914, 2.

55  **"a large and beautiful park":** *News-Press,* Feb. 24, 1914, 2.

55  **"Pretty nearly an earthly paradise here":** *Burroughs Journal,* Feb. 25, 1914.

56  **"good play-fellows":** *Burroughs Journal,* Mar. 10, 1914.

56  **"Really . . . it is animal matter":** Thomas A. Edison, "What Is Life?" *Cosmopolitan Magazine,* vol. 68, May 1920, 26.

56  **"What I believe is":** Edison, "What Is Life?" 27.

56  **"I believe the ultimate life-particle":** Edison, "What Is Life?" 152, 154.

57  **whether, driven by memory, they remained associated:** The physics

of quantum entanglement would now say yes, regardless of where the individual units wind up.

57 **"If they break up":** "Edison's Views upon Vital Human Problems," *Strand Magazine*, vol. 59, Aug. 1922, 162.

57 **"Life is always life":** This and the following quotations are from Trine and Ford, *Power That Wins*, 50, 51, 25.

58 **"He is not puffed up":** *Burroughs Journal*, Mar. 10, 1914.

58 **paper ran banner headlines:** Headlines appeared in the *Atlanta Georgian*, Apr. 29, 1913, 1, 2.

58 **printing an article:** Quoted in Leonard Dinnerstein, *The Leo Frank Case* (New York: Columbia University Press, 1968), 18.

59 **"might possibly result in grave damage":** Dinnerstein, *Leo Frank Case*, 15.

59 **chants of "Hang the Jew":** Dinnerstein, *Leo Frank Case*, 60.

59 **"They are convinced":** *Macon Daily Telegraph*, Aug. 27, 1913; and quoted in Dinnerstein, *Leo Frank Case*, 61.

59 **"distinctive in its attachment":** Dinnerstein, *Leo Frank Case*, xv.

59 **"the most horrible persecution":** *Atlanta Constitution*, Oct. 26, 1913, 1.

60 **An attached story reported:** *News-Press* (Fort Myers, FL), Feb. 24, 1914, 1.

60 **"Justice should be done":** *New York Times*, Apr. 1, 1914, 3.

60 **to see the spectacle:** *News-Press* (Fort Myers, FL), Feb. 25, 1914, 3.

60 **three riders roaring around:** One of the drivers performing at the Motordrome that night was Joseph Dobish, who would go on to build the Wall-of-Death motordrome in Wildwood, New Jersey, where he pioneered the use of lions in daredevil motordrome performances. In 1938, one of his lions escaped and, after several hours at large, attacked and killed a passerby, seizing him by the neck and snapping it before dragging the body under the boardwalk.

61 **"juggling and drinking":** *News-Press* (Fort Myers, FL), Feb. 23, 1914, 3.

61 **"seven shows in one":** *News-Press*, Feb. 23, 1914, 3.

62 **"Every criminal leaves a track":** *News-Press*, Feb. 27, 1914, 1.

62 **"too much of a religious exhorter":** *New York Times*, Apr. 1, 1914, 3.

62 **"I discussed it frequently":** *New York Times*, Apr. 1, 1914, 3.

62 **"I never heard anyone else":** *John Burroughs Talks*, 329.

63 **"food and the act of eating":** John Harvey Kellogg, *The Living Temple* (Battle Creek, MI: Good Health Publishing Company, 1903), 67.

63 **recommended the avoidance of:** Kellogg, *Living Temple*, 197–98, 203.

63 **Kellogg's visit "a bore":** Madeleine Edison to John Sloan, Feb. 26, 1914,

quoted in Michele Wehrwein Albion, *The Florida Life of Thomas Edison* (Gainesville: University Press of Florida, 2008), 76.

63 **"pounds and pounds of"**: Madeleine Edison to John Sloan, Mar. 31, 1914, quoted in Albion, *Florida Life*, 76.

64 **"just like the rest of the children"**: *News-Press* (Fort Myers, FL), Feb. 28, 1914, 1.

64 **"The aigrettes sell"**: *News-Press*, Feb. 28, 1914, 1.

65 **"Suffice it to say"**: "Shooting Up an Egret Rookery," *Outdoor World & Recreation*, Aug. 1913, 84.

66 **"to hear a panther growl"**: *News-Press* (Fort Myers, FL), Feb. 28, 1914, 1.

66 **"I never can see why"**: Mina Miller Edison to Grace Miller Hitchcock, Feb. 27, 1914, quoted in Albion, *Florida Life*, 77.

66 **"their oldest and toughest looking clothes"**: Madeleine Edison's account quoted in Smoot, *Edisons of Fort Myers*, 118.

67 **"The water was almost up to the floorboards"**: Quoted in Albion, *Florida Life*, 78.

67 **"delicate gray cypress trees"**: These and following quotations are from Madeleine Edison's account, quoted in Smoot, *Edisons of Fort Myers*, 119, 121, 123–124.

69 **"Everybody except Burroughs"**: Interview with Charles Edison, April 14, 1953; quoted in Smoot, *Edisons of Fort Myers*, 124.

69 **"Numerous deer and turkey"**: *News-Press* (Fort Myers, FL), Mar. 2, 1914, 4.

70 **"expressed their delight"**: *News-Press*, Mar. 6, 1914, 3. For more on Cottingham, see University of Michigan, ed., *Michigan Alumnus*, Ann Arbor: Alumni Association of the University of Michigan, vol. 18, no. 4, Jan. 1912, 158.

70 **a boating excursion**: *News-Press* (Fort Myers, FL), Mar. 7, 1914, 6. See also Clarence Swick, "Triangulation along the West Coast of Florida," Special Publication no. 16, U.S. Coast and Geodetic Survey, 70.

70 **"confident that rubber trees can be grown"**: *News-Press* (Fort Myers, FL), Mar. 14, 1924, 1; and May 28, 1924, 1.

70 **"appeal especially to the large number"**: John Burroughs, *Afoot and Afloat* (Boston: Houghton Mifflin, 1907), publisher's note.

71 **"the most vital man"**: Burroughs, *Afoot and Afloat*, 64, 54.

71 **"Mr. Edison always told me"**: *News-Press* (Fort Myers, FL), Mar. 10, 1914, 1.

71 **"I am sure we shall"**: *News-Press*, Feb. 28, 1914, 1.

72 **spent a rainy few days with them**: *Burroughs Journal*, June 23, 1914.

72   **"strange far-off elemental look":** *Burroughs Journal*, July 13, 1914.

72   **"It acted like":** *Burroughs Journal*, July 11, 1914.

73   **Ford was as likely to ask:** *Cincinnati Enquirer*, May 30, 1915, 9.

74   **"Thomas Edison eats less":** *New York Times*, July 8, 1915, 5.

74   **graduate near the end of July:** *Daily Review* (Decatur, IL), July 24, 1915, 7; and *Pittsburgh Daily Post*, July 11, 1915, 18.

74   **bringing out a new edition:** *Pittsburgh Post-Gazette*, Apr. 18, 1915, 44.

74   **"If you smoked":** "The Reminiscences of Mr. F. W. Loskowske," Nov. 1951, p. 96, Oral History Section, Ford Motor Company Archives, THF (hereafter FMCA).

75   **"snap" he had felt:** *Burroughs Journal*, Apr. 24, 1915.

75   **"shot from the end of a torpedo":** *Burroughs Journal*, Mar. 4, 1915.

75   **buoyed his spirits "like music":** *Burroughs Journal*, Apr. 29 and Apr. 24, 1915.

76   **"distinguished services and achievements":** "All Call Edison World Benefactor," *New York Times*, May 7, 1915, 13.

76   **"seer, wizard, and master":** "All Call Edison World Benefactor," *New York Times*, May 7, 1915, 13.

76   **"Edison hates all the talk":** *Burroughs Journal*, May 6, 1915: "the whole thing a bore to him."

77   **house doctor for Vassar College:** "Johanna E. R. Von Tiling," *Cliff Island Seagull* (Cliff Island, ME), Summer 2002, 6.

77   **"a little sluggishness in the liver":** *Burroughs Journal*, May 7, 1915.

77   **"horrible war," "terribly upset":** *Burroughs Journal*, Feb. 15 and May 7, 1915.

78   **"Well, they were fools":** George Sylvester Viereck, *American Weekly*, vol. 7, no. 10, July 24, 1918, 399.

78   **"I am too shocked":** *New York Times*, May 9, 1915, 7.

78   **Edison had vowed to rebuild:** *Courier-News* (Bridgewater, NJ), Dec. 10, 1914, 6.

78   **working twenty-four-hour days:** See, for example, *New Castle Herald* (New Castle, PA), May 12, 1915, 1.

79   **"Modern warfare is more a matter of":** *Detroit Free Press*, May 30, 1915, 71.

80   **driven from New Jersey:** *Akron Evening Times*, July 8, 1915, 5.

80   **"To Theodore from mother and father":** *Akron Beacon Journal*, July 7, 1915, 1.

81   **bringing about a lasting peace:** *Detroit Free Press*, July 15, 1915, 3.

81   **Edsel Ford and his friends were discovering:** The story of Edsel's trip

is drawn from the photo-illustrated logbook compiled by H. J. Caulkins Jr.;
a copy is held in the collection of the Antique Automobile Club of America
in Hershey, Pennsylvania, under accession number 10-SP-F0148.

85  **drinking "his own health":** *Detroit Free Press*, July 31, 1915, 1.


## 4. The Palace of Industry and
## the Garden of Earthly Treasures

87  **Edison advertisements maintained:** See, for example, *Ithaca Journal*,
Sep. 24, 1915, 6.

87  **Fagan had sprung into action:** *Pacific Motor Boat*, vol. 13, 1920, 32;
and *Railway Signal Engineer*, vol. 14, no. 2, Feb. 1921, 82.

87  **asked to plant a tree:** Letter from J. M. Hill to Henry Ford, Sep. 21,
1915, Folder X001B2-F, Document X001B2EG, Thomas A. Edison Papers,
School of Arts and Sciences, Rutgers University, New Brunswick, NJ
(hereafter Edison Papers).

87  **one "of but very few requests":** Minutes of the Thirty-First Annual
Meeting of the Association of Edison Illuminating Companies (New York:
Burgoyne's "Quick" Print, 1915), 283.

88  **whether he would be free to travel:** Letter from William Henry Meadowcroft to Ernest Gustav Liebold, Sep. 22, 1915, Folder X001B2-F, Document X001B2EH, Edison Papers.

88  **had his secretary send a telegram:** Telegram from William Henry
Meadowcroft to Ernest Gustav Liebold, Oct. 9, 1915, Folder X001B2-F,
Document X001B2EP, Edison Papers.

88  **taking up that job himself:** Lee A. Craig, *Josephus Daniels: His Life
and Times* (Chapel Hill: University of North Carolina Press, 2013), 216,
221.

89  **addressing incoming enlisted men:** Josephus Daniels, *The Wilson
Era: Years of War and After, 1917–1923* (Chapel Hill: University of North
Carolina Press, 1948), 273.

89  **"a cup of Josephus Daniels":** Craig, *Josephus Daniels*, 245.

89  **relying on Daniels to guide:** *Wall Street Journal*, May 18, 1915, 1.

89  **critics in the press:** See, for example, *Evening World* (New York), June
15, 1915, 6.

89  **"The fleet is deteriorating":** Craig, *Josephus Daniels*, 225.

90  **"self supporting":** *Washington Times*, June 30, 1915, 5.

90  **"the natural inventive genius":** Daniels, *Wilson Era*, 491.

90  **"You will need more":** Daniels, *Wilson Era*, 491.

91 **Edison was recognized:** *Star-Gazette* (Elmira, NY), Oct. 15, 1915, 1.

91 **"I feel like a prince":** *Akron Beacon Journal*, Oct. 16, 1915, 14.

91 **"the mystery" of life:** John Burroughs, *The Breath of Life* (Boston: Houghton Mifflin, 1915), v.

92 **left the city by train:** Leon Pinkson, "Firestone Chief Due Here Today," *San Francisco Chronicle*, Oct. 20, 1915, 9.

92 **Ford was back aboard:** Ford's train stop is described in *Windsor Star* (Windsor, Ontario), Oct. 16, 1915, 1; and *Omaha Daily Bee*, Oct. 16, 1915, 1.

93 **set out for the Chronicle Building:** My description of Ford's visit to the Chronicle and the quotations that follow are from *San Francisco Chronicle*, Oct. 19, 1915, 9.

94 **schoolchildren came aboard:** *San Francisco Examiner*, Oct. 19, 1915, 4.

94 **"I believe that in time":** *San Francisco Chronicle*, Oct. 19, 1915, 9.

94 **"the dawn of vitality":** *San Francisco Examiner*, Oct. 19, 1915, 4.

95 **"Science is greater than any fairy tale":** This and the following quotations are from *San Francisco Examiner*, Oct. 19, 1915, 4.

95 **"I see you are traveling like a prima donna":** This and the following quotations are from *San Francisco Examiner*, Oct. 19, 1915, 4.

97 **"He peered into the pumps":** *San Francisco Examiner*, Oct. 20, 1915, 13.

98 **"Well . . . they are where all such things belong":** *San Francisco Chronicle*, Oct. 20, 1915, 11.

98 **a sociological exhibit:** Details of the various Ford exhibits are drawn from "Ford at the Panama-Pacific Exposition, San Francisco, 1915," Object ID 64.167.951.3, THF.

98 **"How about running some pipe?":** "The Reminiscences of Mr. Frank Vivian," Nov. 1955, 4ff, Owen W. Bombard Interviews series, 1951–1961, Acc. 56, Nov. 1953, THF.

98 **"They were holloing and shoving":** "Reminiscences of Mr. Frank Vivian," 8, THF.

99 **"They are coming out faster":** *San Francisco Chronicle*, Oct. 20, 1915, 11.

100 **"Great Scott, Ford":** *San Francisco Chronicle*, Oct. 20, 1915, 11.

100 **an array of forty-five phonograph machines:** Details of the Panama Canal exhibit are drawn from Frank Morton Todd, the Panama-Pacific International Exposition Company, and the Burndy Library. Todd, *The Story of the Exposition: Being the Official History of the International Celebration Held at San Francisco in 1915 to Commemorate the Discovery of the Pacific Ocean and the Construction of the Panama Canal* (5 vols.), vol. 2 (New York: G. P. Putnam, 1921).

100    **compared his estimate:** *San Francisco Chronicle,* Oct. 20, 1915, 11.

101    **"But both gray-haired men":** *San Francisco Examiner,* Oct. 20, 1915, 13.

101    **"From the start I found":** Thomas A. Edison, *Diary and Sundry Observations,* ed. Dagobert D. Runes (New York: Philosophical Library, 1948), 48.

102    **"The word 'Yes' is an easy one to send":** Edison, *Diary and Sundry Observations,* 55.

102    **her hand on Edison's knee:** Edison, *Diary and Sundry Observations,* 55.

102    **Tonight was different:** My account of the dinner draws on reporting in the *San Francisco Chronicle,* Oct. 20, 1915, 1.

103    **"the first time he had ever made a speech":** *San Francisco Examiner,* Oct. 20, 1915, 14.

103    **Mina stroked Edison's hand:** *San Francisco Examiner,* Oct. 20, 1915, 14.

104    **"jeweled bracelet of light":** *San Francisco Examiner,* Oct. 20, 1915, 13.

104    **"whimsical" shake of his head":** *San Francisco Examiner,* Oct. 20, 1915, 14.

104    **Once aboard the *South Dakota*:** My description of the party's visit with Admiral Fullam draws on reporting in the *San Francisco Examiner,* Oct. 21, 1915, 7.

105    **"in order to pay his respects":** *San Francisco Chronicle,* Oct. 20, 1915, 9.

106    **"This first one":** This and the following quotations are from the *San Francisco Examiner,* Oct. 22, 1915, 3.

107    **"Mr. Edison is the man of the century":** *San Francisco Chronicle,* Oct. 22, 1915, 11.

107    **"From the day that he first made":** *San Francisco Chronicle,* Oct. 22, 1915, 11.

107    **"Hello! Mr. Edison":** Edison's phone call was reported in the *San Francisco Examiner,* Oct. 22, 1915, 14.

109    **uttered the word "Die":** *San Francisco Chronicle,* Oct. 22, 1915, 5.

109    **"They'll die":** *San Francisco Examiner,* Oct. 22, 1915, 1.

110    **"The course of human history":** *New York Times,* May 27, 1915, 10.

111    **"Isn't that delicious":** *San Francisco Examiner,* Oct. 23, 1915, 5.

111    **"Let's take some and have it prepared":** *San Francisco Examiner,* Oct. 23, 1915, 5.

112    **"I intend to get at work":** *San Francisco Chronicle,* Oct. 23, 1915, 4.

113    **"Who will be the one":** Luther Burbank is quoted in Jane S. Smith, *The Garden of Invention* (New York: Penguin, 2009), 245.

114    **written simply, "Everything":** Henry Ford, with Samuel Crowther, *Edison as I Know Him* (New York: Cosmopolitan, 1930), 80.

115  **register all the moons of Jupiter:** My account of work at the observatory draws on F. J. Neubauer, "A Short History of the Lick Observatory," *Popular Astronomy*, vol. 58, no. 5, May 1950.

115  **"This is what I like to see":** *San Francisco Examiner*, Oct. 24, 1915, 10.

115  **take up the issue in their correspondence:** See, for example, William Wallace Campbell to Thomas Alva Edison, Feb. 29, 1916, Folder X162-F, Document X162V, Edison Papers.

116  **"When the fights started":** Account of Edsel's night out is drawn from "Reminiscences of Mr. Frank Vivian," 19, THF.

117  **"Have you had lunch yet?":** This account is also drawn from "Reminiscences of Mr. Frank Vivian," 14, THF.

118  **Dinner that evening:** See *San Francisco Chronicle*, Oct. 26, 1915, 5.

118  **"It has really been a wonderful vacation for me":** *San Francisco Chronicle*, Oct. 27, 1915, 3.

118  **"I don't know yet":** *San Francisco Chronicle*, Oct. 27, 1915, 3.

118  **"That suited Mr. Edison exactly":** This and the following quotations are from Harvey S. Firestone, with Samuel Crowther, *Men and Rubber* (Garden City, NY, 1926), 191, 192.

## 5. Separate Ways

121  **"my old trouble":** *Burroughs Journal*, Jan. 8, 1916.

122  **"I will do everything in my power":** This and the following quotations are from the *Free Press* interview—*Detroit Free Press*, Aug. 22, 1915, 1—which is reproduced in the *Ford Times*, vol. 9, Sep. 1915, 55–60, from which I am quoting.

123  **"It's a good joke":** *Ford Times*, vol. 9, Sep. 1915, 59.

123  **"Ford is a victim":** *Detroit Free Press*, Aug. 30, 1915, 2.

124  **"While due honor is granted":** *New-York Tribune*, Aug. 27, 1915, 3.

124  **Daniels eventually denied:** *Washington Herald*, Sep. 10, 1915, 3.

124  **Ford had come out for peace:** *Wall Street Journal*, Sep. 9, 1915, 1.

124  **"Should the statues":** *Evening Star* (Washington, D.C.), Aug. 29, 1915, 16.

124  **"The European war":** *Californian* (Salinas, CA), Oct. 18, 1915, 1.

125  **"something of the cloak-and-dagger":** Burnet Hershey, *The Odyssey of Henry Ford and the Great Peace Ship* (New York: Taplinger, 1967), 15–16.

126  **"International Jews":** Hershey, *Odyssey of Henry Ford*, 18.

127  **"time is apt to hang heavy":** *Boston Globe*, Nov. 28, 1915, 6.

127  **"thoroughly versed":** David Starr Jordan, "David Starr Jordan to

Henry Ford, January 3, 1916," *Jane Addams Digital Edition*, https:// digital.janeaddams.ramapo.edu/items/show/11438.

128    **"They have called in Thomas Edison":** *Ford Times*, vol. 9, Sep. 1915, 60.

128    **"It was very good of you":** This and the subsequent quotations are from John Burroughs to Henry Ford, Nov. 29, 1915, reproduced in Barrus, *Life and Letters*, vol. 2, 227–28.

129    **"Ford is sanguine":** Quotations here are from *Burroughs Journal*, Dec. 4, 1915.

131    **"He seemed to have a fear":** *New York Times*, Dec. 5, 1915, 1.

131    **"Tom, will you take a million dollars":** Hershey, *Odyssey of Henry Ford*, 9.

131    **"I know Edison well enough":** *New-York Tribune*, Dec. 5, 1915, 1.

131    **One group had demanded:** *Standard Union* (Brooklyn, NY), Dec. 8, 1915, 1.

132    **"the thorough preparation of the nation":** *New York Times*, Dec. 8, 1915, 4.

132    **"were inappropriate":** Hershey, *Odyssey of Henry Ford*, 120.

132    **"philosophy of life":** Hershey, *Odyssey of Henry Ford*, 122.

132    **"Guess I had better go home":** Hershey, *Odyssey of Henry Ford*, 122.

133    **"cost the price of one horse":** *Alexandria Gazette*, Dec. 23, 1915, 1.

133    **"Norway is like every other country":** *Alexandria Gazette*, Dec. 23, 1915, 1.

133    **ran a story headlined:** *New York Times*, Feb. 22, 1916, 7.

133    **a full-page advertisement appeared:** Quotations are from the *New York Times*, Feb. 23, 1916, 7.

134    **reading "war books":** *Burroughs Journal*, Mar. 1, 1916.

134    **"I am well these days":** *Burroughs Journal*, Mar. 28, 1916.

135    **"How the old days":** *Burroughs Journal*, Mar. 31, 1916.

135    **"Do not remember so many birds":** *Burroughs Journal*, Apr. 2, 1916.

135    **"Looks as if we might break":** *Burroughs Journal*, Apr. 19, 1916.

136    **"An hour's walk":** *Burroughs Journal*, Apr. 29, 1916.

136    **first bobolink of the season:** *Burroughs Journal*, May 11, 1916.

136    **"fear she is not really mending":** *Burroughs Journal*, May 26, 1916.

136    **"The tree nesting bird":** *Burroughs Journal*, June 5, 1916.

137    **"a house one could live in":** *Burroughs Journal*, June 7, 1916.

137    **"to give the impression":** For these and other details about Fair Lane, I have drawn on Lacey, *Ford: The Men and the Machine*, 149–50.

138    **"Grass and clover knee-high":** *Burroughs Journal*, June 8, 1916.

## 6. Sunburned and Full of Vim

140   **"Hope you will not disappoint"**: Telegram from Harvey Samuel Firestone to Henry Ford, Aug. 28, 1916, Folder X001B3/FX001B3CM, Edison
Papers.

141   **"We settled it"**: Samuel Crowther, "My Vacations with Ford and Edison,"
*System: The Magazine of Business*, vol. 49, no. 5, May 1926, 722.

141   **"I lived from day to day"**: *Burroughs Journal*, Sep. 29, 1916. This entry
is a summary of events from the middle of August to the end of September.

141   **"When the paper comes"**: *Burroughs Journal*, Aug. 2, 1916.

141   **"He said he was too old"**: Crowther, "My Vacations with Ford and Edison," 722.

141   **"a campers' extemporaneous village"**: *Burroughs Journal*, Aug. 29,
1916.

141   **"There was no convincing Burroughs"**: Crowther, "My Vacations with
Ford and Edison," 722.

142   **"They've been there thousands of years"**: *Roxbury Times*, Sep. 2,
1916, reproduced in *John Burroughs in Roxbury*, n.p.

144   **"Natural Places to Pass the Night"**: Ten Eyck advertisement, in *The
Official Automobile Blue Book, 1916, Volume 1: New York and Canada*
(Chicago: Automobile Blue Book Publishing Company, 1916), insert facing
p. 719.

144   **"Mr. Edison . . . who is looking"**: Quotations in the paragraph are from
the *New York Times*, Sep. 1, 1916, 9.

145   **"They had an air of possession"**: Firestone and Crowther, *Men and
Rubber*, 197.

146   **"The doctors think"**: John Burroughs et al., *In Nature's Laboratory* (Privately printed, 1916), unpaginated; the passage refers to events of August 31.

149   **"Waldorf" and . . . "Astoria"**: See, for example, *Republican-Journal*
(Ogdensburg, NY), Sep. 7, 1916, 6.

149   **"It is the largest"**: *Godey's Magazine*, vol. 107, no. 637, July 1883, 95.

150   **illuminated with electric light**: See Alfred Lee Donaldson, *A History of
the Adirondacks*, vol. 2 (New York: Century, 1921).

151   **"They take the conceit"**: Burroughs Letter, in Burroughs et al., *In
Nature's Laboratory*, n.p.

152   **"He made them interlock"**: Burroughs to Firestone and Edison, in Burroughs et al., *In Nature's Laboratory*, n.p.

153   **"a deep gash"**: *Burroughs Journal*, Sep. 29, 1916 (summary of Aug. 29–
Sep. 29).

154   **"You're a tenderfoot":** Crowther, "My Vacations with Ford and Edison," 723.

155   **"suddenly changed ends":** Quoted in Burroughs's letter to Firestone and Edison, in Burroughs et al., *In Nature's Laboratory*, n.p.

155   **to avert a railroad strike:** *New York Times*, Sep. 4, 1916, 1.

156   **"Dressed for camping":** *Malone Farmer* (Malone, NY), Sep. 6, 1916, 1.

156   **a telegram was waiting:** Telegram from Ernest Gustav Liebold to Harvey Samuel Firestone, Sep. 2, 1916, Folder X001B3-F, Document X001B3CT, Edison Papers.

156   **to spend the morning:** *Plattsburgh Daily Press*, Sep. 6, 1916, 7.

157   **underway by 8:30:** *Barre Daily Times*, Sep. 11, 1916, 7.

157   **stopped for lunch:** *Montpelier Evening Argus*, Sep. 8, 1916, 5; and *St. Albans Daily Messenger*, Sep. 8, 1916, 2.

158   **"Of the three automobiles":** *Rutland News*, Sep. 9, 1916, 4.

158   **"We took a great slice":** Burroughs Letter, in Burroughs et al., *In Nature's Laboratory*, n.p.

158   **"They were sadly in need":** *Boston Post*, Sep. 9, 1916, 12.

158   **"Burroughs never shaves":** *Boston Post*, Sep. 9, 1916, 12.

159   **Charles Dieterich estate:** The Dieterich house would in the 1960s become the site of Timothy Leary's Millbrook experimental community.

159   **"The whole party looked":** *Evening Enterprise* (Poughkeepsie, NY), Sep. 9, 1916, 1.

160   **"sunburned and full of vim":** *Buffalo Times*, Sep. 11, 1916, 5.

160   **"a good time was enjoyed":** *New York Herald*, Sep. 10, 1916, 6.

161   **"If he thought my stick was":** *Burroughs Journal*, Oct. 20, 1916.

161   **"a block away":** *Burroughs Journal*, Oct. 24, 1916.

161   **"a much stronger man":** *Burroughs Journal*, Nov. 7, 1916.

162   **"forward movement among womankind":** *New York Herald*, Oct. 25, 1916, 1.

## 7. At Sea

163   **raided by poachers:** See *Bird Lore*, vol. 18, Nov. 1916, 420.

164   **"the great bard":** *Burroughs Journal*, Sep. 27, 1883.

164   **"Woods deserted":** *Burroughs Journal*, Nov. 8, 1916.

164   **a clove-scented mixture:** *Merck's Archives*, vol. 6, Jan. 1904, 30.

164   **"as if it oiled all my machinery":** *Burroughs Journal*, Dec. 3, 1916.

165   **"I stood by her bedside":** *Burroughs Journal*, Feb. 19, 1917.

165   **"and that it would be an ideal place":** *Sun* (New York), Feb. 19, 1917, 3.

165   **meet with Milton S. Hershey:** "M. S. Hershey and Henry Ford in Cuba,"
      *Semi-Weekly New Era* (Lancaster, PA), Mar. 10, 1917, 3.

166   **constructing a railroad:** See Michael D'Antonio, *Hershey: Milton S.
      Hershey's Extraordinary Life of Wealth, Empire and Utopian Dreams* (New
      York: Simon & Schuster, 2006).

167   **like "the real thing":** *Burroughs Journal*, Feb. 22, 1917.

167   **"too fine for a Slabsider like me":** *Burroughs Journal*, Feb. 21, 1917.

167   **"coarse, dirty, ugly":** *Burroughs Journal*, Feb. 21, 1917.

167   **"What jolly, sportive creatures":** *Burroughs Journal*, Feb. 25, 1917.

167   **"Why is 'Lemon" less dignified":** Quotations in this paragraph are
      from *Burroughs Journal*, Feb. 25, 1917.

168   **"Flocks of boat-tailed grackles":** *Burroughs Journal*, Mar. 2, 1917.

168   **"the cane coming in by car-loads":** *Burroughs Journal*, Mar. 2, 1917.

169   **"We both need the publicity":** D'Antonio, *Hershey*, 166.

169   **"The paper here said":** *Burroughs Journal*, Mar. 3, 1917.

170   **"Here in this peaceful harbor":** *Burroughs Journal*, Mar. 7, 1917.

170   **"a slim, brown warbler":** *Burroughs Journal*, Mar. 8, 1917.

170   **"Capital title!":** *Burroughs Journal*, Mar. 9, 1917.

171   **"Ten days of my life":** *Burroughs Journal*, Mar. 10, 1917.

171   **"to pay tribute to Old Neptune":** *Burroughs Journal*, Mar. 11, 1917.

171   **found the speed . . . "exhilarating":** *Burroughs Journal*, Mar. 13, 1917.

171   **"Very sad, but very glad":** *Burroughs Journal*, Mar. 18, 1917.

171   **"I knew it was our last":** Clara Barrus typescript note, Burroughs 7.2,
      edited transcript of John Burroughs's Journals by Dr. Clara Barrus, p.
      989A, John Burroughs Papers, Archives and Special Collections Library,
      Vassar College Libraries.

172   **to be shipped to Florida:** Thomas Edison, handwritten note to secre-
      tary on Firestone letter, dated Jan. 15, 1917, Edison General File, E-17-69,
      Edison Papers. (Edison's replies to letters are often preserved as hand-
      written notes scrawled directly on the letters to which he is replying.)

172   **"I must confess":** Harvey Firestone to Thomas Edison, Feb. 1, 1917, Edi-
      son General File, E-17-69, Edison Papers.

173   **"my best gift today":** *Burroughs Journal*, Apr. 3, 1917.

173   **newspapers were reporting:** See, for example, *News-Pilot* (San Pedro,
      CA), Apr. 4, 1917, 3.

173   **an induction balance:** *Edison Monthly* (New York: New York Edison
      Co.), vol. 8, no. 9 (Feb. 1916), 335.

175 **"The buoy . . . contains tables":** Lloyd N. Scott, *Naval Consulting Board of the United States* (Washington, D.C.: U.S. Government Printing Office, 1920), 172.

175 **"While watching in the daytime":** Scott, *Naval Consulting Board*, 173.

177 **make the United States appear weak:** Josephus Daniels and Edmund David Cronon, *The Cabinet Diaries of Josephus Daniels, 1913–1921* (Lincoln: University of Nebraska Press, 1963), 191.

177 **went on to detail schemes:** See Daniels and Cronon, *Cabinet Diaries*, 193ff.

177 **more overtly offensive schemes:** Scott, *Naval Consulting Board*, 184.

178 **"Edison full of subject":** Daniels and Cronon, *Cabinet Diaries*, 222.

179 **uncharacteristically "severe":** Daniels and Cronon, *Cabinet Diaries*, 240. Daniels describes the officer as "Wiley Fort of Pikeville of the Confederate navy."

180 **"wearing it in a closed room":** Scott, *Naval Consulting Board*, 183.

180 **statement warning of "riot and anarchy":** *Poughkeepsie Eagle*, Feb. 24, 1917, 1.

181 **U-boat net was tightening:** See, for example, "Rochester Sunk," *New York Times*, Nov. 9, 1917, 8.

181 **"It is believed that most":** "All Hope Abandoned for Alcedo Missing," *New York Times*, Nov. 9, 1917, 8.

182 **"so as to take full advantage":** Frank A. Cianflone, "The Eagle Boats of World War I," *Proceedings of the U.S. Naval Institute*, vol. 99/6/844, June 1973, 74.

182 **Armament included:** See Cianflone, "Eagle Boats," 76, 78.

182 **"the crying need of this hour":** Cianflone, "Eagle Boats," 76.

182 **"this dripping, almost sunless spring":** John Burroughs to Thomas Edison, June 12, 1917, Edison General File, E-17-69, Edison Papers.

183 **"For sometime past":** Thomas Edison to John Burroughs, June 16, 1917, Edison General File, E-17-69, Edison Papers.

183 **"I was in Pittsburgh yesterday":** Harvey Firestone to Thomas Edison, July 14, 1917, Edison General File, E-17-69, Edison Papers.

184 **story was . . . "a fake":** Thomas Edison, handwritten note on Firestone's letter of July 14, 1917, Edison General File, E-17-69, Edison Papers.

184 **"very anxious to get out":** Harvey Firestone to Thomas Edison, July 30, 1917, Edison General File, E-17-69, Edison Papers.

184 **might be able to join them:** Thomas Edison to Harvey Firestone, Aug. 1, 1917, Edison General File, E-17-69, Edison Papers.

185 **"At last minute I find it impossible"**: Thomas Edison, handwritten note, Aug. 18, 1917, Edison General File, E-17-69, Edison Papers.

185 **"I often wish I had never seen"**: *Burroughs Journal*, Sep. 19, 1917.

## 8. A Great Slice of Our Geography

186 **"When the river first freezes over"**: *Burroughs Journal*, Jan. 2, 1918.

186 **"More easily tired"**: *Burroughs Journal*, Jan. 1, 1918.

187 **"very little wildlife"**: *Burroughs Journal*, Mar. 1, 1918.

187 **"All day we hear the boom"**: *Burroughs Journal*, Mar. 1, 1918.

188 **"Such a clean and salubrious land"**: *Burroughs Journal*, Mar. 12, 1918.

188 **"Memory's geese"**: Clara Barrus note to *Burroughs Journal* entry, Mar. 12, 1918.

188 **"Mr. Edison expects to make a trip"**: W. H. Meadowcraft to W. D. Wirt, July 30, 1918, Edison General File, E-18-12, Edison Papers.

188 **a copy of the *Automobile Blue Book***: See handwritten note, July 30, 1918, Edison General File, E-18-14, Edison Papers.

189 **Fred Ott wrote to Firestone**: F. Ott to H. S. Firestone, July 31, 1918, Edison General File, E-18-14, Edison Papers.

189 **Firestones' car rolled over**: *Akron Evening Times*, July 31, 1918, 1.

190 **"It distresses me"**: Telegram from Josephus Daniels to Thomas Alva Edison, Aug. 5, 1918, Edison General File, E-18-14, Edison Papers.

190 **caught the afternoon boat**: Western Union Telegram, John Burroughs to Thomas Edison, Aug. 15, 1918, Edison General File, E-18-14, Edison Papers.

190 **"furious speeds" it made possible**: John Burroughs, *Our Vacation Days of 1918* (Akron, OH: n.p., 1920), unpaginated.

191 **"an opportunity to note"**: Lincoln Highway Association, *The Complete Official Road Guide of the Lincoln Highway* (Detroit: Lincoln Highway Association, 1918), 39.

191 **turned down an officer's commission**: *Kansas City Kansan*, Aug. 17, 1918, 3.

192 **"Mr. Edison, I want the privilege"**: *Gettysburg Times*, Aug. 17, 1918, 1.

193 **"at the foot of those long, winding"**: This account and the following quotations are drawn from John Burroughs, "A Strenuous Holiday," in *Under the Maples* (Boston: Houghton Mifflin, 1921), 110, 111, 112.

196 **"We have about 300 women"**: This and the following quotations are from *Pittsburgh Post-Gazette*, Aug. 18, 1918, 1, 2.

198 **"You can get back by railroad":** Thomas Edison to Edward Hurley, Aug. 6, 1918, Edison General File, E-18-14, Edison Papers.

199 **join the "distinguished group":** Edward Hurley to Thomas Edison, Aug. 6, 1918, 5:34 p.m., Edison General File, E-18-14, Edison Papers.

199 **"when the sun begins to shine":** Quotations in this paragraph are from *Pittsburgh Post-Gazette*, Aug. 19, 1918, 2, 1.

200 **Clara Ford had hired Sato:** See Ford R. Bryan, *Clara: Mrs. Henry Ford* (Detroit: Wayne State University Press, 2001). The receipt Clara Ford received for her purchase of a referral for Mr. Sato is in the collection of the Benson Ford Research Center, THF.

201 **Sato had garnered a reputation:** "The Reminiscences of Dr. W. H. Alexander," Oct. 1956, p. 26, Oral History Section, FMCA.

201 **"I will be glad to let you camp":** Edward Hurley, *The Bridge to France* (Philadelphia: Lippincott, 1927), 227.

202 **"The camp was in an ideal place":** Burroughs, "Strenuous Holiday," 112. Also quoted in Hurley, *Bridge to France*, 229.

202 **Firestone pronounced "delicious":** Harvey S. Firestone, "Roughing It with My Good Friends, Messrs. Edison, Ford, Burroughs, Hurley, De Loach, and My Son, Harvey," Edison Family Records, Edison Papers, p. 1 (hereafter *Firestone Narrative*).

203 **"How . . . could we help freeing our minds":** Hurley, *Bridge to France*, 230.

203 **"Building new ships":** Quotations in this paragraph are from Hurley, *Bridge to France*, 45, 48, 49.

204 **"An Eagle a Day Keeps the Kaiser Away":** Lacey, *Ford: The Men and the Machine*, 158.

205 **"as if they were just so many 'Flivvers'":** Frank Parker Stockbridge, "Warships Built While You Wait," *New York Times*, July 7, 1917, Section 3, 1.

205 **"No man wanted to do his bit":** Hurley, *Bridge to France*, 225.

205 **"Hurley, why did that farmer hesitate":** The dialogue appears in Hurley, *Bridge to France*, 228–29.

206 **reporting this anecdote:** See, for example, "Burroughs Saves the Day," *Public Opinion* (Chambersburg, PA), Aug. 22, 1918, 3; and "Brains on Tour on Motor Truck," *Washington Times*, Aug. 21, 1918, 8.

207 **"Just because he was insistent":** Hurley, *Bridge to France*, 228.

207 **"He was as nimble and lively":** Hurley, *Bridge to France*, 228.

207 **"Folding cots":** Burroughs, "Strenuous Holiday," 112–13.

209 **his friend's "mechanical genius":** *Firestone Narrative*, 2.

209 **"shook their heads":** Burroughs, "Strenuous Holiday," 113.

209 **"I can understand why"**: Hurley, *Bridge to France*, 231.

210 **oversaw the necessary repairs**: *Pittsburgh Press*, Aug. 21, 1918, 4.

211 **"I will join you in anything"**: *Firestone Narrative*, 2.

212 **"dared" anyone present**: *Pittsburgh Post-Gazette*, Aug. 21, 1918, 4. Newspaper accounts of this evening report that the cigar was Ford's, but given his opposition to smoking, that is almost certainly wrong. Although Edison shared Ford's antipathy toward cigarettes, he did enjoy the occasional cigar.

212 **"You can't kick that"**: *Daily News* (Lebanon, PA), Aug. 22, 1918, 6.

212 **"calmly landed his shoe"**: The story and accompanying quotations are from *Pittsburgh Post-Gazette*, Aug. 21, 1918, 4.

213 **the campers paused**: See photo in Norman Brauer, *There to Breathe the Beauty* (Dalton, PA: Norman Brauer, 1995), 69.

214 **two surveying teams**: This story is recounted in the *Official Automobile Blue Book, 1918, Volume 3: New Jersey, Pennsylvania, Maryland, Delaware, District of Columbia, Northern Virginia and W. Virginia* (New York: Automobile Blue Book Publishing Company, 1918), 717.

215 **"shining eyes"**: Burroughs, "Strenuous Holiday," 115.

215 **"This displeased Mr. Ford"**: *Firestone Narrative*, 3.

216 **"very winding and hilly roads"**: *Official Automobile Blue Book, 1918, Volume 3*, 841.

216 **"the rough, grassy margin"**: Burroughs, "Strenuous Holiday," 114.

217 **"wild Nature"**: Burroughs, "Strenuous Holiday," 114.

217 **"the fall was complete"**: *Firestone Narrative*, 3. The emphasis is Firestone's.

217 **"a very rough looking crowd"**: *Firestone Narrative*, 3.

217 **"Thereupon . . . we went out"**: *Firestone Narrative*, 4.

218 **world's largest train set**: See photo in Brauer, *There to Breathe the Beauty*, 74–75.

219 **"If it was mine"**: *John Burroughs Talks*, 298.

220 **"large, clear mountain trout-brook"**: Burroughs, "Strenuous Holiday," 116.

220 **"Every mountain we crossed"**: Burroughs, "Strenuous Holiday," 116.

221 **established a makeshift courthouse**: See Homer Floyd Fansler, *History of Tucker County, West Virginia* (Parsons, WV: McClain, 1962).

222 **"She had been on a train"**: Burroughs, "Strenuous Holiday," 115.

223 **"Ford is our greatest drawing card"**: Barrus, *Life and Letters*, vol. 2, 280.

223 **elliptical leaf springs**: See *Horseless Age: The Automobile Trade Magazine*, vol. 38, Dec. 1, 1916, for more on the Simplex suspension.

224 **on the road again:** *Firestone Narrative,* 4.

224 **"While we were happy to see him":** *Firestone Narrative,* 5.

225 **"the old-time campers":** *Firestone Narrative,* 5.

226 **"They were not rubbed down":** Quotations in the paragraph are from Burroughs, "Strenuous Holiday," 117.

227 **"a splendid place":** *Firestone Narrative,* 5.

227 **"applicable to a wide range of diseases":** *Highland Recorder* (Monterey, VA), Aug. 9, 1918, 4.

228 **"We went up to the hotel":** *Firestone Narrative,* 5.

228 **"Before you do anything these days":** *Evening Public Ledger* (Philadelphia), Aug. 22, 1918, 8.

229 **"so we took great care":** *Firestone Narrative,* 5.

229 **"holding his hand in front of his face":** Barrus, *Life and Letters,* vol. 2, 279.

229 **"What scenery we have beheld!":** Barrus, *Life and Letters,* vol. 2, 279.

231 **"we had this bread":** *Firestone Narrative,* 6.

231 **"are several springs whose waters":** *Automobile Blue Book, 1918, Volume 6: Southeastern States,* 308.

232 **dangled his feet in the water:** See photo in Brauer, *There to Breathe the Beauty,* 82.

232 **"a gentleman," as Firestone saw him:** *Firestone Narrative,* 6.

232 **"Match King," O. C. Barber:** For details of Barber's biography and business operations, see Quentin R. Skrabec Jr., *Rubber: An American Industrial History* (Jefferson, NC: McFarland, 2014).

233 **"the most modern plant in the south":** *Firestone Narrative,* 6.

234 **"It is the most popular resort":** *Automobile Blue Book, 1918, Volume 3,* 546.

235 **"probably brought on by Spanish influenza":** *New York Times,* Aug. 16, 1918, 6.

236 **"just like most of the other ills":** *New-York Tribune,* Aug. 22, 1918, 12.

236 **"will chalk up one more":** *Philadelphia Inquirer,* Aug. 23, 1918, 10.

236 **"not to kiss except":** *Adams County Independent* (Littlestown, PA), Aug. 23, 1918, 5.

236 **"probably the best fed persons":** *St. Albans Weekly Messenger,* Aug. 22, 1918, 5.

236 **"The person who sleeps":** Quoted in Ralph Parlette, *Pockets and Paradises* (Chicago: Parlette-Padget, 1922), 225.

236 **"Most of their energies":** Edison, *Diary and Sundry Observations,* 178.

237 **"Most of our physical ills":** *John Burroughs Talks,* 293.

237  **not sure eggs were good for you:** *John Burroughs Talks*, 294, 295.

237  **"whether unsuitable food":** *John Burroughs Talks*, 294.

237  **"I think this theory":** Edison, "What Is Life," 150.

238  **designed by Thomas Jefferson:** See Ed Robinson, *Historic Inns of Southern West Virginia* (Charleston, SC: Arcadia, 2007).

238  **"looked as if the frogs had been bathing":** *Firestone Narrative*, 7.

239  **"rough and uncivilized":** *Firestone Narrative*, 7.

240  **"After a week of motoring":** Quotations here and in next paragraph are from John Burroughs to Clara Ford, handwritten letter, Wolf Camp, West Va., Aug. 25 [1918], Acc. 1, Fair Lane Papers, Box 111, 106-G-1, Folder 111-2, THF.

241  **"Your best friend is the one":** See photograph in [Letters], Acc. 1, Fair Lane Papers, Box 111, 106-G-1, THF.

242  **"Sato was not in a good humor":** *Firestone Narrative*, 7.

244  **small, enclosed valley:** *Clinch Valley News* (Tazewell, VA), Aug. 30, 1918, 4.

244  **"I gave Harvey a lesson":** *Firestone Narrative*, 8.

245  **"the only man in Michigan":** Quotations here and in next paragraph are from Watts, *People's Tycoon*, 243.

245  **"presence of business men":** *New-York Tribune*, May 19, 1918, 10.

246  **"to become our party candidate":** *Atlanta Constitution*, June 13, 1918, 1.

246  **"Republican in his leanings":** The *Brooklyn Eagle* dispatch is quoted in the *Washington Post*, July 15, 1918, 2.

246  **"My father is too busy":** *Wichita Beacon*, July 18, 1918, 7.

247  **"What do you want to do that for?"; "I'm too deaf":** *John Burroughs Talks*, 337.

247  **"It isn't what you hear":** Burroughs, *Vacation Days*, n.p.

247  **"But if I did go"; "That's so":** *John Burroughs Talks*, 337.

247  **paid a visit to a farm:** *Clinch Valley News* (Tazewell, VA), Aug. 30, 1918, 4.

248  **"the Germans had built the road":** *Firestone Narrative*, 8.

248  **at the Hotel Bristol:** Firestone, in his account of the trip, says the party lunched at a "Hotel Virginia," but newspaper reports make it clear that this was in fact the Hotel Bristol.

249  **"I think he cooked the meal himself":** *Firestone Narrative*, 9.

249  **"tanks, submarine chasers and Liberty motors":** "Thomas Edison and Henry Ford Are Visitors Here," *Bristol Herald Courier*, Aug. 27, 1918, 3.

250  **called the automaker "disloyal":** George Harvey, *North American Review's War Weekly*, vol. 1, no. 31, Aug. 10, 1918, 1.

250  **"I do not know the gentleman":** Quotations in this paragraph are from

"Thomas Edison and Henry Ford Are Visitors Here," *Bristol Herald Courier*, Aug. 27, 1918, 3.

251 **"Mr. Ford always thinks":** Burroughs, "Strenuous Holiday," 122.

251 **"One plant will turn out":** All quotations in the paragraph are from *Knoxville Sentinel*, Aug. 27, 1918, 10.

251 **invitation to inspect a farm:** *Johnson City Staff*, Aug. 26, 1918, 1.

252 **"one of the best tracts of land":** "Edison and Ford Visit Maplehurst," *Bristol Herald Courier*, Aug. 27, 1918, 3.

252 **the town's leading citizens:** *Johnson City Staff*, Aug. 27, 1918, 5.

253 **"to pitch their tents"; "to shake hands":** *Johnson City Staff*, Aug. 27, 1918, 3.

253 **"His father . . . had said":** *Firestone Narrative*, 10.

253 **was later offered five dollars:** *Johnson City Staff*, Aug. 27, 1918, 3.

253 **"Mr. Ford," he asked:** *Johnson City Staff*, Aug. 27, 1918, 3.

257 **"Sonny," he asked:** There were several versions of this story in circulation at the time. See, for example, *Johnson City Staff*, Aug. 28, 1918, 8; and *Journal and Tribune* (Knoxville, TN), Aug. 28, 1918, 5.

257 **Another local boy:** *Johnson City Staff*, Aug. 29, 1918, 8.

258 **first abolitionist organ in the country:** Oliver Perry Temple, *East Tennessee and the Civil War* (Cincinnati: R. Clarke, 1899), 91.

258 **his law practice there in the county court:** See Thomas Edward Watson, *The Life and Times of Andrew Jackson* (Thomson, GA: Jeffersonian Publishing, 1912), 49ff.

258 **ghost of Jackson:** See Charles Edwin Price, *Haunted Jonesborough* (Johnson City, TN: Overmountain, 1993), 25.

258 **"big folks are easy to get to":** *Journal and Tribune* (Knoxville, TN), Aug. 28, 1918, 5.

259 **"Everyone was happy":** *Firestone Narrative*, 11.

260 **"gasless Sunday" policy:** *Topeka Daily Capital*, Aug. 28, 1918, 8.

260 **"Irish bridges":** Burroughs, "Strenuous Holiday," 120.

261 **"explained how greatly we regretted":** *Firestone Narrative*, 12.

262 **"She was more interested in Mr. Burroughs":** *Firestone Narrative*, 13.

262 **"I had forgotten it was today":** *Journal and Tribune* (Knoxville, TN), Aug. 28, 1918, 5.

262 **"I will pitch a penny":** *Asheville Citizen-Times*, Aug. 28, 1918, 3.

264 **"suggestive of Old Heidelberg":** "German Prisoners in America," *Asheville Citizen Times*, Mar. 3, 1918, 13. This richly descriptive full-page article provides the details that follow.

265 **"those that one might hear":** "German Prisoners in America," 13.

265   **"They all looked well-kept":** *Firestone Narrative*, 13.

266   **"I took no chances":** *Firestone Narrative*, 13.

267   **"in his gallant way":** *Firestone Narrative*, 14.

267   **"had been specially talcumed":** *Asheville Citizen-Times*, Aug. 28, 1918, 1.

267   **"probably the largest reception":** *Firestone Narrative*, 14.

267   **"Firestone, you make a speech":** *Firestone Narrative*, 14.

267   **"the greatest man in the scientific world":** Quotations from *Asheville Citizen-Times*, Aug. 28, 1918, 3, 1.

268   **leaving the Model T abandoned:** *Asheville Citizen-Times*, Aug. 29, 1918, 12.

268   **"pretty rough":** *Asheville Citizen-Times*, Aug. 28, 1918, 1.

268   **"Man's foolishness":** *Asheville Citizen-Times*, Aug. 28, 1918, 3.

269   **"beached his ark of peace":** *Greensboro Daily News*, Aug. 28, 1918, 1.

269   **"The only soldier":** *Billings Gazette*, Aug. 28, 1918, 4.

269   **"I don't believe in the flag":** *Atlanta Constitution*, Aug. 28, 1918, 7.

269   **"had made no such statement":** *Asheville Citizen-Times*, Aug. 29, 1918, 12.

269   **"he was most congenial":** *Firestone Narrative*, 14.

270   **"a high-class line of films":** *Firestone Narrative*, 14.

270   **Seely had built it:** For details and photographs of Seely's estate, see Sue Greenberg and Jan Kahn, *Asheville: Vol. 1, A Postcard History* (Dover, NH: Arcadia, 1997), 99.

271   **Edison took his place:** The departure of the party is described in the *News Leader* (Staunton, VA), Aug. 31, 1918, 8.

271   **"Both Victor and Vanquished":** *Lansing State Journal*, Aug. 28, 1918, 1.

272   **offered to donate one:** *Twin-City Daily Sentinel* (Winston-Salem, NC), Aug. 30, 1918, 14.

272   **take home a specimen:** *Winston-Salem Journal*, Aug. 30, 1918, 2.

272   **Edison's theories:** See Thomas A. Edison to C. P. Bollman, Aug. 15, 1918, Edison General Files, E-18-20, Edison Papers.

272   **a set of dentures made:** *Firestone Narrative*, 17.

273   **"They were doing much good":** *Firestone Narrative*, 17.

275   **"happy thoughts":** *Firestone Narrative*, 19.

275   **"beauties and wonders":** This and subsequent quotations are from Barrus, *Life and Letters*, vol. 2, 281, 280.


### Epilogue

280   **"Mr. Ford is a splendid man":** *Lake County Star* (Chase, MI), excerpted in *American Economist*, July 1918, 27.

280   **"Ford Is an Anarchist":** *Chicago Tribune,* June 23, 1916, 6.

281   **"Has Henry Ford ever heard of":** *Fort Wayne Sentinel,* July 17, 1919, 4.

281   **"Henry Ford, sitting in court":** Quoted in Watts, *People's Tycoon,* 271.

281   **"You have done more good":** This letter and several others like it are reproduced in Watts, *People's Tycoon,* 270.

281   **as jurors sat listening:** *Greeneville News* (Greeneville, TN), Aug. 5, 1919, 3.

282   **"being allowed to escape unharnessed":** *Buffalo News,* June 26, 1923, 19.

282   **the power plant and factory would be in operation:** My description of the power plant and factory draws on sources including *Engineering News Record,* vol. 88, no. 1, Jan. 5, 1922, 24; and *Ford News,* vol. 2, no. 22, June 22, 1923, 1, 5.

284   **"For beauty":** Quoted in John Tobin, "Henry Ford and His Village Industries in Southeastern Michigan," unpublished thesis, 1985, Eastern Michigan University, Ypsilanti, 31.

284   **turbines visible to passersby:** Tobin, "Henry Ford," 32.

284   **"We built these plants to run":** Tobin, "Henry Ford," 30.

284   **employed 1,500 workers:** *Pittsburgh Press,* Nov. 8, 1988, 34.

284   **increased to 48 megawatts:** U.S. Federal Energy Regulatory Commission, Green Island Power Authority, Project No. 13-023 Order Issuing New License, Aug. 17, 2012.

285   **"Not any drift boulders":** *Burroughs Journal,* Aug. 13, 1919.

286   **"If we could only tree all the multimillionaires":** *Burroughs Journal,* Aug. 7, 1919.

286   **"clasp him firmly":** *Staunton Daily Leader,* Dec. 17, 1912, 7.

286   **"He told us, among scores of":** *Burroughs Journal,* Aug. 13, 1919.

286   **"Mr. Ford attributes all evil":** *Burroughs Journal,* Aug. 7, 1919.

287   **"My folks didn't cultivate":** *John Burroughs Talks,* 11.

287   **"Well, if he'd gone up the road":** *John Burroughs Talks,* 309.

288   **"small and slight":** Charles Francis Adams, *Chapters of Erie, and Other Essays* (New York: H. Holt, 1886), 105. Note: It is widely reported that Adams elsewhere referred to Gould as a "complex Jew," but this is a misreading of a passage in *The Education of Henry Adams* in which Adams, again struggling to understand the gold conspiracy, writes of President Grant that "neither Jay Gould nor any other astute American mind—still less the complex Jew—could ever have accustomed itself to the incredible and inexplicable lapses of Grant's intelligence." Henry Adams and Henry Cabot Lodge, *The Education of Henry Adams: An Autobiography* (Boston: Houghton Mifflin, 1918), 272.

288   **"plain facts"**: H. S. Firestone to E. G. Liebold, Jan. 20, 1919, Acc. 1, Fair Lane Papers, Folder 121-3, THF.

288   **"economy, service and practicability"**: Firestone to Liebold, Jan. 20, 1919, THF.

289   **"Take the paper as a whole"**: Typewritten letter from Thomas Edison to E. G. Liebold, Jan. 17, 1919, Acc. 1, Fair Lane Papers, Folder 121-3, THF.

289   **"It is surprisingly good"**: Typewritten letter from John Burroughs to E. G. Liebold, Jan. 17, 1919, Acc. 1, Fair Lane Papers, Folder 121-3, THF.

289   **"the decisive anti-Semitic book"**: Schirach is quoted in Max Wallace, *The American Axis: Henry Ford, Charles Lindbergh, and the Rise of the Third Reich* (New York: St. Martin's, 2003), 42.

290   **"Ford's friends and associates"**: Wallace, *American Axis*, 17, 18.

290   **"He inveighs against cane sugar"**: Quotations in this and the next paragraph are from *Burroughs Journal*, Aug. 7 and Aug. 4, 1919.

291   **"they had been beaten all over"**: Alfred W. Crosby, *America's Forgotten Pandemic: The Influenza of 1918*, 2d ed. (New York: Cambridge University Press, 2003), 39. Crosby's richly researched account of the 1918 pandemic informs much of this paragraph.

291   **"German submarines have traversed"**: *Philadelphia Inquirer*, Sep. 19, 1918, 1.

291   **"As soon as through marching"**: *Chicago Tribune*, Oct. 13, 1918, 17.

291   **five thousand Chicagoans would die of the flu**: See chart in Crosby, *America's Forgotten Pandemic*, 60.

292   **killed nearly 675,000 Americans**: Crosby, *America's Forgotten Pandemic*, 206.

292   **"cosmic origin"**: *Burroughs Journal*, Aug. 13, 1919.

292   **began manufacturing ventilators**: David E. Sanger, Zolan Kanno-Youngs, and Ana Swanson, "Slow Response to the Coronavirus Measured in Lost Opportunity," *New York Times*, Mar. 25, 2020, 9.

293   **"I was astounded at the knowledge"**: Firestone and Crowther, *Men and Rubber*, 222.

293   **had "no doubt"**: Quoted in Mark R. Finlay, *Growing American Rubber: Strategic Plants and the Politics of National Security* (New Brunswick, NJ: Rutgers University Press, 2009), 76.

294   **"sprung from our own country"**: Harvey S. Firestone Jr., *The Romance and Drama of the Rubber Industry* (Akron, OH: Firestone Tire and Rubber Company, 1932), 104.

294   **"unique little republic"**: Firestone, *Romance and Drama*, 101.

294   **some 375,000 tons of rubber**: *Baltimore Sun*, Mar. 3, 1928, 2.

295    **underlining key passages:** See Finlay, *Growing American Rubber*, 59.

295    **was "having good luck":** Finlay, *Growing American Rubber*, 59.

296    **"With his accustomed thoroughness":** William Meadowcroft, quoted in Olav Thulesius, *Edison in Florida: The Green Laboratory* (Gainesville: University Press of Florida, 1997), 89.

296    **"the extraction of rubber":** "Processes for Recovering Rubber from Natural Rubber Latex," U.S. Patent 1,740,079A, Dec. 1929.

296    **"to convince the Federal Government":** A. G. Batchelder to Thomas A. Edison, Aug. 28, 1918, Edison General Files, E-18-06, Edison Papers.

297    **"It is my opinion":** Thomas A. Edison to A. G. Batchelder, Sep. 4, 1918, Edison General Files, E-18-06, Edison Papers.

297    **Eisenhower . . . transcontinental convoy:** For details of Eisenhower's experiences, see Memorandum from Lt. Col. Dwight D. Eisenhower to the Chief, Motor Transport Corps, with attached report on the Trans-Continental Trip, Nov. 3, 1919, DDE's Records as President, President's Personal File, Box 967, 1075 Greany Maj. William C., NAID #1055071, Eisenhower Presidential Library.

298    **"Christmas is always":** *Burroughs Journal*, Dec. 25, 1918.

298    **"I trust I shall get much good":** *Burroughs Journal*, Dec. 25, 1918.

298    **"Hope we shall get on well together":** *Burroughs Journal*, Dec. 28, 1918.

299    **"The little beast":** *John Burroughs Talks*, 349.

299    **"The donkey is no good":** *John Burroughs Talks*, 349.

300    **"dumped off the train":** Ford, *Edison as I Know Him*, 122.

300    **"I had found an ax":** Trine and Ford, *Power That Wins*, 153.

301    **"October 26, 1920. Leave Today":** These last words are as attested by Burroughs's Roxbury neighbor Oliver A. MacLaury in *John Burroughs in Roxbury*, n.p.

302    **died, outside Kingston, Ohio:** Details here are from *New York Times*, Mar. 30, 1921, 9.

302    **"beside the rock on the hill":** Reproduced in *John Burroughs in Roxbury*, n.p.

302    **all present at the funeral:** *Beatrice Daily Sun* (Beatrice, NE), Apr. 3, 1921, 1.

302    **"There was no sadness":** Ford and Crowther, *My Life and Work*, 239.

302    **"Life seems worth living again":** *Burroughs Journal*, Feb. 4, 1921.

303    **"Henry was a man of sudden impulse":** Clancy and Davies, *Believer*, 160.

303    **"Mr. Ford has enough":** Clancy and Davies, *Believer*, 159.

303   **"Yes, he's a remarkable man":** *Chicago Tribune*, Feb. 12, 1922, 7.

303   **"Ford missed the quartet":** John Côté Dahlinger and Frances Spatz Leighton, *The Secret Life of Henry Ford* (Indianapolis: Bobbs-Merrill, 1978), 143.

304   **"dilatory and meandering":** The quotations here and in the following paragraphs are from *Burroughs Journal*, Sep. 1, 1911.

305   **"My faith as a naturalist":** *Burroughs Journal*, Feb. 20, 1920.

# Selected Bibliography

In addition to the sources enumerated below, the narrative draws upon hundreds of newspaper reports; these are cited individually in the notes, as are individual documents from archival sources.

## Archival Sources
### The Henry Ford (Dearborn, MI)

Acc. 1, Fair Lane Papers, Box 111, 106-G-1

Acc. 1, Box 14 (includes, in addition to camping notes, jacket of Oxford edition of Emerson's *Essays*, with page numbers noted by Henry Ford)

Acc. 1, Box 34 (in addition to notes on various Ford residences, contains material related to Henry Ford's reading habits)

Acc. 1, Box 104 (includes Panama–Pacific Exposition materials)

Acc. 1, Box 112 (material related to Luther Burbank, Thomas Edison, Harvey Firestone)

Acc. 1, Box 121 [1917–1919] (includes letters from John Burroughs, Thomas Edison, and Harvey Firestone concerning the *Dearborn Independent*)

Acc. 1, Box 135 (material related to Ford's Peace Ship)

Acc. 1, Oversize Box 193 (Peace Ship)

Acc. 62, Box 80, Camping trip 1918

Acc 62, Box 80, Camping trip 1919

Acc. 423, Box 1, "Camping Thesis: The Four Vagabonds," by B. Johnson, Dartmouth College, 44 pages with sources and bibliography

Acc. 1660, Boxes 64, 65; Acc. 34: Topical Albums for Henry Ford (contain annotated photographs that provide details about trip atmosphere, visitors, and itinerary)

Vertical File: Ford, Henry—Camping (contains several folders that collect correspondence, clippings, and other material related to Ford's camping trips, including information about participants and vehicles)

"Our Happy Days of 1919 and 1920" (a typewritten reminiscence of two camping trips, most likely by Harvey Firestone)

"Reminiscences of Dr. W. H. Alexander," Oct. 1956, Oral History Section, Ford Motor Company Archives

"Reminiscences of Mr. W. L. Hughson," Apr. 1955, Oral History Section, Ford Motor Company Archives

"Reminiscences of Mr. F. W. Loskowske," Nov. 1951, Oral History Section, Ford Motor Company Archives

"Reminiscences of Mr. C. J. Smith," Owen W. Bombard Interviews Series, 1951–1961, Acc. 65, Nov. 1951

"Reminiscences of Mr. Frank Vivian," Owen W. Bombard Interviews Series, 1951–1961, Acc. 56, Nov. 1953


### Berg Collection, New York Public Library (New York, NY)

John Burroughs, Holograph and Typewritten Notebook [1918]–1921


### Thomas A. Edison Papers, Rutgers University (New Brunswick, NJ)

Edison General File Series Reel 269:
    E-15-37, Exhibitions
    E-15-60, Naval Consulting Board
    E-16-63, Personal
    E-17-69, Personal
    E-17-82, Submarines
    E-18-06, Automobiles
    E-18-12, Map Request
    E-18-14, Camping Trip (1918)
    E-18-20, Cigarettes
    Vagabond Letters, 1917
Edison Family Records Series Reel 284:
    Harvey S. Firestone, "Roughing It with My Good Friends, Messrs. Edison,

Ford, Burroughs, Hurley, De Loach, and My Son, Harvey." (This account of the 1918 trip, which Firestone "dictated from memory" and sent to Edison, is cited in the notes as *Firestone Narrative*.)

## Archives and Special Collections, Vassar College Library (Poughkeepsie, NY)

John Burroughs Papers, Series I. Writings: Journals and Notebooks
  8.8, Entries for June 1, 1910–Dec. 31, 1912
  9.1, Entries for Jan. 1, 1913–Jan. 6, 1916
  9.2, Entries for Jan. 7, 1916–Sep. 4, 1917
  9.3, Entries for Sep. 6, 1917–July 2, 1919
  9.4, Entries for July 3, 1919–Feb. 4, 1921

References are cited in the notes as *Burroughs Journal*, with the date of the entry.

## Published Sources

Ackley, Laura A. *San Francisco's Jewel City: The Panama–Pacific International Exposition of 1915*. Berkeley, CA: Heyday, 2015.

Adams, Charles Francis. *Chapters of Erie, and Other Essays*. New York: H. Holt, 1886.

Adams, Henry, and Henry Cabot Lodge. *The Education of Henry Adams: An Autobiography*. Boston: Houghton Mifflin, 1918.

Albion, Michele Wehrwein. *The Florida Life of Thomas Edison*. Gainesville: University Press of Florida, 2008.

Baldwin, Neil. *Edison, Inventing the Century*. 1st ed. New York: Hyperion, 1995.

———. *Henry Ford and the Jews: The Mass Production of Hate*. New York: PublicAffairs, 2003.

Banning, Pierson Worrall. *Maker, Man and Matter*. Los Angeles: International Book Concern, 1924.

Barr, James Adam, Joseph M. Cumming, Oscar H. Fernbach, and C. C. Moore, eds. *The Legacy of the Exposition: Interpretation of the Intellectual and Moral Heritage Left to Mankind by the World Celebration at San Francisco in 1915*. San Francisco: Printed for the Exposition by J. H. Nash, 1916.

Barrus, Clara. *John Burroughs, Boy and Man*. Garden City, NY: Doubleday, Page, 1920.

———. *The Life and Letters of John Burroughs*. Boston: Houghton Mifflin, 1925.

———. *Our Friend John Burroughs*. Boston: Houghton Mifflin, 1914.

Beeson, Emma Burbank. *The Early Life and Letters of Luther Burbank*. San Francisco: Harr Wagner, 1927.

Belasco, Warren James. *Americans on the Road: From Autocamp to Motel, 1910–1945*. Cambridge, MA: MIT Press, 1979.

Brauer, Norman. *There to Breathe the Beauty*. Dalton, PA: Norman Brauer Publications, 1995.

Buck, Glen. *Quirks and Quadrates*. Chicago: Buck & Hammesfahr, 1919.

———. *Trademark Power: An Expedition into an Unprobed and Inviting Wilderness*. Chicago: Munroe & Southworth, 1916.

Burbank, Luther, and Luther Burbank Company. "The Burbank Seed Book." Santa Rosa, CA: Luther Burbank Company, 1913.

Burroughs, John. *Accepting the Universe*. Boston: Houghton Mifflin, 1920.

———. *The Breath of Life*. Boston: Houghton Mifflin, 1915.

———. *Camping and Tramping with Roosevelt*. Boston: Houghton Mifflin, 1907.

———. *Field and Study*. Boston: Houghton Mifflin, 1919.

———. *The Last Harvest*. Boston: Houghton Mifflin, 1922.

———. *The Summit of the Years*. Boston: Houghton Mifflin, 1913.

———. *Time and Change*. Boston: Houghton Mifflin, 1912.

———. *Under the Maples*. Boston: Houghton Mifflin, 1921.

Burroughs, John, and Julian Burroughs. *My Boyhood*. Garden City, NY: Doubleday, Page, 1922.

Burroughs, John, with Harvey S. Firestone, Thomas A. Edison, and Henry Ford. *In Nature's Laboratory: [Commemorating Our Vacation Trip of 1916, August 28th to September 9th]*. Privately printed, 1916. Unpaginated.

———. *Our Vacation Days of 1918*. Akron, OH: n.p., 1921.

Burroughs, John, with Clifton Johnson. *John Burroughs Talks: His Reminiscences and Comments*. Boston: Houghton Mifflin, 1922.

Burroughs, Julian, and Elizabeth Burroughs Kelley. *Recollections of John Burroughs*. West Park, NY: Riverby Books, 1991.

Clancy, Louise B., and Florence Davies. *The Believer: The Life Story of Mrs. Henry Ford*. New York: Coward-McCann, 1960.

Craig, Lee A. *Josephus Daniels: His Life and Times*. Chapel Hill: University of North Carolina Press, 2013.

Crosby, Alfred W. *America's Forgotten Pandemic: The Influenza of 1918*. 2d ed. Cambridge: Cambridge University Press, 2003.

Dahlinger, John Côté, and Frances Spatz Leighton. *The Secret Life of Henry Ford*. Indianapolis: Bobbs-Merrill, 1978.

Daniels, Josephus. *Tar Heel Editor*. Chapel Hill: University of North Carolina Press, 1939.

———. *The Wilson Era: Years of War and After, 1917–1923*. Chapel Hill: University of North Carolina Press, 1946.

Daniels, Josephus, and Edmund David Cronon. *The Cabinet Diaries of Josephus Daniels, 1913–1921*. Lincoln: University of Nebraska Press, 1963.

Davies, Pete. *American Road: The Story of an Epic Transcontinental Journey at the Dawn of the Motor Age*. 1st ed. New York: H. Holt, 2002.

De Loach, R. J. H. *Rambles with John Burroughs*. Boston: R. G. Badger, 1912.

DeGraaf, Leonard, and Bill Gates. *Edison and the Rise of Innovation*. New York: Sterling Signature, 2013.

Dinnerstein, Leonard. *The Leo Frank Case*. New York: Columbia University Press, 1968.

Dominguez, Henry L. *Edsel: The Story of Henry Ford's Forgotten Son*. Warrendale, PA: SAE International/Society of Automotive Engineers, 2002.

Donaldson, Alfred L. *A History of the Adirondacks*. New York: Century, 1921.

Edison, Thomas A. "What Is Life?" *Cosmopolitan Magazine*, vol. 68, May 1920.

Edison, Thomas A., and Dagobert D. Runes. *The Diary and Sundry Observations of Thomas Alva Edison*. New York: Philosophical Library, 1948.

Emerson, Ralph Waldo. *Essays*. Boston: Ticknor and Fields, 1865.

———. *Essays: First and Second Series*. London: Humphrey Milford/Oxford University Press, 1936.

———. *Nature*. Boston: J. Munroe and Company, 1836.

Emerson, Ralph Waldo, and Lewis Mumford. *Essays and Journals: Selected, and with an Introd., by Lewis Mumford*. Garden City, NY: Doubleday, 1968.

Fansler, Homer Floyd. *History of Tucker County, West Virginia*. Parsons, WV: McClain, 1990.

Finlay, Mark R. *Growing American Rubber: Strategic Plants and the Politics of National Security*. Studies in Modern Science, Technology, and the Environment. New Brunswick, NJ: Rutgers University Press, 2009.

Firestone, Harvey Samuel. *The Romance and Drama of the Rubber Industry*. Akron, OH: Firestone Tire and Rubber Company, 1932.

Firestone, Harvey Samuel, and Samuel Crowther. *Men and Rubber: The Story of Business*. 1st ed. Garden City, NY: Doubleday, Page, 1926.

Ford, Henry. *The Case against the Little White Slaver: Volumes I, II, III, and IV*. Detroit: H. Ford, 1916.

Ford, Henry, and Samuel Crowther. *Edison as I Know Him*. New York: Cosmopolitan Book Corporation, 1930.

————. *My Life and Work*. Garden City, NY: Doubleday, Page, 1923.

Ford Motor Company, ed. *Ford Times*. Dearborn, MI: Ford Motor Company, n.d.

Fritz, Florence Irene. *Bamboo and Sailing Ships: The Story of Thomas A. Edison and Fort Myers, Florida*. Fort Myers, FL: n.p., 1949.

Gibbons, Felton, and Deborah Strom. *Neighbors to the Birds: A History of Bird-watching in America*. New York: W. W. Norton, 1988.

Goldstone, Lawrence. *Drive! Henry Ford, George Selden, and the Race to Invent the Auto Age*. New York: Ballantine, 2016.

Greenberg, Sue, and Jan Kahn. *Asheville: Vol. 1, A Postcard History*. Dover, NH: Arcadia, 1997.

Grismer, Karl H. *The Story of Fort Myers: The History of the Land of the Caloosahatchee and Southwest Florida*. St. Petersburg, FL: St. Petersburg Printing, 1949.

Haring, H. A., and John Burroughs Memorial Association. *The Slabsides Book of John Burroughs*. Boston: Houghton Mifflin, 1931.

Hershey, Burnet. *The Odyssey of Henry Ford and the Great Peace Ship*. New York: Taplinger, 1967.

*The Horseless Age: The Automobile Trade Magazine*. New York: Horseless Age Company, 1895.

Hurley, Edward N. *The Bridge to France*. Philadelphia: J. B. Lippincott, 1927.

Josephson, Matthew. *Edison: A Biography*. 1st ed. New York: Wiley, 1992.

Kanze, Edward. *The World of John Burroughs*. New York: H. N. Abrams, 1993.

Kelley, Elizabeth Burroughs. *John Burroughs—Naturalist: The Story of His Work and Family*. 1st ed. New York: Exposition, 1959.

Kellogg, John Harvey. *The Living Temple*. Battle Creek, MI: Good Health Publishing Company, 1903.

Kennedy, William Sloane. *The Real John Burroughs: Personal Recollection and Friendly Estimate*. New York: Funk & Wagnalls, 1924.

Klein, Maury. "In Search of Jay Gould." *Business History Review*, vol. 52, no. 2 (1978): 166–99.

Lacey, Robert. *Ford: The Men and the Machine*. Boston: Little, Brown, 1986.

Lane, Rose Wilder. *Henry Ford's Own Story; How a Farmer Boy Rose to the Power That Goes with Many Millions, yet Never Lost Touch with Humanity, as Told to Rose Wilder Lane*. Forest Hills, NY: E. O. Jones, 1917.

*The Legacy of the Exposition: Interpretation of the Intellectual and Moral Heritage Left to Mankind by the World Celebration at San Francisco in 1915*. San Francisco: n.p., 1916.

Lincoln Highway Association, ed. *The Complete Official Road Guide of the Lincoln Highway*. Detroit: Lincoln Highway Association, 1918.

Markel, Howard. *The Kelloggs: The Battling Brothers of Battle Creek*. 1st ed. New York: Pantheon, 2017.

Morris, Edmund. *Theodore Rex*. 1st ed. New York: Random House, 2001.

Nevins, Allan, and Frank Ernest Hill. *Ford: Expansion and Challenge, 1915–1933*. New York: Scribner, 1957.

Newton, James D. *Uncommon Friends: Life with Thomas Edison, Henry Ford, Harvey Firestone, Alexis Carrel, and Charles Lindbergh*. 1st ed. San Diego: Harcourt Brace Jovanovich, 1987.

Nye, David E. *Henry Ford: Ignorant Idealist*. Series in American Studies. Port Washington, NY: Kennikat, 1979.

———. *The Invented Self: An Anti-Biography from Documents of Thomas A. Edison*. Odense University Studies in English, vol. 7. Odense, Denmark: Odense University Press, 1983.

*Official Automobile Blue Book, 1916, Volume 1: New York and Canada*. Chicago: Automobile Blue Book Publishing Company, 1916.

*Official Automobile Blue Book, 1918, Volume 3: New Jersey, Pennsylvania, Maryland, Delaware, District of Columbia, Northern Virginia and W. Virginia*. New York: Automobile Blue Book Publishing Company, 1918.

*Official Automobile Blue Book, 1918, Volume 6: Southeastern States*. New York: Automobile Blue Book Publishing Company, 1918.

Osborne, Clifford Hazeldine. *The Religion of John Burroughs*. Boston: Houghton Mifflin, 1930.

Parlette, Ralph Albert. *Pockets and Paradises*. Chicago: Parlette-Padget, 1922.

Parsons Brinckerhoff, Tudor, and Bechtel, eds. *Engineering Report to the San Francisco Bay Area Rapid Transit District*. San Francisco: Parsons Brinckerhoff/Tudor/Bechtel, June 1961.

Player, Cyril Arthur. *Highlights in the Life of Thomas A. Edison*. Detroit: Detroit Edison Company, 1947.

Price, Charles Edwin. *Haunted Jonesborough*. Johnson City, TN: Overmountain, 1993.

Renehan, Edward. *John Burroughs: An American Naturalist*. Post Mills, VT: Chelsea Green, 1992.

Robinson, Ed. *Historic Inns of Southern West Virginia*. Illus. ed. Charleston, SC: Arcadia, 2007.

Roxbury Burroughs Club, ed. *John Burroughs in Roxbury*. Roxbury, NY: Roxbury Burroughs Club, 196-?.

Sanborn, Franklin Benjamin. *The Personality of Emerson*. Boston: C. E. Goodspeed, 1903.

Scott, Lloyd N. *Naval Consulting Board of the United States*. Washington, D.C.: U.S. Government Printing Office, 1920.

Sharp, Dallas Lore. *The Seer of Slabsides*. Boston: Houghton Mifflin, 1921.

Skrabec, Quentin R. *Rubber: An American Industrial History*. Jefferson, NC: McFarland, 2014.

Smith, Jane S. *The Garden of Invention: Luther Burbank and the Business of Breeding Plants*. New York: Penguin, 2009.

Smoot, Tom. *The Edisons of Fort Myers: Discoveries of the Heart*. 1st paperback ed. Sarasota, FL: Pineapple, 2011.

Snow, Richard. *I Invented the Modern Age: The Rise of Henry Ford*. Illus. ed. New York: Scribner, 2014.

Stross, Randall E. *The Wizard of Menlo Park: How Thomas Alva Edison Invented the Modern World*. Repr. ed. New York: Crown, 2008.

Swift, Hildegarde Hoyt, and Lynd Ward. *The Edge of April: A Biography of John Burroughs*. New York: W. Morrow, 1957.

Temple, Oliver Perry. *East Tennessee and the Civil War*. Cincinnati: R. Clarke, 1899.

Thulesius, Olav. *Edison in Florida: The Green Laboratory*. Gainesville: University Press of Florida, 1997.

Tobin, John. "Henry Ford and His Village Industries in Southeastern Michigan." Unpublished thesis. Eastern Michigan University, Ypsilanti, 1985.

Todd, Frank Morton. *The Story of the Exposition: Being the Official History of the International Celebration Held at San Francisco in 1915 to Commemorate the Discovery of the Pacific Ocean and the Construction of the Panama Canal*. New York: Putnam, 1921.

Trine, Ralph Waldo, and Henry Ford. *The Power That Wins: Henry Ford and Ralph Waldo Trine in an Intimate Talk on Life—the Inner Thing—the Things of the Mind and Spirit—and the Inner Powers and Forces That Make for Achievement*. Indianapolis: Bobbs-Merrill, 1929.

Wallace, Max. *The American Axis: Henry Ford, Charles Lindbergh, and the Rise of the Third Reich*. 1st ed. New York: St. Martin's, 2003.

Watts, Steven. *The People's Tycoon: Henry Ford and the American Century*. Illus. ed. New York: Vintage, 2006.

Wilder, Laura Ingalls. *West from Home: Letters of Laura Ingalls Wilder, San Francisco, 1915*. Reissue ed. New York: HarperCollins, 1974.

Williams, Cora Lenore. *The Fourth-Dimensional Reaches of the Exposition: San Francisco, 1915*. San Francisco: Paul Elder, 1915.

Williams, Henry Smith. *Luther Burbank, His Life and Work*. New York: Hearst's International Library Company, 1915.

# Illustration Credits

230 The camping party is ferried across the Jackson River in Virginia on
    August 23, 1918. (84.1.1660.P.34.118.18/THF127387)

232 Henry Ford and Harvey Firestone investigate a water-power system in
    the mountains above the O. C. Barber phosphate plant near Healing
    Springs, Virginia. (84.1.1660.P.34.43.18/THF111380)

239 Edison, Firestone, Burroughs, and Ford in camp along Wolf Creek, out-
    side Narrows, Virginia. (84.1.1660.P.34.52.18/ THF122450)

244 Morning in camp on the Witt farm near Tazewell, Virginia.
    (84.1.1660.P.34.71.18/THF122464)

256 The Ford party encampment on the Lee farm outside Jonesborough, Ten-
    nessee, August 27, 1918. (84.1.1660.P.34.72.18/THF122468)

259 Crew members Harry Linden, R. V. Kline, and Thomas Sato take
    a break from changing a tire outside Jonesborough, Tennessee.
    (84.1.1660.P.34.147.18/THF127389)

276 Thomas Edison enjoys an afternoon nap as John Burroughs catches up on
    the war news. (84.1.1660.P.O.702/THF124710)

285 Henry Ford and John Burroughs picking raspberries near Long Lake,
    New York. (84.1.1660.P.34.17.19/THF116233)


### Courtesy of Thomas Edison National Historical Park

55 Thomas Edison at his Florida estate with John Burroughs and Henry
   Ford. (14.225.022)

97 Thomas Edison and Henry Ford at the Panama–Pacific Exposition.
   (14.130.118)

105 Thomas Edison and Admiral William Fullam aboard the USS *Oregon* in
    San Francisco Bay. (14.130.134)

112 Thomas Edison, Luther Burbank, and Henry Ford in Santa Rosa.
    (14.130.94)

128 Thomas Edison at the Brooklyn Navy Yard in 1915. (14.225.156)

184 Thomas Edison conducts smoke-screen experiments aboard a navy vessel
    on Long Island Sound, August 26, 1917. (25.500.78)

283 With the mayors of Troy and Albany in attendance, Ford, Edison, Bur-
    roughs, and Firestone chisel their initials into the cornerstone for Ford's
    Green Island hydroelectric plant. (14.225.136)

301 In November 1920, four months before Burroughs's death, Henry Ford
    records his friendship with Burroughs and Edison on film. (14.225.82)

# Index

Note: Page numbers in *italics* refer to illustrations.
Endnotes are indicated by *n* after the page number.

Accident, Maryland, 214
Addams, Henry, 288, 335*n*
Addams, Jane, 126
Adirondacks and Green Mountains
  trip (1916), 139–62
  Albany, New York, 144–45
  Allen farm, Highland, New York,
    159–60
  Au Sable Forks, New York, 153
  Ausable River, 152–54, *154*
  Behan farm, Plattsburgh, New
    York, 156
  Bennington, Vermont, 158
  Blue Mountain Lake, New York,
    149–50
  Bronson farm, Arlington, Vermont,
    158
  Burlington, Vermont, 157
  Chazy Landing, New York, 156
  Chestertown, New York, 148
  Cohoes, New York, 145
  Corinth, New York, 146–47
  Elizabethtown, New York, 147,
    151–52
  Ellenville, New York, 140–41
  Essex, New York, 152

Great Barrington, Massachusetts,
    159
  Hotel Champlain, Plattsburgh,
    New York, 156
  Indian Lake, New York, 148–49,
    *149*
  Lake Champlain, 152, 156–57, 284
  Lake George, New York, 147, 148
  Lake Placid, New York, 154–55
  Lenox, Massachusetts, 158
  Long Lake, New York, 150
  Malone, New York, 155–56
  Middlebury, Vermont, 157
  Paul Smiths, New York, 155
  Pittsfield, Massachusetts, 157, 158
  Plattsburgh, New York, 156
  Prospect House Inn, Blue Moun-
    tain Lake, New York, 149–50
  Roxbury, New York, 140–41,
    160–61
  Rutland, Vermont, 157–58
  Saranac Lake, New York, 155
  Saratoga Springs, New York,
    145–46
  Schroon River, New York, 151
  Sharow farm, 151–52

Adirondacks and Green Mountains
    trip (1916) (*continued*)
  Tahawus, New York, 151
  Ten Eyck Hotel, Albany, New York,
    144–45
  Warrensburg, New York, 148
  West Orange, New Jersey, 140
  Winooski, Vermont, 157
  *see also specific individuals*
*Afoot and Afloat* (Burroughs), 70–71
Agassiz, Louis, 38
Albany, New York, 39, 72, 136, 144–
    45, 190, 281–82, *283*
*Alcedo* (American patrol boat), 181
Allen, Charlie, 65
Allen, George, 159–60
Alligator Bay rookery, 64, 65–66, 163
Appalachian trip. *see* Great Smoky
    Mountains trip
Arlington, Vermont, 158
Au Sable Forks, New York, 153
Ausable River, 152–54, *154*

Babcock Electric, 1
Bacheller, Irving, 14
Baker Model V, 1
Barber, Ohio Columbus, 232–33
Barber phosphate plant, 232, *232*,
    233
Barberton, Virginia, 233
Barrus, Clara, 171–72, 187–88, 229,
    302
Bartow, Virginia, 226
Bell, Alexander Graham, 76, 174
Bennington, Vermont, 158
B.F. Goodrich, 233
Blake, H. A., 61
Bluefield, West Virginia, 241–43
Blue Mountain Lake, New York,
    149–50
Bolar Springs, Virginia, 227–31
Book, Frank, 48
Book, Herbert, 46–47, 314n
Boone, Daniel, 258, 259
Boosters' Club carnival in Fort
    Myers, 60–61
Braddock, Edward, 213
*Breath of Life, The* (Burroughs), 91

Bristol, Tennessee, 248–52
Bristol, Virginia, 248–52
Brown, John, 33
Bryan, William Jennings, 127, 130
Buck, Glen
  about, 11–12
  in Concord, Massachusetts, 33,
    *35*, 38
  in Dearborn (1913), 18
  Model T delivered to Burroughs,
    11, 12
  Model T logo design, 11, 310n
  Sleepy Hollow Cemetery, 34, 38
  trip to Boston (1913), 29
  at Walden Pond, 34, *35*
  at Woodchuck Lodge, 27, 29
Burbank, Luther
  concerns about World War I, 113
  conversation with Edison on train,
    94–95
  exhibit at Panama–Pacific Exposi-
    tion, 99
  at Firestone dinner party, 118
  Ford and Edison visit at Santa
    Rosa, 110–14, *112*, 293
  San Francisco Bay ferry ride, 95
  Santa Rosa gardens, xvii, 110–14,
    120
  spineless cactus, 99, 111, 113
Burlington, Vermont, 157
Burns, William J., 60, 61–62
Burroughs, Curtis, 22
Burroughs, John
  accidents while driving, 16–17,
    23–24, 30, 61, 171–72
  accomplishments, overview, 7–8
  Adirondacks and Green Mountains
    trip, xvii, 143–46, 148–49, *149*,
    151–58, *154*, 160
  age during 1918 road trip, xiii–xv
  at Andrew D. Gwynne Institute,
    70–71
  arm broken in car accident, 171–
    72, 182, 186
  attitude toward Model T, xv, 9–10,
    15–17, 164, 185
  at Boosters' Club carnival in Fort
    Myers, 60–61